NEW W
AND PE~~RI~~ ~~PHERAL~~ ~~STRAINS:~~
SPECIFYING CULTURAL DIMENSIONS
IN LATIN AMERICAN
AND LATINO STUDIES

Edited by

Michael Piazza

and

Marc Zimmerman

MARCH/ABRAZO PRESS
Chicago

Copyright © 1998 Michael Piazza and Marc Zimmerman

Published by El Movimiento Artístico Chicano (MARCH), Inc.
MARCH/Abrazo Press, P.O. Box 2890, Chicago, IL 60690
Printed in the United States of America on acid-free paper.

U.S. Library of Congress Cataloging-in-Publication Data
New world [dis]orders and peripheral strains: specifying
cultural dimensions in Latin American and Latino studies / Michael
   Piazza and Marc Zimmerman, editors.
        p. cm.–(LACASA Chicago; v. 2)
        Includes bibliographical references and index.
        ISBN 1-877636-16-9 (pbk)
        1.   Latin America--Civilization--20th century--Philosophy. 2.
Social sciences--Latin America.. 3. Postmodernism and Globalization--
Latin American and U.S. Latinos. 4. Cultural Studies--Latin America and
U.S. Latinos. 5. Arts, Literature and Society–Latin America., Central
America, Latino. 6. Arts–Performance, computer graphics. I. Piazza,
Michael. II. Zimmerman, Marc. Includes bibliographical references.

Library of Congress Catalogue Card Number # 97-76210

Cover art: *Oceanic Perspectives*, by Michael Piazza, 1992.
Cover and graphic design by Michael Piazza.
Book design by Patricio Navia.

Publication Project II of MARCH's Chicago Latin American Cultural Activities and Studies Arena Series--LACASA Chicago. General Editor, Marc Zimmerman.

DEDICATION

For those who resisted
--fought, were killed,
disappeared or locked away,
were battered, brutalized
and sometimes forgotten,
sometimes remembered,
as the world
went its way
and all things solid
melted into
--something else.

IN MEMORIUM

Peter S. Piazza
Dorothy Zimmerman Yosepowich
Esperanza Martínez-Mendoza de Solís
Frank Genaro Sánchez
And just as we go to press,
María Milagros López
Concepción Andara-Ubeda.

Fathers, Mothers, Friends
--so many gone this past year--
We miss and will remember them

Diana Solís, *Untitled 1*, from *Intersticios* (installation) 1997.
Silver gelatin print-20"x24"
Courtesy of the artist.

TABLE OF CONTENTS

ILLUSTRATIONS, RELATED TEXTS
AND ACKNOWLEDGMENTS

PREFACE

The essays in this book in one way or another grew out of, or contributed or otherwise related to the discussions and activities which have constituted an ongoing development of Latin American cultural studies coordinated by Marc Zimmerman in the Latin American Studies Program of the University of Illinois at Chicago (UIC).

Zimmerman's own theoretical starting points and progressive syntheses are detailed in his volume, *Tropicalizing Hegemony* (1998); they are anticipated, summarized and in some ways gone beyond in his essay for this volume. But concerns in *New World [Dis]Orders and Peripheral Strains* then move on to the perspectives formalized in the papers of long-term seminar participants and others involved as guests, "friends" or "correspondents" in relation to the overall UIC-based project. Piazza, Curry, Bonnin, Macadar, Navia and Vora are the participants in question; Achugar, then a professor at Northwestern University, presented his paper at a seminar meeting; Elizam Escobar, a Puerto Rican artist and POW, was asked by Piazza to write a paper from his prison cell as Piazza kept him informed about various developments in the seminar. The editors invited a UIC campus visitor, Guatemalan novelist/critic Arturo Arias to add an often marginalized Central American perspective to the effort. To round things out, Piazza also invited UIC Art Professor Silvia Malagrino to contribute a photo-essay; and Marc Zimmerman invited Ileana Rodríguez to draw on her work in applying India's Subaltern Studies Group theories as a means for providing some of the final specifications that might lead beyond the questions central to the other essays.

Constructed in relation to a given intellectual project, this book builds upon and complements some of the other volumes and particular essays on Latin American postmodernity cited in the Introduction. What we have here is an intent to intervene in a kind of "second wave" of discussion of Latin American postmodernity, now in the wake of increasing debates about transnational and globalizing trends. In effect, the texts herein are partial responses to questions raised in the earlier texts of socio-political and cultural developments in the Latin American periphery from a particular site of enunciation which is also (and not coincidentally) one of the key centers of U.S. capitalism, postmodern culture and, to some not insignificant extent, U.S. Latino cultural development.

The place of the "Second City" in the first world implies access to original, partial perspectives which other loci might not be able to provide. However, this is not a fully "Chicago volume," but one in which Chicago, an increasingly Latin Americanized city, is the site for a somewhat different look at the questions posed by postmodernity than found elsewhere. Not incidental to this matter is that the decision to develop the volume out of seminar-related papers was made after a few of the contributors attended Fredric Jameson's lectures on Marxism and culture at the University of Chicago in May 1992; not incidental also is the volume's articulation in the wake of the conference on Latin American Cultural Studies hosted by Néstor García Canclini at the Universidad Metropolitana in Mexico City, the visits of Gómez-Peña and collaborator Coco Fusco to Chicago and the UIC campus, the intense citywide discussions of NAFTA and overall Mexican and Latin American development, and advances in a project on transnational migration involving the Colegio de Michoacán in Mexico, UIC and the latter's recently emerging Great Cities Institute.

These matters affected many dimensions of the text, and especially the question of globalization, articulated in our introduction. Despite all the caveats and qualifications, this volume is quite able to stand on its own. It enriches Zimmerman's own individual efforts, but does not depend on them. It presents a Chicago "slant," but is not limited, damaged or wounded by its particular locus. Presenting a few examples of general theory and work in the social sciences, as well as literary and art criticism, providing tentative projections toward future worlds, this book indeed represents hopes for positive applications of concepts which have often seemed to stifle rather than further Latin American concerns.

The editors would like to give thanks for support, financial or otherwise, to UIC's Latin American Studies Program, John Nuveen Center of International Affairs (especially to director Ariani Friedl and our contributing writer, Nora Bonnin), Institute for the Humanities, Campus Research Board and Great Cities Institute;; to Carlos Cumpián and the Board of the Movimiento Artístico Chicano (MARCH); to Esther Soler and Collage de las Américas; and to Scott Curry and family. We would also like to thank Daniel Bermúdez for his indexing work–and thanks to the students who participated in our deliberations, but whose work could not be represented here. We also wish to acknowledge our debt to the other Latin Americans and Latin Americanists mining the riches of cultural studies, postmodernity, subaltern and globalization studies. Thanks to Hugo Achugar for taking us to the Montevideo website. Thanks to Maureen Connolly for her participation in Diana Solís's work..

With this publication, we formally launch a new program, LACASA CHICAGO, the Latin American/Latino/a Cultural Activities and Studies Arena of Chicago. A branch of MARCH and with UIC roots and ties, LACASA will support and sponsor many activities and publications which flow out of, or are related, to this book. We look forward to meeting our readers in person or in cyberspace in the future which awaits LACASA . Of course it's LACASA CHICAGO--it's our casa, but our house is also yours.

–The Editors, Chicago, August-December 1996; November 1997

INTRODUCTION

By Michael Piazza and Marc Zimmerman
with Robert Scott Curry

As critics, we must retain, not pretend to resolve, a tension between what will remain an unsatisfactorily homogenizing term: postmodernism, and the heterogenous local forms produced within and sometimes against its logic. Something of this motivates Jameson's own seemingly totalizing argument.... [But] perhaps if Jameson successfully projected the "concept of a new systematic cultural norm," it remains for others to "reflect more adequately on the most effective forms of any radical cultural politics today" [1991: 6]...[; and] perhaps the formal articulation of this tension between local difference and global totality constitutes a postmodern politics. One response to Jameson's work might then be to confront his projected concept of global totality with the details for various local forms of cultural politics. In this way, certain global categories operative within Jameson's model (or other global models of postmodernity) can be provisionally rewritten with greater flexibility to assist us in understanding and articulating the heterogeneous forms of resistance culture functioning around the world today. [Santiago Colás 1994: 18-19]

1. Opening Strains

Theorists, writers, and artists know only too well the predicament we face in what we've come loosely to refer to as the late capitalist, postmodern world. The so-called "cool neutralizing gaze" of postmodernism has taken a hegemonic role over previous academic and political discourses now seemingly smashed and scattered across the theoretical terrain. Older ideological constructs no longer seem sufficient to explain the situation, and more importantly, the theoretical appears unable to engage any oppositional praxis. As Jean Franco sees it, "one of the ironies of pluralism is that even commitment becomes marketable" (1992: 69). As a primary byword of ideological accommodation and co-optation, pluralism in turn only reinforces existing unequal power relations in favor of U.S./European hegemony and domination. It is the leveling implicit in pluralism which becomes problematic and mystifying, suppressing the particular behind an imposed universal of disintegration and "pure difference."

Revolutionary hopes and efforts turned to blood and ashes, Latin America ever all the more experiences international patterns of hegemony and continues to be relegated to periphery status. So Nelly Richard questions, "where does this ironic situation leave the periphery when the center is in 'privileged disintegration?'" (1987: 7). Speaking from the U.S./Mexican border, Guillermo Gómez-Peña gives a sense of what this may mean today:

> This being the age of "*la desmodernidad*" (from the Spanish noun *desmadre*, meaning both being without a mother and living in chaos), the great fiction of a state-sponsored order has evaporated, leaving us in a state of meta-orphanhood. We are all finally "hijos de la chingada," citizens of a borderless society. [1992: 86]

In the context of our Latin American and broader concerns, Gómez-Peña provides a sense of the ironic that can easily be lost in the slippages that occur between abstractions within postmodernism's co-optation, leaving only an essentialist universal humanism while Latin America is relegated to struggling in a growingly globalized economy in which the area's place remains increasingly problematic. The critical voices of the peripheries (class, national, gay, ethnic, etc.) that gained new ground through the struggles which peaked in the sixties and early seventies, now become confounded within that universal humanism. The harsh disillusionment that is said to be postmodern in turn only provides another illusion which absolves any responsibility for, and more importantly will never resolve, the inequities and injustices that occur in the peripheries and, as Hugo Achugar puts it, "the peripheries within the peripheries." For the time, perhaps we must settle for "meta-orphanhood," keeping in mind that it is a meta-orphanhood of extreme inequity within the new world order--or "(b)order," as Gómez-Peña has phrased it (1996)--of transnational hegemony.

2. The Haunting Dimension

For the most part implicitly, Latin American transnational processes as central to the area's postmodern strains haunt the analyses presented herein.

Emphasis on these processes had gained considerable ground in relation to Latin American cultural and literary analyses as part of a transforming vision with respect to third world and peripheral formations, as well as recent concerns with modes of postcolonial, post-national and "subaltern" resistance. Dependency and more broadly world systems theories pointed to the impossibility of examining cultural phenomena as mere reflexes of national and local modes of production and market systems, as well as national and state political apparatuses.

The successive, complex and contradictory migration and imposition of structures and forms from one social formation to and on another came to dominate research. But in a period of globalization under the aegis of neo-liberalism and supposed democratization, there was clearly a growing interest in the cultural as well as economic and political implications of the transnational process--in the impact on modes of mass or popular cultural production and distribution, on matters of "everyday life" and questions involving models of hegemony as opposed to ones of domination. In this context, older formulations, such as "cultural imperialism," were criticized for failing to take into account positive, dynamizing and transformative dimensions coming from without or underplaying the way in which given local forms and modes have their "inverse effect"--sometimes "positive," sometimes "negative," usually greatly mixed--on the more global structurations.

The key linkages between economic processes and the "cultural sphere," including such hegemonic "first world" theoretical catchalls as "poststructuralism," "post-Marxism," "postcolonialism" and, above all, "postmodern-sm," have found their maximal expression in Jameson's seminal essay and book (1984 and 1991)--and then, in another way, in Harvey (1989). It is, however, Jameson's critique which is clearly central to what follows herein.

To summarize what has become commonplace to contemporary cultural studies, but which should be at least minimally described in an introduction such as this: Jameson conceives postmodernity and its related theorizations as phenomena which owe their unique characteristics to the shift in the global socio-economic mode of production into a new dominant phase which Belgian economist Ernest Mandel theorized under the rubric of "Late Capitalism" (1972).. For Mandel, late capitalism follows a first stage, characterized by Marx's view of industrial capitalism, and a second,

3

characterized by Lenin's presentation of finance or monopoly capital and imperialism. In economic terms, late capitalism can be said to have as its most important feature, the dominance of multinational corporations as an over-arching feature of a world system; hence Mandel's view of late capitalism as a purer capitalist stage leading to current conceptualizations of economic globalization and its social, political and cultural dimensions. As one of the first thinkers to link views congealing in the Lyotard's theorizing of postmodernism with Mandel's critique, Jameson saw the very emergence of "late capitalism" as spelling a radical problematizing and virtual dis-articulation of the frequently posited order of things between nation-bounded socio-economic, political, ideological and cultural spheres, as well as the very negation of "spheres" as relatively autonomous or viable constructs. The new world order transforms geographies, technologies and identities; it generates an apparent disordering and overdetermination of all social processes, in which, it should be underlined, micro-cultures and micro-politics may themselves have increased efficacy and impact, as in such far-flung examples as Bosnia and Chiapas.

Foucault's analysis of dispersed power, Baudrillard's culture of signs and simulacra, Lyotard's view of an end to modernist and modernizing narratives, and Deleuze and Guattari's views of nomadic, transmigrative, schizoid identities transgressing definitions and borders--all of these emergent constructs from the first world began to find their Latin American articulation in function of a neo-Gramscian rethinking of social and political theory in which there is no inevitable class reference or centeredness and in which cultural articulations, disarticulations, rearticulations and transculturations become central.

For the studies undertaken in this volume, the key socio-historical changes have to do with shifts in global relations (cf. Mandel and Wallerstein) and the overall effects of post-Fordism and globalization (cf. Harvey 1989), the collapse of the supposed alternative to capitalism, and the achieved hegemony of IMF-promoted neo-liberalism and democratization processes in Latin America (cf. Halebsky and Harris, ed. 1995). The key theoretical innovations potentiating a greater weight for shifting trans-national cultural processes, were, as Marc Zimmerman's essay emphasizes, those of Laclau and Mouffe (1985) and Deleuze and Guattari (1987). The key cultural moves may be located beyond Jameson's ongoing opus and cultural studies work best represented by Stuart Hall--but perhaps most

4

crucially now in studies of globalization and culture such as the collective volumes edited by Mike Featherstone and associates (1990 and 1995), and individual efforts like the recent book by Appadurai (1996). We may in this broader context invoke such specifically Latin American cultural thinkers as Roberto Schwarz in Brazil, Jesús Martín Barbero in Colombia, Beatriz Sarlo in Argentina, Nelly Richard in Chile and, perhaps most decisively for the concerns reflected here, Néstor García Canclini in Mexico.

García Canclini's work enters the cultural arena--questions of "folk," popular, mass, elite culture, questions of class, ethnicity, gender, etc. in ever more tenuous and oblique relation to capitalist reproduction. In his seminal work, Culturas híbridas: Estratégias para entrar y salir de la modernidad (1992), he speaks to contemporary, postmodern processes characterized by transculturation, hybridization, articulation, reconversion, de and re-territorialization and all the other terms associated with Laclau-Mouffean and Deleuze-Guattarian critiques. Embodied in his analysis, situated in Mexico, is also a serious concern with border culture as intensely symptomatic of hybrid transnational trends. In this way, his work is a kind of bridge between writers like Roger Bartra and Carlos Monsiváis to border poets like Gloria Anzaldúa and Gómez-Peña. His work charts inter-connections between tradition and modernity, indigenous and transnational cultures, between the evolving life in the great Latin American cities and in smaller rural communities like Ocumicho, Michoacán; between the cultural transformations on the border, and in Mexican and other Latino towns and barrios throughout the U.S. Most recently his work has centered on the cultural effects of globalization and questions of participatory democracy and citizenship in relation to Latin America's emergent neo-liberal civil societies.

The cultural studies emphasis as central to more broadly social and political concerns reached a new point of crystallization at the Rockefeller Foundation-funded conference hosted by García Canclini in conjunction with George Yúdice, in May 1993. The conference brought together several key Latin American and Latino figures in an effort to form an association for future work and to provide a kind of model for regional and local integration into a macro-structural project. The need for regional, more local and rural perspectives apparently carried over into a second conference which piggy-backed the more theoretical one and dealt with the cultural dimensions and effects of NAFTA and Latin American economic integration

5

(cf. García Canclini, ed. 1996). As these conferences showed, the local always has the potential of transforming the whole. The question is that of "specifying"--that of somehow marking particular instances so that they be related fully and viably to the whole, and so that the whole can be modified to account for the specific.

Hence the emphasis on "specifying" in the subtitle of this book. Our work is conceived as a contribution to the growing discussion of Latin American postmodernity as carried on at innumerable conferences like those mentioned above, as well as at several sessions at the Latin American Studies Association and other professional organizations. It takes its place as a response to or continuing discussion of issues central to a few key contemporary Latin American journals (e.g. Nelly Richard's *Revista de Crítica Cultural*, Beatriz Sarlo's *Punto de Vista* and the English publication *Travesia*, recently renamed *The Journal of Latin American Cultural Studies*) as well as to recent collections such as those edited by Jorge Ruffinelli (1990); George Yúdice, Jean Franco and Juan Flores (1992); Arturo Arias (1993); Hermann Herlinghaus and Monika Walter (1994); Alan Rush (1995); Irma Rivera Nieves and Carlos Gil (1995); John Beverley, José Oviedo and Michael Aronna (1995); and Claudia Ferman (1996).

The latter two texts are especially important here, since they present English translations of key interventions by some of the most important writers in the Latin American debate, as well as essays by Neil Larsen and some members of the U.S.-based Latin American Subaltern Studies group, Beverley included. This present volume cuts through, supplements and at times argues with and even deepens positions set forth in the other works, as well as in individual volumes such as those by Celeste Olaquiaga (1992), Claudia Ferman (1994), Santiago Colás (1994), and Raymond L. Williams (1995); its particular contribution rests in a concern for the specific effects of postmodern thinking on a variety Latin American political and cultural developments as grasped from a Chicago/midwestern locus and as filtered through or related to both the Latin American formulations as well as varying paradigms and perspectives emanating from U.S. social science and literary discourses.

In terms of contemporary concerns for the "location of enunciation," our text perhaps seeks to integrate visual arts perspectives and play out Chicago/Latin American (as well as Latino/Latin American) relations in

6

ways that probably most parallel John Welchman's recently published collection on border theory (1996). Our play with the question of "strains", (genetic "varieties," musical "variations" or themes) in the book's title reflects both the partial and specifying nature of our enterprise, our concern with a kind of postmodern crisis of representation.

The question is most specifically one of metaphors, especially biological ones (development and evolution are just the most obvious examples), but also the sense of tensions, discomforts, and even threats of rupture, chaos or *disorder* which the use of postmodern taxonomy, terminology and ontology poses for those, especially among the left, who seek to deal with the multilayered, musical complexity of Latin American non-linear temporalities, rhythms and transformations in the context of post-Cold War societies.

This book traces some of the possible routes in the overall enterprise of cognitive mapping in postmodern geographical space. How Latin America is to deal with "postmodern" situations, impositions and internal developments is the concern of the writers presented as part of the ongoing discussion of the peripheral or excluded status against the postmodern cultural dominant. But the growing emphasis on globalization has led us to join with Appadurai in emphasizing "cultural dimensions" over "cultural dominants" (Jameson) or even "cultural studies," taken as some kind of determinant and self-sufficient field.

Although varied in their emphasis, the contributors aim for a praxis which will, as Elizam Escobar puts it, "pierce through" our predicament, in hopes of a liberated future –but all this without the illusion that we can find much hope in older Marxist-Leninist or *focquista* formulations for third world revolution. García Canclini's question, "how to be radical without being fundamentalist" (1995a: 281) also haunts this text even as we explore the effects of modernization, globalization and neo-liberal hegemony in Latin America.

In this sense, most of the essays seek to explore what Derrida has defined as the "specters of Marx" (1994) now freed from many of our twentieth century illusions and false sightings, reconstituting past developments in function of readings that point toward a living Marx for the future. And here at least some of the essays parallel the efforts by Yúdice (1992) and Colás (1994) in following the path of logic from postmodern critique to its third world and specifically Latin American applications.

7

3. The Essays

We have divided the volume into four major sections. "Theorizing Specificities" combines with this introduction to present some perspectives that enable specific and local analyses in the wake of the incursion of postmodern discourse into the Latin American turf. "Specifying South" shows how Latin Americanist social science and cultural studies concerns relate to frames generated in contemporary U.S. sociology, political science, communications and arts discourses. "Specifying Textualities, Transfixions and Appropriations" highlights Central America and takes us through various parts of Latin America and across the Mexican-U.S. border to raise some vital questions about the relation of postmodern perspectives to literary production and politically committed art. As a way of concluding, "Final Subaltern In(tro)spections and (B)order Specifications" supplements the previous sections and articles with "peripheral" perspectives that confirm, extend, sometimes contradict and round out the field of inquiry stirred by recent Latin American developments and their theorization.

Part I starts with an essay by Zimmerman which gives an overview of the theoretical debates that connected Latin America's democratization processes to the emergence of postmodernism-inflected cultural trends and perspectives. In an approach that both parallels and diverges from the recent effort by Ilan Stavins (1995, especially 156-157]), Zimmerman examines seminal texts on Latin American and Chicano culture by Roberto Fernández Retamar and Juan Gómez-Quiñones to show how postmodern theory helps underline the inadequacies of radical Latin American and Latino cultural studies approaches of the 1970s and helps highlight new theoretical approaches that have a better chance of adequating current processes and tendencies. Zimmerman believes Marxism must be re-defined in the wake of the critique of late capitalism; and he considers Jameson's "cognitive mapping" as a still to be detailed alternative, in relation to emergent practices in popular culture which help to induce what Brecht had characterized as a "slow anger" as a bridge between critical consciousness and new articulations able to engage hegemonic powers as a key dimension of any postmodern political agenda. Zimmerman closes his essay with a meditation on how one crucial European postmodern thinker (Foucault) sets forth theoretical frames which both help and hinder thinking the Latin American present and future. But for all the efforts at theorization he has examined

8

the Latin American present and future. But for all the efforts at theorization he has examined since the fall of the Soviet Union and the consolidation of postmodernist critique (including post-structuralism, postcolonialism, etc.), Zimmerman feels that a fully developed oppositional alternative to capitalist globalization is not possible to theorize at this time of world-historical transition; instead he concludes that any search for "concrete alternatives by which the subaltern can become agents of their own liberation" involves looking "for small openings, possibilities--options" which hold some promise for a future trajectory beyond normative determinations.

Robert Scott Curry's essay is the one which most directly parallels the efforts by Yúdice and Colás to critique Jameson's reading of postmodernity in ways that lead to valid Latin American applications. What distinguishes his effort is his turn to Gayatri Spivak's famous post-Derridean, Subaltern group-inflected essay, "Can the Subaltern Speak?" (1988) and Spivak's critique of Marxist categories of representation and interpretation. Jameson's cognitive mapping as a totalizing construct and means by which we might come to terms with late capitalism and its effects on the world is central to Curry's contribution.

Jameson's accomplishment was to identify postmodernity with the "dominant cultural logic" of a new stage in an ever more complicated capitalist world system in which cognitive mapping (a metaphor for collective, or political, unconscious) could serve as the most adequate basis for representation. Curry examines Jameson's take on postmodernity from a perspective on relations between totality and difference, and the late capitalist shift Jameson identifies in the parallel change in conceptual emphasis from the temporal to the spatial dimension as a basis for explaining the current global situation. This shift explains the continuing importance of Foucault's historicism, which, for Curry (as for Jean-Paul Sartre and Lucien Goldmann so many years ago), denies "the possibility of discursive formations as having historical subjects." The denial of the subject finds its definitive expression in Foucault's negation of any sort of continuity between given historical periods, even as his early work implies a theory of pre-dominating and transforming epistemes as the basis for some kind of periodization or historicization. However, this perspective on history as structurally based synchronic transformation is a denial which nevertheless accommodates the "shift to a spatial, *genealogical* view and its corresponding characteristic of immediacy."

9

To be sure, Foucault's relevance in a spatialization of historical thought (cf. the critique of Soja 1989) is only heightened in relation to third world and specifically Latin American contexts (cf. Ticio Escobar 1984). But Curry emphasizes a more complex route with regard to the relevance of poststructuralism and the question of Latin American postmodernity. So it is in reference to critiques that use difference as a means of masking or ignoring ideology that Curry draws on Spivak's essay to show the relevance and limits of Jameson's approach, and also to show the positive uses of postmarxist Derridian critique in challenging the ideological monopolization of deconstructionism by postmodernist proponents of "pure difference."

For Curry, Spivak's explication of Marx's notion of a divided subject is invaluable in concretely figuring and utilizing Jameson's cognitive mapping. Additionally, Curry points to the importance to a postmodern rereading of Hegel and Marx in relation to the more purely philosophic concerns of Sean Sayers and Richard Norman's *Hegel, Marx and Dialectic* (1980) to establish the relationship of cognition and cognitive mapping to the dialectical process at work within representation. In this regard, Curry follows Spivak in what may be seen as a Derridean deconstruction of Althusser's critique of structural determination and his view of representation as *Darstellung* as a means of separating Marx from the essence/appearance/expressive totality kind of argument which marks Hegel and Marx's own early writings (cf. Althusser 1970).

Spivak does not negate Althusser's emphasis on the overly generalized powers Althusser assigns to *Dahrstellung*, but she "supplements" that emphasis with another representational logic which she finds spelled out, especially in *The Eighteenth Brummaire* and which she considers essential to any particular application of Marx especially to subaltern and third world subjects. This for Curry is a valid approach to "specifying the cultural dominant" of postmodernity in relation to "the Third World" and Latin America, which, parallel to Colás's critique (1994), Curry shows to be far more crucial to Jameson's own constitution of modernity and postmodernity than generally recognized.

In sum, primarily through Spivak's complex intervention (but with help from Aijaz Ahmad and others), Curry indicates how the "third world" and the subaltern, properly specified within a global frame which it helps to constitute and to which it is equally central and not necessarily peripheral,

10

becomes the basis for particular cultural mappings, analyses and actions; and Curry goes so far as to suggest some concrete applications to Guatemala and elsewhere. Through his efforts of theoretical synthesizing and application, Curry's article establishes linkages between Jameson's postmodern meta-narrative and approaches relevant to contemporary Latin American Subaltern Studies critique.

A major participant in the international discussions over Latin American postmodernity and the cultural dimensions of globalization, as well as his native country's role in MERCOSUR and other economic relations, Uruguayan poet-critic Hugo Achugar provides a paper centered on literary and cultural studies within the context of the "notions of modernity, postmodernity and the vanguard in relation to the subject of enunciation in a peripheral situation." Achugar's essay is haunted not only by Marx in the age of globalization but by E.M. Cioran's view of the need for a renewed faith in a "utopian impulse" in the contemporary world; he explores that impulse in relation to the specificity of the Latin American area's "peripheral positionality and status."

Remaining attentive to the particular, Achugar argues that "There is no single postmodernity just as there was no single modernity." Clearly the problems of totality remain crucial for him even into the postmodern era. The key questions he asks have to do not with any "end of history" and diachrony, but with a means of establishing a new ideological arena for the study of relations between modern and postmodern elements and the potential for change on the part of one combination or another. Noting that totalizations achieved through "pure theory" inevitably obscure particulars, Achugar traces utopian totalizations, their implications, variants and oscillations, their tenuous demarcations and multiple slippages occurring in different peripheral formations. Sharing Curry's concern with the cruciality of representation, Achugar takes up the theme in relation to given cultural and artistic forms.

Above all, he focuses on the transposition of avant garde tendencies to and from Latin America; but, parallel to García Canclini (cf. 1995a: 252-258), he also examines popular forms like the contemporary Argentine comic strip. Anticipating a concern for the role of contemporary artists and writers which will emerge especially in the third part of this volume, Achugar, like Curry, turns to Spivak's exploration of representation with respect to the subaltern.

11

Through all of this, Achugar shows how the utopian need persists, as does the need to suspect or even fear that need; and he considers how it is possible for the periphery to probe its own relations when they are set within the multiple discourses emanating from the center.

With the general theoretical frames established in Part I, we turn to four essays that illustrate the workings of contemporary approaches developing in Political Science, Anthropology and visual arts practices in relation to problematics explored throughout this volume. First, Nora Bonnin's essay provides a comparative perspective on modernization in Mexico, Brazil and Argentina as a prelude to a treatment of the latter country's transformation of cultural models in function of a theory of shifting "power gaps" and relations.

In particular, Bonnin provides a conceptually-driven followup to the studies of the Di Tella Foundation by King (1985) and García Canclini (1988), as a means of exploring the questions of combined and uneven development involved in the change from landowning/cattle-growing to industrial hegemony as part of Argentine modernization processes. Commenting on her own effort, Bonnin notes:

> The Di Tella Institute has been the center of a large number of activities and controversies since its opening and after its closing. The Institute became a phenomenon in itself that, despite whether one likes it or not, influenced a decisive segment of Argentina's population. In this paper I was curious about the way different events entangle producing new relations in society. This is the case of the Di Tella that generated activities which ended up mobilizing, in pro or against itself, unthinkable corners of society. [Bonnin. Note to Editors. March 6, 1997]

Remarkable in this brief essay is Bonnin's portrayal of the lag between economic and cultural hegemony, and the contradictory political processes this situation generates; also of great interest is how Bonnin applies contemporary U.S. social theory to conceptualize her study in ways which are different from those employed by King and García Canclini, and that lead her to fill in a relative blank in Sarlo's seminal study of Argentine modernization (1988). In fact, Bonnin's work reveals how Di Tella modernization frames and even helps constitute some of the very qualities which Sarlo has recently posited (cf. 1994 and 1995b) as postmodern dimensions of contemporary Argentine society. No time can be more crucial for examinations such as Bonnin's than the present moment, when the dreams and projects of revolutionary political movements have been discredited as privileged vehicles for seeking social transformation.

Chilean Patricio Navia's contribution looks problematically at the relationship of the periodizations of the modern and the postmodern–above all, how these two seemingly exclusive cultural concepts relate to the development of the structure of the state. For Navia, postmodernity can be viewed as an extension of modernity; and in this light he reviews historical incidents that have transpired in his native country and explores the ideological pitfalls of subsequent analyzes that tend to cloud reality.

Revisiting Chile's entry into modernity, Navia contends that modernity arrived there earlier than previously thought and that different aspects of modernity were either thwarted or developed by the imposed authoritarian culture of the Pinochet regime. Navia analyses Chilean cultural dimensions to distinguish the impact that modernity had on Chile from the impact that the Pinochet regime had. He breaks down the various aspects of present-day Chilean culture, including mass media and fine arts, as well as educational and economic structures, in order to map the changes occurring in recent years.

An explicit dimension of this investigation is a critique of contemporary Chilean social theory, as represented primarily by social scientists and cultural theorists affiliated with the Facultad Latinoamericana de Ciencias Sociales (FLACSO) and/or the *Revista de Crítica Cultural*. FLACSO's studies of popular culture and authoritarianism, military rule, military spending and re-emergence of democracy have been at the forefront of the discussion of modernity in Chile and Latin America; and they are prominently consulted in Navia's research--above all, in his work on FLACSO leader José Joaquín Brunner's view of Chilean modernity. Furthermore, Navia provides a summary of the *Revista*'s editor, Nelly Richard and her influential take on Chilean post-dictatorship and postmodernity. By this means, Navia presents a reading of the role of neo-liberal economic policy, democratization and other processes in Chile's recent transition; in so doing, he plots key theoretical transformations and positionings that have been praised as constituting valuable post-Marxist stances and attacked, as Navia notes, by Hernán Vidal (but others as well-- cf. Petras 1990 and Chilcote 1990a and b) for retreating from a more fully radical oppositional critique. Navia's essay combines analytical rigor with a deeply felt commitment to Chile's future, to provide a valuable application of contemporary U.S.-based political theory.

In a further contribution to this section, Marquesa Macadar brings us from modernity fully into the realm of the postmodern both in subject matter and method, as she presents a vivid portrait of Montevideo in 1992. Weaving in perspectives drawn primarily from contemporary anthropology and communications theories (above all those of Michael Jackson [1994], Anthony Giddens [1990], Jürgen Habermas [1983, 1990] and others), Macadar takes the temperature of her native city's life and ambience, to provide a veritable phenomenology of Montevideo in its postmodern moment as a virtual Husserlian Being-in-the-World. Her effort has been to deconstruct postmodern concepts in relation to cultural and everyday life processes in the urban center of a specific peripheral social formation.

Uruguayan critics like Abril Trigo and Hugo Achugar have also worked this turf, with the latter defining Montevidean postmodernity in function of a metaphor, the "balsa de la Medusa" (1992 and Achugar's essay above). Speaking for a younger generation, Macadar sees Montevidean society as characterized by an "absence of equilibrium," a "stumbling and sinking sensation," stemming from the loss of an illusion of coherence or unifying explanation of the world.

As she notes in an extended meta-critique of this essay, her approach is primarily governed by Jackson's stipulated methodology--i.e. through the "medium of conceptual reflection." This is a description of a society not considered as frozen in a historical moment, but in constant flow. This is why she doesn't try to see what her city is, but tries rather to elucidate the directions, imperatives and tones of its changes, since "the world is always in the making" (Jackson 10).

The postmodern condition, its aesthetics and discourse modes, only have meaning in relation to the practical and social life in which they are engaged. If we believe that postmodernity exists in Montevideo, we do so in the spirit of ... Jameson's view (1984) that the truth of any idea is not a stagnant property inherent in it; that truth happens to an idea. What becomes true, is made true by events. Its verity is in fact an event, a process. I wanted to "undercut the epistemological pretensions" of any claim of postmodernity in Latin America, and especially in Montevideo, in order, as Jackson would say, "to disclose" the "existential implications" (6) of the new cultural dominant and its work in our midst. This is why I decided to go into the streets to read the walls and sense the feelings of Montevideans. I didn't try to take a still photo of Montevideo, with the pretension of saying, "this is it"; instead I sought to provide a space for the different voices that constitute this chaotic social reality. I am aware of the unsystematic, disoriented and intersubjective reality I have revealed. I wanted to explore the existential uses and consequences of these phenomena. As Jackson insists, our emphasis thus shifts "to what [things and beliefs] are made to mean, and what they accomplish for those who invoke and use them." I didn't look for an essence of truth, and in this case, for the essence of the Postmodern, postmodernism and postmodernity, but for its existence in the dynamic relations of everyday life. I looked for the instrumental value it plays in the imaginary of Montevideans.

Macadar says that she uses the word *postmodern* because it plays a role in Montevidean discourse. It is not something she has imposed, not something she has inserted in their vocabulary. And obviously it does not have the same meaning, even if it has a reinterpretation from one group to another. Here she has echoed Jackson's concern with the need to undercut certain popular perceptions that new commodities and technologies are not in themselves determinative or imply irreversible change in third world societies; rather, they are instrumental possibilities whose meaning and use are shaped as much by the conventional wisdom and interests of particular consumers as by the product or technique itself. As she understands the terms, postmodern meanings are shaped and reshaped by the interplay with its needs. In Jackson's terms, she has tried to include

the plurality of all experienced facts, regardless of how they are conceived and classified--conjunctive and disjunctive, fixed and fluid, social and personal, theoretical and practical, subjective and objective, mental and physical, real and illusionary.... I drew on many systems of knowledge ...--as long as they served social and personal uses, without any one of them given a monopoly on "truth." They were used as long as they served to weave the fabric of Montevidean "fantasy and reality, everyday life, habits, crisis, decisive events, and 'indecisive strategies', its ... particularities, its idiomatic and vernacular character"--its lifeworlds.

By mapping out these procedures, Macadar takes us from a generalized postmodern anthropological methodology as in Clifford and Marcus (1983) and Gertz (1986) to one that leads to contemporary postcolonial and

15

subaltern concerns as specified by Ranajit Guha and Gayatri Chakravorty Spivak (1988). As she notes in her metacommentary:

> It was by being there in Montevideo that my knowledge was gained and given expression ..., so that the postmodern was not conceived as an abstract form, but as a presence that exists within ... people who then express it in their own way.... My effort was rather to reconstitute a notion of Montevideo as something urgently of and for the world, rather than something about it.... Something similar to what I have been doing is also indicated by Guha's work in which defiance and rebellion are shown to grow out of forms of resistance and ... everyday life. I tried to depict the lifeworld of subalterns understood as the projection and social continuity for those who, in colonial history, defined themselves as the subjects of their own destiny..., whose modalities of action were marked in hegemonic colonial conditions as transgression, disorder, violence and affective action. Their subalternity made them react not blindly to external domination, but consciously, [with] an ... intentionality, agency, determination and rationality [that were] no less [than that of their] ... oppressor." According to Jackson, what is at issue is the link between discursive suppression and political oppression" (51).

Similar concerns with evoking phenomena and persons targeted for oblivion and with finding new paths to change--and this through contemporary techniques of estrangement, splintering and intertextuality--occur in the work of Silvia Malagrino in her effort to circumvent the dominant or normative truths of discursive practice and show official history as a selective, normalizing ideological process. In "Testimony: Inscriptions from the War Zone," Malagrino draws on her personal experience in Argentina, where state terrorism resulted in the disappearance of thousands of people whose lives and terrible deaths were edited out of the official records.

Malagrino develops an interdisciplinary strategy that attempts to resist this control over history while questioning the adequacy of artists and artistic media (including her own) to reveal and dramatize the truths forgotten in the era of postmodern sublimity. The metaphors implied through the proximity of disparate images and text open new possibilities beyond the ideological. Perhaps it is only through heaping of words on top of one another, fragmenting or reconfiguring image and text that questions can emerge which underline the slippages that occur in normative discourse and point to something more.

So, for Soibhan Somerville, "Malagrino's photographs are never simply referential or documentary, but rather pose fundamental questions about the nature of evidence and documentary photography, about who controls what is seen and what is known" (1996). Through a process of variations, Malagrino often situates her work in the form of an installation which allows viewers to move between electronically generated images and text to conjure their own metaphorical interpretations. As to her art-making process, Malagrino states that it is, "an intuitive experience in which deeper connections are made on the unconscious and subconscious levels which result in images which have fresh symbolic relationships and offer expanded meanings" (in Inselmann 1997). Asserting that "one's interior world is not separate from one's social existence" (ibid.), Malagrino provides us word and image fragments which constitute an intertextual essay and lend our volume a fresh approach to such complex issues as representation and control.

It is, finally, significant that this part of our book and its examination of modernization trends before, during and after an intense period of Southern Cone repressive dictatorships, should conclude with a presentation which reminds of horrors which are not to be forgotten and are in some ways ever present even as we pursue newer trends of Latin American life and representation. It is in the context of such concerns that we can turn to the third part of our volume, which focuses on conceptualizing some of the literary and artistic matters alluded to or seen as part of the picture in the previous parts of our book. Here, the fallacy of Neil Larsen's view of postmodern cultural studies as a fetishization of culture over politics (cf. Larsen 1995) emerges most clearly--as it becomes quite evident that even those most concerned with specific artistic modes of representation see their work as illuminating and affecting, rather than being the end-alls of, more general social processes.

The section begins with Arturo Arias's consideration of Central America's changed situation in the "new world" order and his analysis of the contours of recent novelistic production in this context. The Central American perspectives are important because they are so patently missing in the other works on postmodernity cited throughout this introduction. The exception is Colás's book; and in this context, it is ironic how a Central American like Yúdice and Zimmerman's collaborator on Central American work, Beverley (1990), have tended to occlude or preclude a treatment of

Central America in their discussions of postmodern developments. And this is so, even though their analyses of testimonio-as-postmodern/subaltern/anti-literary discourse have centered on Rigoberta Menchú and other figures connected with recent Central American developments; and even though the efforts by Greg Dawes (1991, 1992) and others provided a context for heated discussion of the possible postmodern character of at least certain forms of Central American writing.

To be sure, the full onslaught of Latin American postmodernity can be dated perhaps not so much with the end of the Cold War, as with the Central American peace process itself, as symptomatic of the close of at least one historical phase of Latin America's conflictive relations with world capitalist hegemony. In this context, finally, how we may configure the continuing Chiapas and overall Mexican struggle as a part of a larger Meso-American drama and a kind of bridge between modern/postmodern, pre-globalization/full globalization phases of Latin American development is a matter that remains open to a full consideration which has not yet been fully attempted on the turf of post-postmodernist studies.

Arias's analysis anticipates such considerations even as he maintains a focus on literary developments. A key Guatemalan novelist, critic and social thinker himself, Arias has written fictional works which, among others, Claudia Ferman (1993) has seen as postmodern. Currently he and fellow novelist Mario Roberto Morales are the primary thinkers about their nation and area's processes of economic and cultural modernization, hybridization, and globalization and the implications of these processes for fiction itself.

In previous essays on Guatemalan and Central American fiction, Arias (see especially 1990b and 1991) focused on formal transformations and qualities that were symptomatic of struggles over modernization in Central America's fragile and vulnerable social formations. This essay is a followup to the other two, in which Arias's fascination with Bakhtin joins with Homi Bhabha, Terry Eagleton and, for Latin America, García Canclini and Doris Sommer, to establish a context for viewing the relation between socioeconomical and fictional transformations in the new historical epoch signalled by the Nicaraguan elections of 1990. Arias looks at the recent writing of Gioconda Belli, Sergio Ramírez, Luis de Lión, and other Central American writers to point toward recent postmodern trends; he suggests certain of the political implications generating and projected by the new formal developments. He thus provides a basis for deeper Central American work in the context of postmodernity and globalization, as well as a model for considering postmodern literary developments elsewhere in Latin America and the postcolonial Third World--a model that seems more deeply political and aesthetic than that found in much of the recent work on Latin American literary postmodernity (see above).

Important recent socially-centered studies of oppositional and specifically Latin American and U.S. Latino visual arts (e.g., Carol Becker, ed. 1994 and Shifra Goldman 1994) find expression in the next two essays in this section, by Elizam Escobar and Michael Piazza, who look at postmodernism from their unique angles as practicing artists with social and political commitments.

Escobar is an island and New York-bred Puerto Rican poet, artist and cultural theorist whose political activism in Chicago led to his incarceration several years ago. As one of the Puerto Rican POWs, he has been the object of an intense international anti-colonialist campaign for their release. During his years in prison Escobar has kept abreast of cultural and artistic developments and has been able to express his own, evolving radical stance and vision in a broad body of work, including his poetry and criticism, but above all his painting.

Piazza is a Chicago-based visual artist and art theorist long concerned with art's social connections, including those with Latin America (above all Central America and Puerto Rico as well as local Latino arts). He was drawn to Escobar's struggle and art several years ago; and the two have maintained a correspondence and interaction which have led to art shows and previous collaborative publications (cf. Escobar and the Axe Street Arena, ed. 1991)--even as they have developed in their own directions, with Piazza deepening his vision and elaborating a series of community-based projects, including ones with Latino artists and with institutionalized "problem children" and young adults.

Both artist/writers come to these pages as representatives of the kind of critical, postcolonial appropriation of postmodern perspectives to be found in the journal they most frequently cite here: *Third Text*, which has brought together original articles by such third world/subaltern studies-inflected critics like Gayatri Spivak and Rasheed Araeen, along with translations of Latin American cultural critics like Nelly Richard. It is *Third Text* but also the particular life and struggles of these two writers as artists confronting

19

the current, relativistic/pluralistic, politically tepid ambience of postmodern hegemony which distinguishes their concerns from the other, more academically oriented contributors to this volume--and makes their effort to constitute an left-activist appropriation of postmodern themes all the more striking and compelling.

Escobar is especially wary of postmodernism as the latest guise and continuation of bourgeois cultural domination with all its ramifications for artistic practice. In this respect, Escobar also points to the prestidigitation of terms which hearken "the end of history" and seek to guarantee the security of privileged social sectors, while trivializing the force of art as "continuation" and reducing it to mere "imitation" of life. Class conflict and praxis get lost among the multiple logics and ideologies of domination. As theorists attempt to develop adequate structures in which to describe certain situations, artists feel the shackles extending from those situations and must then struggle for some means of liberating action.

Drawing on Derrida, Foucault, Baudrillard and Spivak, as well as specifically Latin Americanist thinkers, Escobar seeks to maintain and promote the "subversive permanent force of the political of the imagination"--fending against directly ideological and political art on the one hand and empty formalistic and market art on the other hand--both of which phenomena he sees as aspects of what he has chosen to dub as "Echonarcissism." As noted earlier in this essay, he proposes an anti-theoreticist theory able to break through late capitalist structurations. Interestingly, he also manages to take up a debate between John Beverley and U. of Puerto Rico postmodernist professor Juan Duchesne which brings us back to questions of testimonio in Central America and elsewhere as part of the overall question of postmodernity. Finally, Escobar reveals the strong influence of radical Marxist philosopher Antonio Negri on his mode of anti-theoreticist theory and activism; while his interest in such Puerto Rican writers as Duchesne, and above all poet-critic Iván Silén, shows how he has kept in touch with island postmodern currents, which, manifest in the journal *Postdata* and more recently in *Nómada* and *Bordes*, both challenge and deepen the direction of his own "prison notebooks."

With regard to Elizam's participation in Puerto Rican postmodern discussions, *Postdata* editor Irma Rivera Nieves notes that his essay

exposes two debates and responds to them. In the first place it presents the debate over whether postmodernity really exists, as a superation of modernity's political, philosophical and historical agenda. In the second place, it analyzes the debate between two different conceptions of art: on the one hand, art as simple reflection of the material circumstances of life (as in the figure of Echo), and, on the other hand, art as eternal self-representation that continually desires and repeats itself (the figure of Narcissus). This is, nevertheless a feigned battle. Escobar responds to these debates ... in the first place, by posing the will of the artist expressed in the double possibility of ... a re-politicization of life by means of ever-renewed symbolic forms; and, parallelly, by situating the resubjectivization of the artist ... not only as creator, but also as interpreter of his or her own work. This proposal demands in and of itself, a renewed space for artistic autonomy beyond all possibility of cooptation of creative practice, whether scientific or philosophical. For Escobar, the antithesis modernity/postmodernity operates as a distraction from what is truly urgent for us: giving back to art its quality of danger. [1995: 37-38]

Piazza takes up the more general concerns expressed in Escobar's work and, applies them to the concrete political situation within the visual art world itself. Drawing on recent neo-Gramscian perspectives from Stuart Hall, Laclau and Mouffe and Nelly Richard, he looks to individual artists who are excluded or are said to have a "dependent" relation to hegemonic forces and how they struggle against them--artists who, as Coco Fusco pointed out in reference to young Cuban practitioners, "reject the implicit paternalism of the assumption that their borrowing [from the cultural dominant] is necessarily a symptom of dependency while similar gestures in the first world [supposedly] enrich the vocabulary of high art" (1988: 31-5).

Fully aware of the difficulties posed to resistance by postmodern theorizations, and aware nevertheless of a possible leftism emergent in postmodernism itself, Piazza begins to close the book's hermeneutic circle by emphasizing the praxis of art as an indirectly subversive mode which, even in the midst and as part of, postmodern cultural dominance, can and should enhance, as Marcuse said, "the power of estrangement and the radical, transcendent goals of change" (1978).

In words that may well sum up the work in this book, however varied the perspectives, approaches and dimensions entertained therein, Piazza argues that students of contemporary Latin American culture "must take advantage of the space opened in postmodern discourse and practice, and nurture the emergence of voices that had previously been silenced."

In our attempt to evoke the new voices and new strains that continue entering in the ongoing debate over Latin American realities and theorizations, we conclude the book with a final section, Final Subaltern (Intro)spections and (B)order Specifications. Here, the first voice (attempting to speak from, of, and about others) is that of Ileana Rodríguez, a Nicaraguan student of Caribbean basin literature whose own involvement in the Sandinista experience of a prior historical moment has led her to work with like-minded thinkers in forming a group which explores the Latin American applicability of Ranajit Guha's Subaltern Studies in the new era marked by the collapse of the traditional left in the face of the hegemony of neo-liberalism and globalizing "late capitalism." Polemical in their borrowings and transformations, Rodríguez's "notes from a subaltern underground" point to recent essays by Jameson that go beyond those cited previously in this volume and that serve as a bridge to current Latin American cultural studies and Rodríguez's own mode of theorization.

Considerable debate has raged about the applicability of Guha's theories to Latin America, and Rodríguez's essay here should stir the pot further as she makes claims which others will question. Can a theory constituted in relation to one postcolonial area be transposed, even with the most careful modifications, to another very different postcolonial area? Do Guha's post-structuralist (post-Gramscian and post-Maoist) decenterings of Marxist theory (from economics and politics to culture, from workers to peasants to "subalterns"--and do these terms even have the same meaning in one context or another?) really show the way to the resolution of the problems inherent in the older Marxisms' third world applications? Did Furtado really offer a response to Gunder Frank that was richer and more totalistic (shades of the old productionist-market debate between Dodd and Sweezy!)? Or is this a hangover CP "hardliner"/sixties view signalling a contradictory fidelity to older positions which may question or undermine subalternistas claims of theoretical renovation? Given Zimmerman's view of a kind of displaced "lack" in Foucault's eurocentric (and francocentric) take on modernization and the configuration of institutions and epistemes that constitute modern subjectiviites, can Foucault's thoughts on ungovernability feed properly into a theory of citizenship and, above all, social movements that points to viable future modes resistance in the Americas?

Finally do subaltern perspectives supplement and deepen the more "mainstream" (and postmodern) cultural studies contributions of García

Canclini, Richard, Sarlo and company, best represented in our text by Achugar's supposedly "Arielist" meditation; or does the subaltern focus, especially as it deconstructs governability and underlines deep strands of resistance, potentially with "post-Calibanic" political articulations, ultimately and decisively contradict and undermine the postmodern cultural studies project?

Rather than attempting to answer such questions definitively, we turn, instead, to a representative of the country of Rodríguez's subalternist inspiration, Kartik Vora, a Joseph Bueys enthusiast who witnessed the performance act of Coco Fusco and Guillermo Gómez-Peña posing as captive savages in a cage outside Chicago's Field Museum, and who then wrote the meditation which we reproduce here as a kind of coda to Rodríguez's essay and our overall book.

Like the border-crossings of Latin Americans into the Anglo-Latino world, the colonial re-enactment of Amerindian imprisonment and exploitation by Fusco and Gómez-Peña extended their concerns with postmodern, Latin American and Latino border discourses into the heart of the first world itself--and this by means of their performance art, which functions as what Appadurai (1996) has termed a "kind of 'transnational anthropology.'" By exploring their art and anthropology, Vora, with very little direct contact with the U.S. Latino experience, but writes an essay in which postcolonial and peripheral strains become central motives in a new world polyphonic order that some consider a cacophony brought about by the collapse of macro-narratives and utopian hope.

Several years ago, Nelly Richard (1987) had called attention to the danger of postmodern perspectives (including her own) with regard to Latin America, by asking how "third world intellectuals" might struggle against the tyranny of modernity if modernity and center/periphery discourse were already deconstructed--and if their geographic areas and problematics were ignored and absented in the process. García Canclini even took this problematic to the U.S.-Mexico border with his own major limitations (mainly the descriptive, fundamentally untheoretical nature of his nomadic hybridizations, re-articulations and reconversions) coming very much to the fore as his work on Tijuana (1989 and 1995) marked what some critics clearly interpreted as a Baudrillardian celebration of border miseries.

Along with Gómez-Peña and his collaborators, Gloria Anzaldúa, David Avalos and many other Mexican-U.S. border thinkers have sometimes underplayed inter-latino tensions and deep problems in their improvisations, incantations and celebrations of the borderland as a creative space for the forging of postcolonial New World mestizo/mestiza identities. Increasingly, they have had to see how the post-Cold War era has meant a heating up of ethnic enmities, frustrations and ires, leading to efforts to reinforce rather than to negate or deconstruct border walls and watches even as transnational and globalizing processes have developed.

The cultural studies orientation to postmodernity, globalization and the overall border paradigm would seem to involve an inherent minimalization of the brutality and violence over artificially constructed borders which continue to intensify daily. Indeed, as Vora's citation from Bhabha would seem to suggest, growing border violence demonstrates how problematics deconstructed in metropolitan macro-theory can remain quite real but are virtually immunized by the dynamics of postmodern debate; and it is presumably against this immunization that subaltern studies would seek to struggle. The relation of these matters of border theory addressed here (and in Welchman 1996) came forth with some force in a panel on the subject chaired by Chicano critic-artist Santiago Vaquera (with Marc Zimmerman as discussant) at the April 1997 Latin American Studies Association meeting in Guadalajara, Mexico.

At the same conference García Canclini insisted on the questions of border conflicts and crises as fundamental (but previously implicit) to his border vision; he also argued that the subaltern and the local could only have weight in relation to a grasp of overall social and cultural process. In conjunction with Rodríguez's essay and the perspectives set forth in this book, Vora's article may help readers to decide if García Canclini or the postmarxist subalternistas are right in their assessment of future relations among theoretical strands emergent in the Latin America's murky transition to a new millennium.

4. "The Visuals"

Music may well be one of the foods of Latin American/Caribbean love and life (see our Coda); but the visual arts (above all, architecture and the video clip), play a notoriously critical role in virtually all postmodern formations and formulations. The power of the "visuals" in this text stem from their capacity to address a critical potential or subversive level of symbolic exchange–from their ability to undermine, thwart, and question dominant ideological discourses at every turn. The visual art works represent various media--electronic digital montage, assemblage, bricollage, painting, photography, etc.--i.e., many of the forms which more readily translate into the print medium.

All of life may well be flux and flow. Nonetheless, phenomenologically, there is a need to fix images for a process of silent contemplation that leads to forming a poetic language of imagination and memory. When pushed to favor one art form over another, and thereby prioritize the senses, Surrealist poet André Breton paraphrased Poe's remark that "on his death bed, Mozart ... `began to see what might be accomplished in music'" (Breton 1936: 10).

In a sense, European ideology is still being played out in the arena of aesthetics. The visual arts took form and were institutionalized as an ideological control and power over the sensate body and the overall cultural landscape. Positioned between sociability and sublimity (I and Non I), plastic expression achieves its value precisely in its indeterminacy and again recalls Marcuse's utopian hope that the radicality of given art works will emerge and persist in spite of the fact, so accutely affirmed by Adorno, that once articulated, the works are generally accommodated and subsumed within ever-evolving hegemonically dominant discourses--and even claimed as part of those discourses--in "the commodification of critique." Thus, dominant discourses or master narratives give way to micro-narratives which appear as critical but are in turn often realigned in neo-hegemonic formations. However there are poetic potentialities that escape discursive logic and logistics--the illogical gesture, the confounding of binary boundaries in the dialectical overcoming of commodification and encapsulation and in the articulation of radically oppositional discourse.

Instead of being subordinated responses, reflexes of formalizations, supplements or adornments of verbal-centered texts, the works we present are haphazard and dangerous acts which initiate their own theoretical terrain and add critical weight, stress and, yes, strain to prevailing ideologies in the dialectical play of freedom on every imaginable front: critical transculturation beyond acculturation; empowered popular culture intervening in mass culture; collaboration in multiple authorship; interdisciplinary performative tactics opened by postmodern hegemony.

Perhaps all of this is being played out in the realm of the conceptual--in the imaginary--shaking up and frustrating the tyranny of the ideological. But here is the significance and very purpose of the imaginary as it projects historical becoming: a sutured bricollage of thought which transverses the specialized Cartesian categories making their divisions and boundaries inconsequential--an alternative rational or irrational set against the rationale and irrationale of domination.

As artists became disillusioned with highculture modernity or the hegemony of micro-narrative, there still needs to be a more viable approach in face of various poststructuralist, postmarxist, postcolonial and feminist positionings. The need persists for new articulations, new interconnections that can accommodate diversity, or raise questions about our (ir)rational conjugations of concerns, tactics, solutions and meanings. By the artist's use of every medium available, new theory pushes onto the terrain of the non-utopian present beyond individual and collective visions and dreams.

These and similar matters outlined in relation to Malagrino's intertextual essay discussed above can be seen in the works by other artists that appear and indeed give depth to this volume. Many of the images the artists provide deal with the body as it relates to controlled space including the ideological and cognitive underpinnings of mapping as a mechanism of domination and ownership. It may well be that divisions become blurred further, that contradictions add more weight, as printed matter interfaces with electronic media such as the internet.

Two images by Diana Solís, a Chicago-based Mexican photographer and writer (as well as a recent student of Malagrino and Esther Parada), bookend the text proper (see the images following the dedication and closing Part IV) with an old map of the Great Lakes area as charted and demarcated by early French explorers and projected onto the face and body ("Untitled 1") and the legs and feet ("Untitled 2") of a woman. Examining these two works, as well as Solís's overall "Interstices" photo installation, artist-critic Bertha Husband argues that Solís fends against rather than celebrates postmodern fragmentation. Her work is a "mediation about different relations and separations; fissures between imposed frontiers"; it involves matters very much related to contemporary postcolonial discourse (1997: 16). Though the viewer may be unsure as to the subject's European or indigenous origin, the images we present raise questions about conquest, relocation, extermination, migration, and submission.

Above all, Solís's own image appropriation recognizes, examines and ultimately critiques the material and ideological power inherent in geographical mapping--a power imposed and inscribed on American subjectivities and identities. In the two images we present, Solís draws on recent technological innovations associated with postmodern orientations; but to some degree she refuses to be fully caught up in, or restricted by, postmodernity's problematic referentiality and its more trendy art practices, still keeping faith with techniques rooted in Mexican and Chicano, Mexico and Chicago, realities. Indeed, for Husband, Chicago is a place where "cultural divisions[,] ... differences [and] fragmentations" emerge "with great ... emphasis" (ibid.: 17).

If modernity caged the imagination in printed texts and their structured worlds, so, as if to break with print world domination, Piazza's "Method" draws on a news story about the recent discovery of Che Guevara's handless remains and attempts to reread Che's *Guerrilla Warfare* without (how does one turn the pages?) the use of hands. Meanwhile, Esther Parada's "Native Fruits" involves superimposed images and texts, superimposed racial and cultural identifications, superimposed historical times, and, at least implicitly, superimposed life modes and ideological constructs.

Specifically, "Native Fruits" overlays older representations onto a photograph taken when Parada was in Cuba in 1984. She juxtaposes all this with quotations from the 1892 World's Fair Columbian Exposition in Chicago. The authorial voice points to a time of optimism and righteousness unable to look beyond its ideological biases. Truth was inherent in the written word, in rational thought processes addressing and determining issues; but of course truth was only a reflection of a confirmed bias in the service of domination.

By putting a strain on older prevailing rationales through a reassembling of elements, Parada aims at disassembling still-prevailing notions. Crucial to her work is her use of computer technology to digitally generate her photographic and multiply manipulable images. Perhaps the vertigo of potential options associated with this process is in itself metaphoric of present life complexities. Decisions thus limit euphoric potentials leaving one anxious in lieu of other possibilities, all of which are suspiciously restricted and perhaps damaging. We are left in a state of catatonic immobility as if decisions are generated through uncertainty and a fear of mistakes.

27

As for computerized image transmission, we present the home page of the Montividean Museo Virtual de Artes, a project created by Uruguayan art critic and curatorAlicia Haber which has received countless awards including the fifth International Website Competion in Mexico City (1997). Similarly Raúl Quintanilla transmits his "Tripping con Colón" via the established website for *Artefacto*, a Nicaraguan journal of art and writing. The image is an installation which includes a hanging bird cage and hints at the domestication of the "new world" by Columbus. *Artefacto* with its connotations of human endeavor, anthro-pological specimen, or fuse for an explosive device, is a group of Nicaraguan artist dedicated to a critical stance visavis the new dominant (dis)order of transnational capital and globalization. The ironic discrepancies between the staggeringly poor economic conditions existing alongside the availability of sophisticated computer technology are being played out in Nicaragua as well as in the rest of the world. The *Artefacto* group is staking a claim in virtual reality turf as a form of critical transculturation which points up the inherent contradictions of the medium itself. The cage continues its "tripping" around the world as a configuration of bits circulating through fiber optics and looking for a terminal port of entry.

Our emphasis on photo and electronic images in the context of an analysis of divisions and fragmentations should not be understood as giving less weight to more seemingly traditional art forms or suggesting that such forms cannot or are not used to generate important cultural effects and responses.

Discussed somewhat in Piazza's essay, Cuban artist José Bedía draws on long-established methods to present his quest for self-realization in a world which problematizes subject and investigation narratives. In "Llega al pie," we are presented with the traces of a figure that is walking or has walked across a large terrain attempting to come to terms with various cultural, political, and spiritual issues that must be grappled with. Then too, Piazza's essay presents works by Julian Schnabel, Eduardo León, Elizam Escobar and Jimmie Durham which reiterate perspectives found in other visual work in the book--though here we should simply add that the way Durham inscribes words of the colonizer on a lifesize cutout portrait of himself is at least somewhat parallel to how Solís maps over a body or how Gómez-Peña writes "Don't Discover Me" on his own chest (see below).

28

Although known for his large canvases, Elizam Escobar also experiments with other media. He reconfigures his own face on photographs taken of him in prison as an exploration of domination through a poetic erasure of authority. In "Heurística uno" and "El terrorista," Escobar uses the avenues available to him within the restrictions of the penal institution while subverting the rules (in this case photos to be sent home to loved ones) to create turbulent self images. There are of course other, more complex and painful modes of interpreting Escobar's portraiture in relation to Puerto Rico's insertion in postmodern consumption patterns and discourse which has simultaneously fascinated and troubled him. Thus according to fellow Puerto Rican Carlos Gil, co-founder of *Postdata*:

> What sums up these terrible [works] of Escobar is ... transfixion, a dual act that can signify the overcoming, or the impossibility, of fixation, in time. The central problem of the work of Escobar ... is the problem of time. [1995: 238]

For Gil and other Puerto Rican postmoderns, the new cultural dominant means the end of the island's macro-narratives of independence and nation-building seen as a utopia in the name of which one resisted U.S. powers of hegemonic cooptation. So, his view of Escobar's problem:

> Escobar has been deprived of his liberty for the last fourteen years. But there is a suffering even greater than this a dimensionless suffering because it lacks the profundity which consolation provides; a unidimensional suffering, a flat suffering: that of the loss of utopia.... But why has this incredible thing happened to Elizam Escobar, to him, alleged member of the FALN, standard bearer of a prefiguration of a better world, a future of transparency.... Because the utopia of Elizam Escobar, the utopia of our generation, lost its time and the clock kept ticking.... And it was not a question of time as an empty sequence... but the time of the martir, the time of prefiguration. [ibid.]

In relation to the goals of this volume, it is pertinent to note that Escobar sees his fate and function in ways quite different from those which Gil and others have articulated. Escobar refuses to be limited or imprisoned within a discourse which credits a particular enunciation of his only to the degree it can be construed as being in conformity with postmodern practices. For him, sitting, pacing, reading and creating in his prison cell, the emergence of postmodernist perspectives and their particular Puerto Rican turn has represented a fascinating adventure and challenge, raising questions which he has felt he has had to answer, and challenges he has had to meet.

Dealing with postmodernity has become this prisoner's mode of being in the world, his mode of freedom as artist and intellectual, militant and human being. Thus he has been able to enter the discussion and sustain positions.

If, as in the case of Juan Duchesne and others (1997), the logic of Puerto Rican postmodernity leads to a renunciation of nationalist and independentista positions and the assumption of a posture designated as "radical statehood," Escobar has positioned himself to be able to critique this stance and answer with his own (cf. his three-part essay on this matters in *Claridad*, summer 1997).

To bring these matters fully home to Chicago, we introduce Kartik Vora's essay with a collage image, "Caged--Sin Fronteras," combining two works by Chicago Chicano artist and poet, Carlos Cortez, of the Movimiento Artístico Chicago (MARCH), the very Chicago Latino Arts organization which has taken this project under its wing (see the final note in this book). What we have are a woodcut and collage that Cortez prepared for us in relation to Fusco and Gómez-Peña's Chicago visit of 1993; but the two images are further collaged and subjected to superimpositions by Michael Piazza in his search for a signifying field related to the other images and issues in our text. In the parodic mode of Cortez's Chicago Mexican imaginary, the Afro-Cuban features of Fusco are rendered as an Indian icon, squat and stout. Fusco, much taller than Gómez-Peña, becomes shorter even when he's sitting down. The Mexican male looms large in his transformation as a gendered indigenous presence. Piazza plays with the image, provides variations on sizes and dimensions as an expression of Chicago postmodern logic and his search for an image which can represent Latino border art and the contribution Fusco and Gómez-Peña make (through the mediation of Vora, Cortez and MARCH) to this Chicago-centered book.

It is in this context that Piazza's "Oceanic Perspectives," may be said to frame but also contend with all the other images in the text--as well as with other possible interpretations of the images. In its initial presentation and fragmented reappearances, Piazza's piece highlights Latin America's cartographic inscription in relation to the themes of measure, scale and identity that are indeed central to contemporary postmodern and globalization theory and to every section of this book. Piazza uses a dangling perspective device which attempts to get a fix on a location somewhere between Sicily and Cuba from a stack of maps that float on a field of oceanic blue. The maps are a metaphor for control of the unknown both real and imaginary. Projections of terrain is in this sense related to projections onto the body which lead ultimately to the domestication of the anthropophagi cyclops who were once said to inhabit Sicily, to the domestication of Calibán in the Caribbean.

Piazza's images and indeed all the graphics and essays in this volume are presented as a heterogeneous but somehow unified answer to the collapse of utopian thinking, and to the distortions of vision by those who no longer can feel secure with their earlier points of view. The overall combination of materials constitutes an effort, then, to grasp past and present with realism but also humor--an intent, as well, to move in the direction of reconstructive action.

5. Coda

Of course, the new spatialities of postmodern thought traverse and at times deny the very borders between theory and application, social sciences and the humanities, linguistic and visual discourse, that seem to undergird this volume. In this sense, to the degree that the borders between disciplines, forms of knowledge and discourses continue to exist and guide the structuration of materials presented herein, our own discourse may be said to belong to a conceptual universe that is coming to its end even as we transcribe these words or are ventriloquized to enunciate the cultural dimensions of our present field of study. In this emergent post-postmodernist moment of new or effaced borders and nomadic logistics, in the new world order with its new world strains, [dis]orders and (dis)harmonies, a critique of this book could well center on the supposed periodizing shift from a modern to a postmodern sentiment that Achugar evokes in his description of periphery/center relationships of power, as well as in his treatment of the utopian impulse. From that point, one might challenge the wholesale use of the concept of postmodernism, especially by particular segments of the left intelligentsia worldwide, to show how its origins in European thought of the sixties relate to the current debates over

31

the concept in specific areas of the world, and especially in Latin America. In this regard such early critiques like those by Callinicos (1989) and Norris (1990 and 1992) were useful, if overly reductive, in helping thinkers to grasp the dangers of wholeheartedly embracing postmodernism.

It seems imperative, then, to note that most of the materials presented in the essays that constitute this volume were drafted pre-NAFTA and pre-Chiapas; they represent a moment, shared by Jorge Castañeda's *Utopía desarmada* (1993) in which the end of the cold war confirmed postmodernity's marginalization of Latin America and when the struggle for neoliberal or more deeply participatory democracies spelled a virtual decline in revolutionary possibilities and theories as understood in an earlier period. NAFTA and other economic integration projects constituted the means to put Latin America once again on the U.S. cognitive map; but NAFTA also fed quite specifically into the rebellion which while evidently postmodern (since the goal was not a question of state power but a negotiation of political space) at least problematized postmodernity's questioning of standard and Marxist theories of resistance.

Reference to these matters leads us to some final notes about globalization--first that globalization perspectives have already overtaken postmodernity itself as the center of theoretical debate even at the cultural level (cf. King, ed. 1991; Robertson 1992; Featherstone, Lash and Robertson, ed. 1995; and Appadurai 1996) and in the Latin American turf itself (cf. García Canclini 1995b and García Canclini, ed. 1996); and second, within this context, contemporary studies by García Canclini and others do not indicate any narrowly conceived homogenization of culture. This position, alluded to by Beverley and Oviedo in the introduction to their collection with Aronna (1995), and also by Appadurai throughout his book, is well articulated by Santiago Colás (1994: 10-12) under the rubric of "dynamic heterogeneity." Drawing on economic and social theorists from Marx to Michael Speaks and Arturo Escobar, Colás develops an argument which he sees as running contrary to Jameson's Adorno-like vision of a postmodern cultural homogeneity against which third world narratives and actions stand as last gasp modes of resistance:

Capital requires differences, an exterior, to survive. If contemporary capital has consumed all difference, then it will, in effect, run out of gas. But ... capitalism engages in a constant self-refueling. As it consumes difference in one place, it regenerates it elsewhere. [10]

32

In effect, heterogeneity, otherness and difference are necessary for the expanded reproduction of capital. Capitalism can only thrive on the commodification of varied use values. Most pointedly, the most varied areas of Latin America will continue to count on the reproduction of otherness for tourist and export dollars as well as social ordering, just as U.S. capital has counted on racial, ethnic and cultural differentiation in its division of labor. Ironically now, otherness can only have weight and can only survive within the circuit of capital--that is, as "cultural capital." This term itself cannot be taken in uncritically as some kind of economistic reduction of cultural practice. However, it points to the accumulated repository of possibilities from which new political scenes and scenarios can develop. In this sense, such notions as transnationalization, globalization and post-colonialism, post-Marxism and postmodernism do not imply the erasure of colonialism, neo-colonialism, imperialism and Marxism, but rather their re-articulation in relation to new global and local interrelations.

To be sure, "hybridization," "deterritorialization," and other terms that are part of the recent arsenal of Latin American cultural studies are not innocent of existing relations and hierarchies of power and control, no matter how transformed they may be by new post-Cold War and post-dictatorial contexts. Those new contexts, however characterized, may well imply that the commodification of otherness, while fully dangerous, offers a space for oppositional articulation otherwise not available. In this sense, as globalization increases, so do the spaces for potential resistance; new social movements may emerge and lead to crises in civil society and citizenship, in governability and, yes, hegemony. Chiapas registers the first post-NAFTA note of discord in the new world disorder. And what of the rest of Latin America and the hemisphere?

The themes articulated throughout the book engage Latin American specificities in terms of controversies that will repeat and echo as this century comes to an end and as Gómez-Peña's "new world (b)order" continues to configure itself on the horizon of our fears and expectations. As such this book can provide no comfortable answers to the questions it raises; but the questions themselves will help to frame the discussions which will continue on into the future. It is relation, finally, to Jameson's evocation of Van Gogh's modernist shoes and the feet, walking, mapping, and bodying that this book makes its most significant contribution. So our book goes beyond its own parameters and points to the kind of globalistic logic required by recent developments; so it joins in the music of contemporary discourse in an effort to find some remedies for the strains and veritable pains of the postmodern condition, to find some new keys, some new strains and even (is it plausible?) some dynamic harmonies, that may be part of this world's future music and its non-homogeneous but thoroughly globalized cultural directions. In this sense, perhaps, our book is transitional, as it reconfirms but also renegotiates its spatial and visual emphasis, so much the "cultural dominant" of cosmopolitan postmodernity; and even as it draws on and then transforms a musical conceit that, as in the cases of Benítez Rojas's book and the *Polifonía salvaje* collection from Puerto Rico, may well represent an Afro-Latino rearticulation internal to our overall positioning in the Latin American debates over the applicability of postmodern. post-colonial and globalization theories.

34

I. Theorizing Specificities

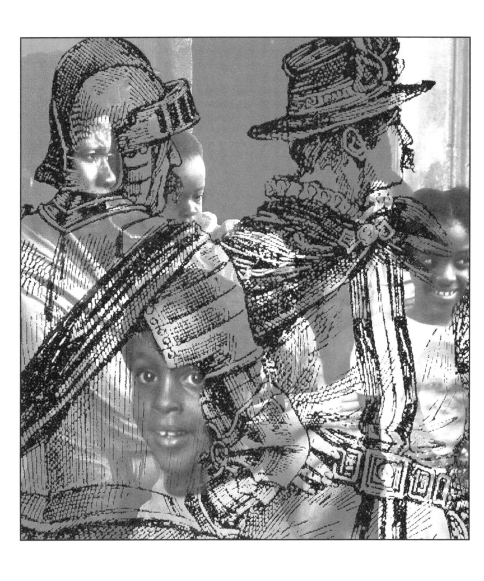

"While lying at anchor in LaCruz (Cuba) Columbus was visited by many natives who manifested the same friendly disposition as those whom he first met..

"It was not til the last quarter of the 18th century that England, who never surrenders, surrendered to her own, thus losing   the mortification of failure in the proud reflection that she alone could produce the race that could conquer her.... Then it was that the New World opened wide its golden gates — a virgin hemisphere — and presently to the continent for whose discovery Italy had lent the patient explorer and Spain the vital succor, England brought her contingent of a sturdy race...."

...and generously supplied the expedition with fruits...."

LATIN AMERICA, LATINOS AND POSTMODERNITY: FRAMES OF REFERENCE AND POINTS OF ENTRANCE

Marc Zimmerman

1. Postmodernist Counter-Hegemony

In recent debates about the present and future of Latin America, there is no doubt but that the new post-structuralist and postmodernist discourses have had a crucial role to play. One only has to leaf through the first issue of Nelly Richard's *Revista de Crítica Cultural* (May 1990) published in Santiago de Chile to have an idea of how the discussion throughout the first half of this decade would go. There we have Néstor García Canclini speaking of the transformations of Latin American culture through a look at situations on the border between Mexico and the U.S.; there are also articles by Beatriz Sarlo, Hugo Achugar and Julio Ortega on transitions in their own countries. There's a key interview with José Joaquín Brunner about the Chilean transformation, as well as an article on women in the transition by Adriana Valdés. Almost all contributions speak of postmodernity, post-dictatorship, post-Marxism.

Just to cite three symptomatic examples:

1.) Postmodernity is for some the exhaustion of Marxism and the necessity of a new social and economic pact which achieves a certain version of modernization in the country. For others, on the other hand, it is a problem belonging to postindustrial societies that has little to do with the underdeveloped reality of Latin America.... It is a question of a grey, mediocre, middle class desperation, which... emerges... as an effect which the economic crisis, dictatorship and the lack of a dynamic project have produced in the dreams of the average citizen. [Achugar 1990a: 18]

2.) In Latin America, the discussion of postmodernity can help us to reconsider, with greater intellectual rigor, our most contemporary theme, which is that of modernity in peripheral conditions, of the international market, of the crisis of the populist state, of cultures in process of massification, of emergent democracies.... We find ourselves now, in a situation in which the multiple social rationalities can no longer unify themselves under one sole discourse, whether it be that of progress, that of communism or that of religion. [Brunner 1990: 25]

3.) For a radical democracy, it is necessary to amplify the political horizon; and amplify it even beyond the political order of the segmented left, moving us toward a practice of democratic (egalitarian, emancipatory, solidary) relations in everyday life... In the economy of discourse, a radical democracy recognizes the necessary diversity of positions; it exercises an inclusive will of persuasion which supposes a plural subject, not one singular discourse, and that promotes mutual tolerance; it awaits from the new cultural agents (women, ethnic groups, marginals) a renewed enunciation of demands. [Ortega 1990: 27]

Several years later, it has of course become a commonplace to argue that postmodern perspectives have penetrated the cultural discourse of key Latin American intellectuals and that dimensions of the postmodern have penetrated mass and even popular culture, so that Latin America, however unevenly, is simultaneously continuing its struggle to enter modernity and to resolve all the problems which its "peripheral history" of dependency, underdevelopment and oppression has imposed at the same time that it has had to relate to and deal with imperatives stemming from the overlays of postmodern culture and ideology as they became part and parcel of Latin American thinking and being. The difficulties in configuring structures of socio-economic and cultural domination are compounded by those in configuring the specificities of subalternity and viable resistance.

The first question arising from these circumstances is that of the transformation of theoretical frames with which they might be examined. And here, ironically, we have had to face the fact that postmodernist cultural penetration has been increasingly studied in terms of postmodern perspectives and theorizations which predetermine the results. What this implies is a critical distancing by most of the cultural left from older perspectives such as dependency theory and Althusserianism, and the virtual hegemony of the post-discourse in the taking on of theoretical perspectives which, no matter how one might criticize this or that aspect, ultimately find their symptomatic expression or basis in the work of Ernesto Laclau and Chantal Mouffe (1985) and/or Gilles Deleuze and Félix Guattari.

Ironically, the linkages forged by Fredric Jameson (1984) between Lyotard's *Postmodern Condition* (1984) and Mandel's *Late Capitalism* (1978) and then Jameson's effort to move from this equation to one between a Mandelian-Wallersteinian view of peripheral social formations and a perspective on "Third World" cultural production (and particularly narrative) as part of a largescale cultural or "cognitive" mapping, have been widely criticized as far too mechanistic, far too caught up still in an ultimate base/superstructure formulation, far too caught up in an ultimate economism and compensatory "third world romanticism," then, to provide a fully satisfactory frame for understanding Latin American phenomena. Nevertheless, some of the core bridgework has indeed held; and Latin American variations have at least been sketched out (cf. Larsen 1991, Yúdice 1992, and Colás 1994, etc.).

Contemporary discourse on the status of peripheral formations and the articulation of politics therein has required rethinking earlier historical phases and of course the older categories. Here, we can think of the catalogue of core texts cited in the introduction to this book. Above all, the question is one ultimately of agency and its potential articulation into actual politics. And here, as well, the usual complaints: what could postmodernism mean in a world which has not experienced full modernization--if not the complete ascendancy of a mode of ideological domination? "We haven't even experienced nationhood when they claim that nation-centeredness is another false logo-centrism," so many Latin Americans have complained. It is certainly dangerous to be seduced by new critical languages, new definitions which may have a very different meaning and effect in underdeveloped countries than they do in developed ones. Nevertheless there is *little* possibility of resistance unless hegemonic patterns are acknowledged and engaged.

In earlier Marxist formulations, alienation in the guises of commodity fetishism and more general reification were simultaneously symptoms of the development of productive forces that could lead to their supersession (or *Aufgehebung*) in revolutionary consciousness. However, we should no longer have many illusions on this score. Reification, or whatever more postmodern name we give to the diffuse, endlessly transformable but seemingly unchangeable refunctioning and rearticulating of signs and simulacra that characterize Baudrillard's vision of contemporary life provides no clear mechanisms for creative resistance and transformation. We no longer have illusions about a lost plenitude to which we can return; we no longer can project an alienated species being or sing praises to supposedly less alienated modes of being under one or another precapitalist system. We could speak of alienation from future possibilities. However, we would have to locate the bases for our sense of future, knowing that the ubiquitous processes by which we replicate structures of hegemony in no way imply a clear possibility of resisting or transforming social frustration and disarray, when indeed the very sites of resistance now seem, as Nelly Richard (1991) tells us, part of the very system against which those suffering under it are contending.

In the 1990s, when the dreams of the grand narratives of global Marxist or dependency theories, national liberation struggle and happy socialism are all but fading into a nebulous horizon, when nothing seems external to or able to resist the system of constraints, when nationalist illusions persist in the third world only to combine with postmodernist patterns of transculturation and transformation, we are still seeking a framework which provides a consideration of past, present and future offering some possibility for transformative change.

The cultural arena is a key one--not a completely hopeful one but the site of some of the few hopes we might still foster. On this front now, instead of decrying transculturation as another word for acculturation, we accede to the inevitable and seek positive moments and possibilities in the pores of what we used to call (with such blithe spirit) "cultural imperialism." We speak of struggles over semiotic appropriation, consumption and re-signification; we point to hegemonic oppositions with respect to expressive and communicative systems (including the mass media, etc.). We point to how globalizing and transnational trends point to new scenarios for subaltern social movements and even class-based or class-inflected struggles.

Of course some are bored by a kind of romantic search for oppositions and oppositional discourse structures in the pores of a capitalism that has now achieved a new stage of power and determination. There are also some who in function of one or another posture would debunk all the new postmodernist and "culturalist" theorizations that seem indeed "relativist and effete" in their utter fragmentation and lack of any grounding (cf. Larsen 1995). The means to analyze the cultural field, its multiple positions and contradictions, its yet-to-be-constituted sources of action require us to rethink the fundamental terms of our critique and our engagement.

And why should we continue to seek looking for such theorizations and solutions? Why do we keep hovering around Marx in any event? Why in spite of all the characterizations of contemporary society, in terms of information and other technologies, in terms of whatever else one might point to, do many of us, at least, continue to return to seeing it as capitalist in terms that are not too remote from those Marx used? And why do we look for solutions down the roads Marx suggested we go?

Very simply because the problems of socio-economic and particularly what Marx came to call "capitalist" development persist and have in fact deepened; precisely because the world's prospects for human pain, human destruction and human exploitation persist, even as the critique of sources and possible solutions created, at least in previous twentieth century formulations, problems at least as great as the system they purportedly opposed. Furthermore these problems persist when, as we have noted, in the postmodernist scheme of Late Capitalism, Latin America and the so-called "third world" have less importance than in the previous period of revolutionary hope and seeming possibility. The matters at hand then are of great importance for those concerned with future hopes and possibilities, when the vision of continental blight is indeed quite credible, and the need to seek possibilities that lead to a better future has become a matter of life and death for far too many.

2. *The Quick Decline and Rise of Latin America in the New World Order*

In the macro-political changes signified by the end of the Cold War, as well as in the theorization of the contemporary world marked by the emergence of postmodernist critique, what we have come to call "the third world," and particularly Latin America has been redesignated as an area of less importance. This leads to the feeling of abandonment noted in the first section of the Introduction above--a feeling especially strong in those places like Grenada or Panama where the U.S. intervened, virtually without effectual opposition. Middle-Eastern and more recently domestic problems have been center-stage in the U.S. and elsewhere; newspaper coverage of Latin America consists of events, with little sense of process.

With respect to the theoretical question, Lyotard's critique first of all specifies the end of narrative and narrative logic resulting from the rise of information technologies. In this sense, postmodernism replicates a first world/third world dichotomy that is greater than in previous historical moments, though here it should be further noted that the dichotomy also spreads to questions of class and gender in each geo-political space. Second, the end of master narratives spells the end of modernizing myths (capitalist and socialist) which had seemed to represent paths for Latin America's future. Revolution is less imaginable in terms of geo-political dominations, and it is less possible, also because in terms of postmodern constructs (here, reshuffling Parsonian logistics), resistances tend to contribute to the functioning, rather than the overturning, of hegemonic systems. In addition, in a world dominated by technology and communications, those countries, peoples, and groups less advanced in these fields will tend to lag further and further behind, ever becoming recipients and yes, potential victims, of forces not generated by, and therefore frequently foreign to, their own geo-political space and state (but not *stage*, because such heuristic devices as periodization categories may no longer exist) of development.

While reception may never be passive (as it tends to be in the older models of cultural and communicative imperialism as generated by Schiller, Dorfman and Mattelart, etc.), and while postmodernist-influenced theorists reject the over-simplistic dichotomy of authentic original and inauthentic influence, nevertheless, in postmodern circumstances and the ever-greater difficulties of "catching up with" or countering an ever-expanding dominion of "first world" technocratic culture, the so-called third world (now denied even easy access to being so named or categorized) is more inclined to produce elite/urban social sectors gradually deprived of their original tribal and geographic cultural bases and now relatively in tune with the changing world and a social mass which, no matter how diversified in ethnic, class and other dimensions, persists in an otherness dominated, regulated or encapsulated by postmodern patterns which neutralize or diminish the significance of their alterity.

The peripheral status accorded the varying polities constituting Latin America means less potential capacity for producing autonomously functioning systems and states. The fragility and vulnerability of Latin American social formations tend to make them open for penetration and intervention. Now, under current post-war circumstances, Latin America is more subject than ever before to postmodern interventions. Thus in a world of image proliferation and copying, Latin America, like other parts of the "third world" is primarily reduced to producing copies of copies, simulacra of simulacra. We are thus into an area of critique most articulated by Nelly Richard in Chile (1988), Roberto Schwarz in Brazil (1992) and, most particularly, Beatriz Sarlo in Argentina (1994).

Now, when according to contemporary orientations, the metropolitan countries have been relegated to the margins which ontologically and epistemologically only the underdeveloped countries occupied before, now the previously marginal, rather than entering as full participants in the functioning of contemporary life, tend to lose the very edge for marginal oppositionality which they previously held.

The threat of revolution, the return of the repressed, the rebellion of the mimic men and women, the revolt of the subaltern, etc., etc., have apparently faded; and the bases upon which forms of oppositionality or resistance, and the political articulation thereof have seemed virtually unforeseeable if not genuinely untenable given current patterns of hegemonic control and acceptance and, what may be more alarming, given the ideological inability at this present historical juncture to think and imagine beyond the given.

To be sure, the very decline in Latin America's significance in the overall system during a period of globalization was the basis for the effort to formalize transnational processes in terms of the North American Treaty Agreement and other, related trends or intents throughout Latin America. New economic relations potentiate political and cultural modes of conformation and resistance, with the Chiapas rebellion in Mexico perhaps signalling the kinds of movements and directions that will emerge in the next century.

In these circumstances, we seem to have two dominant tendencies emerging from among those who persist as "left" ideologues. First, there is the persistent effort by figures like Hernán Vidal and Neil Larsen (in Beverley, Oviedo and Arrona 1995) to show that the current episteme is merely a mirage of capital, and that the older concerns with class, politics and revolutionary parties, presently lost in an acceptance of the new controlled, "limited" or "delegated" democracies, of a post-revolutionary ethos and a rejection of previously vaunted struggles against cultural imperialism, are still absolutely valid even if requiring some adjustment in the present period. Second, there is the position of those who feel that, while class and politics are still viable concerns, still they are so radically transformed in the current period that they may no longer be explored according to their older categorizations and pathways.

These matters are explored in depth in my book, *Tropicalizing Hegemony* (1998). But here let me state that my own position, to a degree shared by critics like Yúdice (1992) and Beverley (1995), is that old politics and political epistemes failed in the Third World and Latin America; and that it is just as likely that they are virtually bankrupt, as it is that they just need some creative tinkering. We are basically in accord in asserting that whatever validity there may be in the dangers that the critics point to, their arguments are structured in terms of conceptions that are no longer operative. Our perspective is also not to deny economic inequalities as fundamental in Latin America, but to deny that articulation of class constitutes the fundamental or only fundamental basis of oppression and struggle in Latin America, to deny that Marxism is the only basis of oppositional or even revolutionary energies.

The question for me ultimately is not whether or to what degree Marxism may be helpful in understanding and transforming the current cultural field, but whether a given theory or body of theories can grasp Latin American processes in such a way as to change them in a direction that is more affirmative for human survival and development. This could mean class struggles, gender or ecological struggles. Marxism should not be assumed as the end all of analysis even if it remains an important contributant to overall critique.

Before, all modes of thought, what was valid or useful in them useful in them. totalized inevitably in Marxism. This was the strategy of Fernández Retamar in his critique of Latin American and Caribbean resistance, of Martí and other non-Marxist currents; and it was the strategy of many of us of the Latin Americanist left: to appropriate what was valuable in Martí, Sandino or Mariátegui, as a contribution toward the truly proper critique (ours!). The standard procedure was much the same: Complain bitterly about Eurocentrism. Attack the reactionary or "aestheticist" and elitist *criollo* intelligentsia, etc. But what critique could be more Eurocentric than one rooted in a European Marxism that could not adequately explain Europe, let alone any place else? How can we construct Latin American versions of world theoretical frames? By denying authentic/inauthentic, European/Latin American dichotomies and looking for the obscured truncated and distorted possibilities for radical opposition.

The new critique is not easy to come by. The elements of the present leading toward some dynamic, hopeful future are not at all clear in the present juncture. Yet exploration and speculation must continue until some valid roads are discovered. It is in this context that the sections which follow are dedicated--those dealing with questions of Latin American popular culture and literature, and even of U.S. Latino culture and literature, as sites for potential subaltern resistance and new historical becoming. Of these latter areas, our comments here should help indicate their points of insertion in the overall discussion of social theory, postmodernity and popular culture in Latin America.

3. Calibán and Changes in Cultural Production

A key aspect of contemporary research on Latin American development and modernization, as well as oppositional projects, has been the effort to try characterizing certain of the essential changes in Latin American cultural life since the installation of the dictatorships and the petroleum crisis in the early the 1970s, when a new context began to emerge. From this point on, efforts directed toward revolution or other modes of social renovation were structured and limited, at least in part, by the inexorable costs of development, the overwhelming reality produced by debt crisis and the search for alternative economic and government models, especially as the search reached its extreme in the wake of the reasserted U.S. ambition, articulated by Ronald Reagan, to restore and reassert its hegemony throughout all that was considered to be its "sphere of influence."

Especially in the wake of renewed U.S. hegemony, affecting the Central American countries where dimensions of Cuban revolutionary culture lived on the 80s in relation to liberation theology and other forces of resistance, the new processes in progress throughout most of Latin America implied a rupture with the overtly anti-imperialist and anti-bourgeois cultural models which emerged in the course of the Cuban Revolution. The new transformations have not necessarily reflected old dichotomies of left/right, national/cosmopolitan, etc.; rather they have signaled the growing consolidation of a new socio-political macrostructure.

The ethos generated by the Cuban revolution and dispersed throughout the Latin American world in the 1960s and into the 1970s has been greatly modified by newer currents that emerged in the region and have come to dominate the times. But to speak of "change" and a "move away from" an older revolutionary cultural model, it would do well to recall and articulate here however so briefly what indeed that model was, what orientation toward Latin American culture was embedded in the Cuban Revolution, what role culture and its theorization played in the Revolution and its consolidation, and what effect these matters had on Latin America and on those who would be called upon to characterize and theorize Latin American culture over the years. This will provide some bases for seeing where things are today, and where the initial and subsequent dimensions of Cuban cultural theorization stand vis-a-vis recent developments.

It is still relatively easy to recall the effect of Cuba's cultural revolution throughout the Americas. Cuba reminded many young intellectuals of black cultural roots in Latin America, the Caribbean but also the U.S. and of course Africa. The young intelligentsia read Aimé Césaire, discovered the Harlem Renaissance, discovered Amílcar Cabral, Frantz Fanon, Albert Memmi, the critiques of colonialism and neo-colonialism, such constructs as Régis Debray's *foco* theory and André Gunder Frank's original version of dependency theory. Through the Revolution, popular images (of Ché, of Castro) became virtual icons of a new cultural orientation; the example of Nicolás Guillén, and his *poesía negra*, joined with the images of bearded revolutionaries as variant versions of "*el nuevo hombre.*" The "New Song Movement," new political poetry, new popular theatre, new dance, new art, new narrative genres such as the testimonio, and above all a new cinema surfaced as part of an overall emerging system of Cuban and more broadly Latin American/Caribbean left popular culture that incorporated and yet challenged more exclusively elite cultural models and posited a pre-history that linked Martí to Mariátegui and Sandino, to Cuban left writers of the 1930s and 40s, and to a wide range of writers, cultural producers and revolutionaries who developed in the fifties and on into the sixties.

Indeed a genealogy of revolutionary culture and revolutionary ethos emerged linking *el nuevo hombre* to the indigenous struggle against the Spaniards, to moments and movements of Indian and Black resistance and then mestizo, mulatto and overall worker and poor people's struggle throughout the centuries in the Caribbean and Latin America. Martí was heralded as the father of a modern movement that had roots in Tecún Umán, Toussaint L'Ouverture and Bolívar; and the Revolution's ideologues fought

47

over his image against his liberal and rightwing champions and interpreters, to posit him as the forerunner of the Sierra Maestra revolutionaries who were in turn seen as heirs to Sandino and all prior liberation fighters, and as the predecessors of a veritable new wave of revolutionaries that would emerge very quickly throughout Latin America, the Caribbean and the Third World.

Summing up this overall perspective in the cultural sphere (and then applying the perspective to his own literary specialty) was Roberto Fernández Retamar in his *Calibán* essay (1985 and 1990). Here, the Cuban critic overturns Rodó's old *modernista* identification of Latin America as a spiritual Ariel opposed to a materialistic U.S. Calibán in function of a view which takes on the colonial vision of Latin America as Calibán (a barbarous malcreant--indeed a Caribbean cannibal) to be "tamed" and controlled by white European civilization, and transforms the image to posit a future in function of the resistance and revolt of the oppressed African, Indian and "half-breed" or mestizo masses of Latin America. Fernández Retamar then traced the cultural expressions of this revolt seeing in them the bases for the emergence of a new revolutionary ethos through a creative cultural *mestizaje* in fulfillment of Latin America's particular nature as the most westernized sector of the colonial or third world.

Inevitably, Fernández Retamar sought to see all cultural forms and works in relation to his overall theory; he sought to develop his own work and that of other Cuban and Latin American cultural producers in this direction. Indeed, even long before writing *Calibán* and as director of *Casa de las Américas*, he had made the values underlying this work essential dimensions and criteria in promoting and granting prizes to works submitted to his *Casa* journal and its annual literary contests. On the whole, *Casa de las Américas* joins with the overall Ministry of Culture program in promoting the specific developments in new song and the new film industry and the institutionalization of all these advances in function of international competitions and festivals, as a prime force in the generation of the cultural image fostered by the Cuban Revolution for internal and external consumption.

This orientation has much to tell us about the importance of cultural production and theory for Latin America as a whole. To the degree revolutionary ideologues were able to go beyond orthodox paradigms, they projected a long-term situation in which Cuba's underdeveloped economy would not lead the way in transforming consciousness; rather, cultural and ideological structures and their institutionalization would have to provide the concrete practices that would in turn sustain revolutionary élan through hard times and would in fact help in the ultimate socio-economic and political transformations required by the revolution. Since resistance to powerful structures of domination had frequently been centered in, or displaced to, cultural and ideological expression, and since, then, cultural resistance could also become a mode of opposition to the Revolution itself, great attention was given to these aspects of social life as essential to the revolutionary process. Culture became a prime site of struggle against resistance to the Revolution.

At first, Cuban cultural production was pluralistic and explosive. In painting, sculpture and photography, the older artists were encouraged; and new artists working in new media with a wide range of techniques, were helped along. In poetry, the Afro-Cuban forms of Guillén were heralded, and taken up too by a new generation of writers like Nancy Morejón. But Black revindication and recuperation, so central to Guillén's work, were not promoted as the only national way. Non-Marxist Catholic "progressives" such as Cintio Vittier and Fina García Marruz were promoted; and a kind of "conversational poetry" more indebted to Vallejo and Nicanor Parra than to Neruda or Guillén was championed by Fernández Retamar and became the prime model. As for narrative, Alejo Carpentier was seen as the national model, though many continued to recognize Lezama Lima as the nation's greatest writer, and his views about the Revolution, and his relation to the process (including questions of his sexual orientation) became the subject of continued commentary. Among the younger writers, Herberto Padilla, Roberto Desnoes and Antonio Benítez Rojo won praise, even, for a time, when their work showed some severe questioning of the Revolution. As policies began to tighten up, when Padilla was jailed and his work censored, when Vargas Llosa and other Latin American Boom writers began to question Cuba's cultural policy and the Revolution as a whole, the official response was to point toward the generation of more "popular" modes as essential to the needs of the people.

Miguel Barnet's *Autobiography of a Runaway Slave* launched the new testimonial genre, which, as theorized by Barnet, Margaret Randall and others, came to be seen as a literary form expressing the oppressed and subaltern (the black slaves, the abused Indians, women, workers, etc.) opposing the modern boom novel in essential ways and having a certain traditional base in the Caribbean. Then of course there were the developments in song, theater and film. The new song movement foregrounded older artists and musical forms obscured by commercialism, and opened the door to new poets, musicians and singers in the creation of the new Latin American music. In addition to reviving older Afro-Caribbean musical traditions, the musicians also sought new fusions of afro-, jazz, tropical, popular, classical and other musical modes, creating some of the more exciting experimental music work in the hemisphere.

The cultural ethos of the revolution led to institutional efforts promoting the discussion and creation of new plays and theatrical forms. Yet, while many agit-prop plays developed, it should be noted that one of the first acclaimed plays, dealing with problems of domestic adjustment to the revolutionary process, *Noche de los asesinos*, by José Triana, was modelled more on Jean Genet than on Bertolt Brecht, and that the kind of theater most encouraged, the kind which developed in the countryside by the Escambray theater group, drew on a wide range of popular and "high culture" forms in trying to find dynamic ways of portraying and participating in the new social process that was under way.

Along with the literacy program and other forms of popular outreach, the film industry developed, producing not only a wide range of educational and propaganda films of high quality, but also new feature film forms seeking new ways to link history and narrative, collective and individual experience. From the documentaries of Santiago Alvarez, to *Lucía*, to masterpieces by Tomás Gutiérrez Alea (*Memórias de subdesarrollo*, *La última cena*, *La muerte de un burócrata*, etc.), Cuban filmmakers working with low budgets and under often primitive conditions followed the lead of a few other predecessors in Latin America (a few key directors in Mexico, Argentina, Brazil, etc.) in linking popular indigenous traditions with elements of Italian neo-realism, surrealism and the world revolutionary cinematic tradition to further develop "the new Latin American Cinema."

Of special relevance was the film industry's concern with national history and culture, with some special emphasis on folk traditions and slavery. In productions such as *El otro Francisco*, the film industry sought to present and critique previous Cuban ideological-literary constructs; Sara Gómez's *En cierta manera*, shows various dimensions of transformed

African and Spanish culture to be in conflict with the Revolution's social and productive ethic, and the film remarkably projects a series of continuing and future conflicts that would plague the Revolution over the years. Cuban cultural developments and their institutionalization had a marked impact on Caribbean and Latin American cultural production throughout the sixties and into the 1970s--partially through imitation, partially because national social forces dictated parallel developments and partially because young revolutionary artists saw the situations as similar or wished them to be so. In art and theater, many young radical artists followed the Cuban lead; and in some cases, they developed forms paralleling Cuban "models," but speaking to distinct national contexts and possibilities. For many, the Revolution and its cultural achievements constituted a new phase in a long history of Caribbean struggle and resistance. The institutionalization of the prizes of *Casa de las Américas*, the promotion of Caribbean cultural conferences and investigation, the development of international cultural competitions created vehicles for spreading Cuban cultural influences. Revolutionary poetry, testimonios and new novels appeared throughout the area, often showing the Cuban impact. Musical forms like salsa and reggae at times captured or reflected certain dimensions of criticism, protest and rebellion that had been given new life with the Cuban experience. In the Caribbean, as in much of the Third World, and even in the U.S., among counter-cultural sectors, and especially among radical Latino cultural workers, what was understood as the Cuban example was a constant dimension of cultural life. Cultural expression and aesthetic criteria became overtly politicized; radical artist groups developed; new journals sprang up; there were even efforts on some islands to follow the Cuban lead and produce socially-oriented feature films.

This is not the place for an in-depth exploration of the achievements and problems of Cuba's cultural revolution (or Nicaragua's subsequent and greatly variant effort in the same direction) in efforts to forge a democratization of the overall Latin American cultural model--and even a democratization of literary modeling in which testimonio and popular conversational poetry were given significant space; this is also not the place to measure the vast effect of that model throughout the rest of Latin America, except to say that for many, the Revolution and revolutionary cultural achievements constituted one of the most significant phenomena in a long history of struggle and resistance.

In the present context, it is more important to underline the limitations and problems with Fernández Retamar's critique which come to the fore today with the greatest clarity. Fernández Retamar's text is haunted by his faith in socialism and his belief that Marxist and non-Marxist Latin American cultural resistance ideologies could be merged into a unified critique. In the process, of course, he tends to homogenize questions of class and ethnicity and all of Latin America and the Caribbean. He collapses third world and working class critiques, too readily equates creole leftism and Marxism with the questions of mestizo resistance and afro or Indian resistance modes. There is a reification and homogenization of all modes and sources of oppression, a reduction of all resistance patterns to one ultimate model. There is a distortion of patterns of social ordering in function of a model too much based on domination as opposed to hegemony and internal patterns of consent and negotiation.

Ultimately, the image of resistance resides only in a model of thorough, transformative revolution marked by gender in terms of Ché's "new man" versus the old—a theme which has sad implications for Cuba today. In fact, if we understand gender questions as central to future Latin American life, we may simply say that Fernández Retamar's model required not only a "sea change," but a sex change--perhaps one in which Miranda's brave new world disorder would lead to her emergence not as a Boticelli Venus, but as a some kind of transexed *"Calibana."* But even this stipulation is metonymic, in that today the effort would seem to be to assert *Calibán/a* not only against traditional criollo elite critics, but also against the seemingly oppositional sub-elites and even their transvaluation of the Shakespearean monster of nature into some kind of romantic, hoped for, but never adequately achieved linkage between themselves and subaltern sectors who somehow stand in as some Latin American equivalents for Marx's history-transforming proles.

These matters are undoubtedly a result of historical limitations, which also tell about the problems with Latin American revolutionary culture as a whole. Indeed the sad story of Cuba and of the Latin American left in general may well be that Fernández Retamar's Calibán, like Che Guevara's "new man," is a construct in the name of which vast numbers of historical subalterns were measured, reified, marginalized and indeed victimized.

Suffice it to say here that few texts are so marked by their historical moment than Fernández Retamar's. For his work is not simply a summary of a radical cultural model that has been evolving over the years since the revolution, but in fact the actual crisis of that model in the midst of defeats among Latin American leftwing movements and a decline in the prestige of the Cuban Revolution marked by Cuba's economic and political problems, most significantly signalled in the cultural sphere by the Padilla case. The overall revolutionary decline, but now a new hope in the electoral victory of Allende (cf. Fernández Retamar 38) makes *Calibán* an embattled, defensive and nevertheless hopeful argument marking a bifurcation between what Fernández Retamar considers revolutionary culture and the elite culture of those Latin American cultural super-stars who, excepting Borges, Vargas Llosa, Paz and a few others, had, up to this point remained on friendly terms with the Revolution.

In this context, it is ironic to read Fernández Retamar's blistering pages with respect to Carlos Fuentes, who, while highly critical of the Padilla case and never fully affirmative about the Revolution from that point on, nevertheless would maintain an open, basically "progressive" anti-interventionism with respect to Cuba and the emergent Central American crisis that would belie the fierceness of Fernández Retamar's attack. Nevertheless, the value of Fernández Retamar's anti-Fuentes diatribe is that it anticipates the arguments that the left and the radical cultural model represented by *Calibán* would have in the future not only with elite writers and critics but with the emergence of subsequent cultural attitudes readily associable with the contemporary postmodern ethos.

Most specifically the final pages of Calibán point to an opposition between historical and linguistic orientations to literature which is then transcribed into socialism versus capitalism and is seen as a site for a struggle over the future.

Fernández Retamar describes how in *La nueva novela hispanoamericana* (1969), Fuentes puts forth structuralist oppositions to historicism, and the reduction of recent Latin American narratives to strictly Latin American social concerns, which he sees as secondary to more general or "universal" literary and "human" values which the narrative texts may lay claims to achieving. In effect, new Latin American literature claims to be and is part of a cosmopolitan totality.

Fernández Retamar asks if Fuentes doesn't also value Latin American difference within the totality. And he points to how Fuentes, in an effort to have his cake and eat it, shifts gears to speak of the deep role of Latin

American literature in creating an alternative language to that which has oppressed and distorted Latin American realities.

Attempting to unmask Fuentes's ideological project, Fernández Retamar quotes a passage in which the Mexican novelist actually anticipates the emergence of postmodernity and its implications for Latin America:

> In proportion to the widening of the abyss between the geometric expansion of the technocratic world and the arithmetic expansion of our own ancillary societies, Latin America is being transformed into a world that is *superfluous* ... to imperialism. Traditionally, we have been exploited countries. Soon we will not even be that. It will no longer be necessary to exploit us, for technology will have succeeded in--to a large extent it has already-- manufacturing substitutes for our single-product offerings. [Fuentes in Fernández Retamar 90: 35]

In answering this statement, Fernández Retamar scoffs at Fuentes's view as based on the assumption of a reasserted U.S. and rightwing hegemony which will make a second Cuba, and implicitly even a first one, impossible. In a remarkably prophetic way, we see him flail at Fuentes's technological and political perspective linking it to--among other things-- "the neo-Barthean flutterings of Severo Sarduy" (ibid. 36).

Fernández Retamar furiously assails a view that Latin America doesn't exist except as a resistance that must be overcome. He insists that Latin America, through the Cuban Revolution, is just coming into its own, and that the resistance culture of Calibán is winning. Resistance is the essence of Calibán; and indeed Fernández Retamar would seem to win the day here because revolutionary hope has been reborn with Allende, and it will be sustained over the years with Central American insurgency. The deeper structures of world and hemispheric changes would only become evident much later.

It would of course be faulty to suggest that Fuentes's prediction is quite on the mark, but his emphasis on the world of discourse and new technologies marks his views as symptomatic of an increasingly post-structuralist and postmodernist orientation emerging among progressive Latin American thinkers. Now Latin America looks to the free market and free trade within the uncontested structure of U.S. hegemony; capitalism has reasserted its global position, and postmodernity implodes on areas struggling to achieve modernity.

54

The cultural model of Calibán, based on radicalizing *mestizaje* and patterns of resistance rooted in a history of efforts of control and discipline first saw itself clearly at odds with the growing ethos. And so it would be portrayed by many Latin Americanists and others in the years to come. So Jameson, already in his postmodernist phase, became interested in *Calibán* in relation to his vision of a global cognitive mapping of primary modes of cultural opposition within, but on the periphery of, postmodernity.

Nevertheless, whether Calibán and Latin American resistance culture, either in literary or more popular, non-literary forms, remained oppositional to postmodernism (as in Yúdice's first formulation 1985), or stood as a kind of left wing, progressive alternative *within* it (as in Beverley and Zimmerman 1990 and, somewhat differently, Larsen 1990 and 1995), would be a point of contention for at least some critics. Within postmodernism, that cultural model, however modified, might still have some effect, but of course it might also be absorbed. Outside it, it might survive in some kind of ideological or material enclave only to be readily targeted and destroyed at some future time. In the terms of Laclau-Mouffe (1985) and Hall (1986), the question has remained that of the articulation of what remains of the Calibanic tradition--again, to evoke Spivak's so evocative title, the question of the conditions under which the subaltern might indeed be able to speak (1988b). This question becomes further complicated by developments in subaltern studies (cf. Guha and Spivak, ed. 1988) which problematize the situation of those seeking to constitute a critical perspective visavis recent phases of Latin American cultural being and becoming (cf. the Latin American Subaltern Studies Group 1995 and Rodríguez's essay in this volume).

4. *Latin American Literary Culture in Postmodern Context*

Turning to literary concerns perse, we face the common cliche of our times: Latin American literature was postmodern *avant la lettre*; Latin American writers achieved a form of high modernism which then deconstructed both their literary and extra-literary value and projected the very *postmodern* qualities which characterize the "cultural dominant" of lived experience in an ever more global society. Clearly those who say this (Ruffinelli [1990: 32-33] cites Ihab Hassan 1987, Linda Hutcheon 1988,

55

etc.) may or may not know what they're talking about, or may simply be referring to a handful of works which they willfully interpret in conformity with the image they wish to foster.

Above all, it is clear that they are not referring to all of Latin American literature, but rather to those works (almost exclusively those by Borges and the boom writers of the 1960s and beyond) which fit their definitions and desires. And they then falsify Latin American literary history and its conceptualization by reconstructing it in function of a genealogical line which seeks predecessors and contemporary analogues to the exclusion of all else (cf. Colás 1994: 1-5; but see Sommer and Yúdice 1986 as well as Williams 1995).

If we seek a tradition of elite innovations without direct concern with socio-cultural origins, relations or references, then we exclude all works centered on them, and all tendencies within the works which point to dialogism, to "structured-outs" beyond the dominant patterns emphasized, projected and even more indirectly implied. And yet a goal of many left literary critics, myself included, has been to point to just these elements and in effect to use some of the theoretical baggage of postmodernism to point to subaltern dimensions which would ultimately challenge the upper and middle sector elites and their appropriation of cosmopolitan dominants inscribed in the literary field.

In one sense of course, to speak of Latin American literature is to speak of a beast that is at once many headed and non-existent. As if in anticipation of encroaching cultural imperialism, some critics write as if there is no such systemic reality as Latin American literature, but rather a series of national or regional literatures, related in some ways yet different in others, in Latin America.

However in addition to national, regional and subregional forces at work on the various Latin American literatures existing often within the same contiguous geographical or politically discrete space, there are also forces of homogenization and diversification stemming from the two major systems affecting the area, one global, the other far more local (though both now circulate through the new technologies: 1.) the predominantly western (Madrid, but preferably Paris, sometimes New York or even London, and now perhaps L.A. or Miami) culture of the cosmopolitan, urban or urbanized elites; and 2.) the various indigenous popular cultures, transformed by the impact of modernization from the conquest on, but still existing, especially in those less urbanized and less "whitened" areas of Latin America.

To the degree that they survive, these latter cultural strains impact the literature of the elites, even if it is only by conditioning, if not determining, a desperate denying cosmopolitanism common throughout Latin American literary history. For many they are much the continuing source of Latin America's residual "otherness," what remains of the non-Western tradition in America, the source of non-instrumental, magical and mystical energies some look to in the area--forces that are threatened, and even dying, perhaps, and transforming certainly, but which have somehow at least partially eluded "Latin America's dependent, peripheral capitalism" and which continue to incite concern, and sometimes, even provide bases for hope, and for change (even when and if they themselves begin to take on monstrous hybrid, cosmopolitan-influenced forms) in a world whose horizon of possibility seems more reduced than even under the old dictatorships and older forms of domination.

In effect, as advanced capitalist cosmopolitan forces impact Latin American literary work, they are met by pre-capitalist cultural residues which largely limit and characterize their disposition and "season," "tropicalize" or in the last analysis profoundly transform the very patterns which seek to encapsulate them.

Ironically, it is this very situation of hybridization or transculturation which constitutes Latin American literature's oblique relation to modernizing, Eurocentric traditions, and which positions at least some Latin American work as "postmodern" even in the context of social formations which are primarily "pre-modern" in virtually every other way.

There is no doubt but that the peculiar synthesis which characterizes Latin American literature and its own problematic relation to literary modernism--in sum, the equation of at least some key works of the Latin American literary boom and postboom with postmodernism--is the source of the continued intense interest in the literature even in this age of electronic media. There is also little doubt that this is where an effort to understand the social basis of Latin America's literary development might find its clearest contemporary path to explication; it is also where Latin Americanists have found themselves gradually turning to questions of Latino culture and literature within the U.S.

5. *From Gómez-Quiñones to Gómez-Peña and Beyond: Prelude to Presentday Chicano/Latino Cultural Studies*

For Guillermo Gómez-Peña (1987), Gloria Anzaldúa (1987), García Canclini and Patricia Safa (1990), Emily Hicks (1992) and others, the questions of modernity and postmodernity, Latin America and the U.S., come together in the Mexico/U.S. border areas, where new cultural trends affecting both sides of the border are said to be in a state of creative dynamic transformation. Here the themes of displacement, decentering, hybridization, deterritorialization, etc. come forth with great intensity and variety. Here identity class and transformations shift, slide, collide and divide; and new combinations, new collective and individual subjects, emerge.

One of the major themes of contemporary Latin American studies begins its story in what are the border areas, and that theme may in fact have things to tell us about what is going on both sides--how north hits south, how a now transformed south responds and in turn transforms itself; how outward and return, limited and extended, transnational migrations, as well as the deterritorializations and identity shifts involved, may speak to and anticipate new constellations, new relations both in our hemisphere and elsewhere throughout the world, as the planet heats up and as ethnic identifications and enmities grow in the interstices of the postmodern world.

But we should be clear that, while the story may begin and much of it take place at the border, and while border, as metaphor may dominate much postmodern discourse today, nevertheless, if our subject is Latino people and culture, the metaphor dangerously becomes overly fixed, so that southwestern patterns, certainly a predominant U.S. Latino experience, come to "colonize" other ones, so that non-Mexicans and Mexicans in the Midwest (many of whom arrived from their homebase without touching the Río Grande or the Tijuana fence), are virtually subsumed in the metaphorical operation.

So, even New York-based theorists like Juan Flores and George Yúdice (1989) pick up on the metaphor and apply it to the overall Latino experience; so *Latino* itself becomes a dangerous generalization, concealing regional, class and ideological differences, causing us to forget how different urban experiences may make very different people and groups even of people from the same town or region of origin, to the point that a terminology designed to both designate diverse peoples as having points of unity comes to obviate, cancel and yet simultaneously structure experience. So a Latino event is really a Mexican or Cuban one; a Cuban one a "Caribbean" or "Latin American" one, etc.

And yet we know that such terms, "Latino" or even that term so despised by the "politically correct," including myself--Hispanic--and the term, "borders," are very useful, even as we know we must resist their totalizing and colonizing tendencies. So too, the recent, if still-to-be-detailed, effort to explore postmodern dimensions of U.S. Latinization (cf. Olalquiaga 1992) or the largely still-to-be-written story of the "Miamization" of Latin America in past several years are important to the overall question of emergent Latino identities in relation to postmodernity and its impact in Latin America.

So Latino culture and literature must be studied as part of Latin American postmodernity and part of the new postmodern world in the Americas (cf. Zimmerman 1992a). And so too, this discussion will not only mean applying Latin American and Chicano, Puerto Rican and other perspectives to the question of Latino identities, but will mean too a consideration of how the Latino totality affects the overall Latin American and broader world in the Americas. Here, to simply parallel our presentation of *Calibán* earlier in this essay, we may turn to one of the major cultural documents of what was called the Chicano movement, to evoke a sense of the transformations involved in the larger "Latino question.

The document referred to is the essay by Juan Gómez-Quiñónez, "On Culture" (1982), which for some years served as a prime text for understanding and interpreting Chicano culture and literature. Drawing on a construct that alludes to Gramsci in relation to the now mainly abandoned "internal colony" model, grafting onto this the spirit of cultural revolutionism emanating from the neo-colonial world (in Memmi, Fanon, Cabral and Fernández Retamar's *Calibán*), Gómez-Quiñonez sought to project *chicanismo* as the culture of the oppressed, on the road toward liberation and the long march to "*el nuevo hombre.*" For him, Chicanos were, in spite of their internal contradictions and class differentiations, still sufficiently homogenous to constitute a potential bloc which could in turn relate to other oppressed groups in the U.S. and also in the Third World, to thus participate in the still larger coalition of peoples who would somehow coincide in some world revolutionary movement.

59

It was at times hard to know how Gómez-Quiñones precisely positioned his essay. Was it an anthropological study, and was its anthropology sound? Was it a call to action? Was it as directly revolutionary as it seemed? Or was its apparent revolutionism on the other hand simply a heuristic strategy designed to place Chicanos among broader traditions as a means of maintaining the relative weight of progressive if not necessarily revolutionary tendencies among a larger social aggregate whose radical orientations seemed to be turning toward modes of racial nationalism, or pre-Colombian pre-industrial romanticism, if they survived at all?

But whatever Gómez-Quiñones's intention and whatever shortcomings may be found in his articulation of the cultural question and its application to the situation of Chicanos, nevertheless the effect of his essay was first to put that cultural dimensions into the forefront of discussions of the future of Chicanos; second to begin theorizing the question of the left-tending articulation of Chicano cultural concerns in relation to significant Third World and above all Latin American efforts in this direction; and third, to thereby raise the question not only of group unity but also the relationship of group concerns to those of other groups in the U.S. and abroad.

Of course many things have happened in life and theory and in theory since the days of Gómez-Quiñones's essay. It is obvious that his perspective derived from the Calibanic ethos generated by the Cuban revolution and dispersed throughout the Latin American and U.S. Latino world in the 1960s and into the 1970s; and we have already discussed above how this ethos has been modified by newer currents that have emerged in the region and have come to dominate our times. As Marxist and nationalist revolutionary movements suffered setbacks; as many developing Third World revolutions (Cambodia, Iran, Nicaragua) failed and led to deep disaster, what was called the Chicano movement no longer exists as such and certainly the radical ambience and the pressure of Chicanos to "march with" the supposed revolution has largely evaporated.

To be sure, the effort to link Chicanos to some broader "revolutionary subject" (no longer, strictly the "industrial proletariat" or even "people of color") persists in the form of a populist articulation registered in terms of Jesse Jackson's Laclauian "rainbow coalition." But Chicanos have been struggling with regard to the weight of their concerns in a coalition many of them deem to be Black-centered. And of course, many Puerto Ricans and other Latinos feel they are not represented or that they are misrepresented,

60

and grumble about Chicano or Mexicano hegemony. But whatever previous lip service there may have been about a socialist or Marxist agenda, whatever direct effort to establish the superiority of Marxist over, say, "culturalist" concerns--in Aztlán, in tribal blood, in the visions of Don Juan or even the cures of Ultima–have become largely issues of the past, of value more for historical remembering than contemporary probing.

This is a time when a Chicano intelligentsia has been firmly established, but also when Mexican and broader Latin American immigration have taken us from discussions of Oscar Lewis's "culture of poverty" and patterns of assimilation to ones more specifically centered on questions of the "underclass," transnational migration and "effective citizenship." This is a time when Chicanos are not the only oppressed Latinos in many areas and when in fact there is a struggle to maintain or decenter things Chicano in function of a larger (perhaps more diluted and unconcretizable) Latino whole. And of course, this is a time of ever-more sophisticated feminism, when in fact the older struggle against the external other (the Anglo, the *gabacho*, *bolillo* or *quién sea*) has been turned inward, when the very issue of cultural affirmation and change has been complicated by the critique of gender oppression as part of culture. Chicano and Latino culture are being deconstructed and reconstructed, de-centered and re-centered, as we seek to plot what to hold onto, what to lose, how can we retain X as a value when it is tainted by class privilege, or sexist oppression.

Identities and identifications have been transforming in relation to the global economy and global perspectives. Immigration surveillance and English-only movements, Proposition 187, Welfare reform, attacks on Affirmative Action, bilingual education--these and other issues-- spell the reintensification of anti-Mexican and anti-Latino feelings, as well as splits in Latino communities. But ongoing economic crisis continues to send thousands north; and the explosion of mass media (and especially Spanish-language television) now gives Spanish a stronger foothold north of the border with Mexico.

The possibility of a Latinized U.S., of a reconquest by the older peoples of America (transformed, of course in varying degrees by U.S. modernist and now postmodern cultural hegemony) looms before us as a millennial prospect that could make all previous Chicano history and all previous critiques and theories of Chicano identity and culture into mere phases and aspects of the pre-history of a remade cultural hemisphere.

But in all this picture, of course, the question of the world of gangs and drugs, of informal economy and drug-running enclaves, of continuing and extending anomie, of dropouts and welfare dependency, of growing parental absenteeism, growing and deepening racial conflicts, and intensifying gender conflicts, class differentiation and the like have prevented Chicanos, Chicanos and Latinos, Latinos and Blacks, Latinos, Blacks and others, from forming a bloc, from struggling in the most meaningful ways. Now, bereft of older revolutionary illusions and horizons, and without a sure sense of new ones, the whole world and all of Latin America in or out of what is legally Latin America dance to the rhythm of postmodern commodity logic; and those who can't go with the flow and who can't get with the diffused, de-centered, post-industrial universe are doomed to live in its back alleys, unable to adjust or react creatively to new cultural transformations, and only able to hold on to the most questionable aspects of the "older cultural bases--precisely those which may best conform to and then lend themselves to becoming transformed by the logic of the informal economy and underclass patterns, the bartered communalism of gang and druggie loyalties, the nostalgic feudalism that feeds on as it fends off of advanced capitalist marginalization, a misplaced, communally destructive *compadrazgo*--even as a new Latino middle class intelligentsia takes shape and as young professors find themselves lucky to have their problems to deal with even as they scurry to their conferences in Santa Barbara or San Juan, publish their articles and go about their lives.

Here, as in the case of cultural studies in general, world changes inevitably affect our views with respect to things Chicano and Latino, just as thoughts about Chicano and Latino culture as the life form of a significant subaltern population may potentially affect the overall theoretical field.

Recent anthropological, historical and literary studies (cf. the work of Renato Rosaldo, Mario García, Rosaura Sánchez, Norma Alarcón, Ramón, José David and Sonia Saldívar, etc.) point to dimensions crucial to any overall synthetic perspective on U.S. Latino culture, and especially the matter of counter-hegemonic modes which directly or indirectly express human groups attempting to cope with the various forms of oppression that exist throughout the Americas and affect the very psychology and being of those coming to, or living in, U.S. enclaves. The questions for U.S. Latino, as well as Latin American, culture posed by this perspective have mainly to do with the overlays of postmodern cultural forms and norms. The current task is to draw on contemporary work as a means of articulating an approach to the particularities of U.S. Latino social life in ways, however critical and however respectful they are of the irreducibility of Latino experience, also point to global contexts and link up with broader theorizations in expressing present realities and future potentialities.

The goal in contemporary and future work in Latino studies, then, will be to consider some dimensions of the theoretical revolution to see how they make us rethink Latino cultural questions since the Chicano intervention of Gómez-Quiñones. This consideration will inevitably take place in the shadow of our deliberations over post-Marxian and Gramscian currents which point to a cultural emphasis as implicitly given space by the work of Jameson, Laclau/Mouffe, etc. Clearly, we should add here that this cultural focus is especially valuable for Chicanos and more broadly, Latinos, among whom the question of culture or "cultural dimensions" in the midst of and even at times opposed to civilization, is more central than it is for the more modernized peoples sharing the American landscape.

In dealing with such theoretical concerns (see Zimmerman 1992b), I would like finally to suggest that Chicano and more broadly Latino resistances and accommodations will be important to the future of U.S., Latin American, and even more broadly international configurations in which humanity makes or does not make its future. In this frame, it is of course important to examine the effects of contemporary patterns of immigration, settlement, acculturation and the like (cf. Schiller, Basch and Banc Szanton 1992). As Flores and Yúdice (1992) have been pointing out, Latino identity with all its previous characteristics and contours, crosses over in postmodern culture as posing some combination of the most retrograde and progressive possibilities for future patterns of resistance and creativity, posing some of the most dynamic points of convergence and alliance with other, non-Latino groups in a broader field of new oppositions internal to and at least possibly transformative of the entire social system.

6. Concluding Perspectives

Let me move toward cloture by drawing on my more extensive discussion of Laclau and Mouffe in *Tropicalizing Hegemony* and citing one

63

of many passages from their book that are especially germane to the subject at hand:

> From the point of view of a hegemonic politics, ... the crucial limitation of the traditional left perspective is that it attempts to determine a priori agents of change, levels of effectiveness in the field of the social, and privileged points and moments of rupture. All these obstacles come together in a common core, which is the refusal to abandon the assumption of a sutured society. Once this is discarded, however, there arises a whole set of new problems: How do we determine... *surfaces of emergence* and the... *forms of articulation* of the antagonisms? To what extent is [theoretical] ... pluralism ... compatible with the effects of equivalence which are ... characteristic of every hegemonic articulation? [Laclau and Mouffe 1985: 178-180]

In the spirit of these problems, I should like to anticipate the logic of other essays in this collection by invoking a moment at the beginning of the post-structuralist challenge to Marxist thought--from one of Foucault's crucial early books, translated as *Madness and Civilization* (1973). Here, Foucault reveals how the emergent Absolutist regime in France established categories of reason and unreason, mind and body, mental and physical work, etc., as basic to the social order, and the effort to forge a modern social formation.

In this construction, Foucault shows how the logic instituted in houses for the mad was also applied to the workhouses for the rural poor as they came into the city. He completes thereby a post-structuralist version of the Weberian conversion of Marxist categories (something he will make more explicit in the more rigorous *Les mots et les choses*), whereby the emergent episteme of reason in fact generates the structure of capital and labor, work and workforce.

Of course any contemporary critique of Foucault would point to the hiddens and absences in his analysis--the division of mind/body extending to questions of gender, region, etc. Cutting across such questions and what is especially germane for us at this juncture is the fact that what is hidden in Foucault's portrayal of the new social categories is how even the inscription of what will be the beginnings of a new urban proletariat was made necessary by the uprisings among these sectors (most notoriously the displaced rural "rabble" now rooting in Paris, and their role in La Fronde of

1650)--and of course these are the very sectors that would come forth in 1789. As such, madhouses and workhouses are structures of containment (so too neo-classical architecture, theater and literary modes themselves), in relation to very real forces of underclass resistance.

To push this argument further, if we remember that one of the goals of Absolutism was to create a domestic basis for pursuing foreign mercantalist goals (as France battled with Holland to catch up with Spain, England and Portugal to make a run at New World riches), we can understand that in addition to the structured-in emergent proletariat, we have, unacknowledged by Foucault, a structured-out, an absence, which would be the still unurbanized Old World sectors and, above all, New World social actors, who find only the most marginal and exotic representations in 17th Century French ideology or iconography.

It is in fact this structured-outedness vis-a-vis the Amer-Indian world which has its parallel in the Latin and Anglo-American experience. In the first case, contemporary Native Americans, are almost structured out of an episteme which their antecedents helped pressure into being. In the second case, it is the Latinos (including Indians and Blacks of Latin American background) who are structured out.

In Latin America indigenous oppression by Spaniards, creoles and those who identified with them lives internalized in the very psyche of many Latin American peoples; however, it is often not even a living memory, but something shunted off to the reservoir of the unconscious.

To the degree that the Latin American Indian, mestizo and mulato poor internalize dominant categories articulated in colonial society and the formation of what Severo Martínez Paláez called *La patria del criollo*, they exclude themselves as a fundamental fact and make their resistive action one fraught with internal negations.

In the U.S., Latinos are also effaced in a variant "cognitive mapping" which came to be configured through a dominant opposition of Anglo-White and Anglo-Black. While this structuring out is perhaps no more severe than Latin American anti-Indian or anti-African racism and the group (and self) deprecation it generates, nevertheless, the internal U.S. Latino process., ever more compounded with newer, renewing and transnational Latin American "residues," is one of a kind of self-obliteration and othering which makes the articulation of effective, transformative resistance very difficult to realize (cf. Sandoval 1991 and Oboler 1995).

In both cases, the further psychic obliteration fostered by global, homogenizing multi-national postmodernist culture is only countered, it would seem, by the particular articulatory processes inherent in larger patterns. If, through Foucault, we can speak of historical obliteration as well as structural obliteration occurring in the very episteme of postmodernism itself, here we may also point to García Canclini's effort to emphasize certain modes of non-apocalyptic resistance as theorized by de Certeau (1984).

Regardless of recent uprisings in Chiapas and elsewhere in Mexico, we should not be misled by any shortterm optimism about revolutionary possibilities among the obliterated, oppressed and subaltern in Latin America. It must be said here that plotting future cultural and political struggles will obviously be no easy matter, and that the movement from subalternity to cultural resistance to the actual constitution of political struggle in function of class, group and other necessary alliances is extremely difficult to conceptualize and actualize. Indeed, in warning against Eurocentric resistance/conformity dichotomies, William Rowe and Vivian Schelling, note that "there is no automatic translation of cultural resistance into political change" --to say nothing of political organization, "new social movements" or any other modes of postmodern political articulation. People may develop modes of symbolic oppositional expression without necessarily seeing or articulating themselves as subjects or agents of an alternative political project. "To give cultural difference an automatic connotation of oppositional politics is to indulge in romanticism or populism" (1991: 119). If fully opppositional politics are not viable at this time, if powerful oppositional currents are unable to achieve an effective total articulation, if we lack concrete alternatives by which the subaltern become the agents of their own liberation, if this is indeed the contemporary trend and challenge, then we must look for small openings, possibilities-- options: we have no other viable choice.

Oppositional forms emerge giving symbolic expression of an alternative world which is wished for and imagined but not yet realized. It is true that cultural expression may provide a release which does not incite but rather pacifies opposition (this Aristotle's answer to Plato--the fear haunting Brecht's "anti-Aristotlean" aesthetics). Nevertheless, as de Certeau (1984) emphasizes, the non-immediate politicization of cultural resistance patterns kept alive in newer cultural practices maintains them as sources for political

66

resistance at later, more propitious historical junctures--and, we suggest, may help to bring such junctures into being. Supposed cultural utopianism could provide models for future construction.

This is of course an item of hope and faith guiding cultural studies and this particular effort. In this regard, I wish to take a position between those who find and exaggerate oppositions in the most superficial of daily practices and those who deny the significance of any stance unless it is already tied to a party practice leading to the overthrow of the state in the name of the working class. It is clear that what many of us considered romantically and falsely as the era of Latin American revolution has come and gone with great loss of life and without any resolution of the deep problems facing the peoples of the hemisphere. Clearly there is much rethinking to be done, and premature cloture, suture or whatever is just as dangerous and destructive to possibility as mindless utopianism. In this sense, I opt for Brecht's aesthetics of "slow anger" as opposed to what I have found in the work of several theorists who attempt to leap to premature political articulations and condemn anything which does not move in the direction of their prejudices, desires and dreams.

This essay is dedicated to the prospect of a continuing search for the means to properly define the Latin American situation and the nature of Latin American struggles (which are also broader, more hemispheric "American" ones) in a none-too brave and postmodern new world in which new modes of opposition and resistance are still in the process of formation and discovery.

José Bedia, *Llega al pie*, 1994.
Acrylic on canvas- 14''x199½''
Photo courtesy of George Adams Gallery, New York.

JAMESON'S POSTMODERN LOGIC
AND ITS THIRD WORLD APPLICABILITY:
COGNITIVE MAPPING AND THE PERSISTENCE
OF THE DIALECTIC

Robert Scott Curry

> Without a conception of the social totality (and the possibility of transforming a whole social system), no properly socialist politics is possible. [Jameson 1988: 354-355]

1.

This paper centers on the problems of applying "first world" concepts to "third world" cultures. Above all, the paper, first conceived within the problematic conceptualization of postmodernism specific to Latin America, supports Jameson's appropriation of Ernest Mandel's view in establishing postmodernism as the cultural dominant of late capitalism--as well as Jameson's insistence that this cultural dominant must be thought through in terms of a geopolitical and geocultural conception of totality. In this regard, a reading of Immanuel Wallerstein's *Geopolitics and Geoculture* (1991) has reinforced my original attraction to the theories of Mandel and Jameson, although from a somewhat different angle and with a somewhat different terminology.

It is in function of the conceptions of totality and difference, and especially their role in the conceptualization of a discursive formation of historical/class subjects--in this case the "third world"--that my assessment of a global condition of postmodernity begins and ends. I argue against current theoretical claims that totalizations such as "the third world" or "capitalism" in themselves lead to totalitarianism; I assert that in fact totalities are necessary to conceptual adequacy, and that they have their basis in the real material conditions of existence. This is not to say, however, that such concepts are absolute, and may be constituted uncritically; but rather that they are mediated by the material specificities of given situations, and must be constantly modified in a Marxist-Hegelian dialectical fashion. Hence, I have come to understand the relevance of a second Jamesonian concept, that of *cognitive mapping*, as a key step in the methodology needed to understand the current phase of capitalism and to provide a framework for a contemporary Marxist understanding of the world.

The need to work through such problematized concepts as totality and difference, and how they relate to the conceptualization of discursive subject formations, casts a shadow on contemporary theory. I am thinking here of applications and extensions of Foucault's approach to history, as well as particular apolitical applications of Derridean deconstructionism and post-structuralism in general.

In Jameson's work, post-structuralist and contemporary historicist approaches are useful in their being symptomatic descriptions within the "cultural logic" of late capitalism rather than being wholly valid conceptualizations above or beyond historical determinations. Two of the most striking symptoms of contemporary theory and life Jameson describes are the shift from an aesthetic based in temporality to one based in spatiality, and the positing of the end of ideology. Both symptoms register in this paper in relation to the problematic of the representation of the third world subject. In fact, by the late 1960s, the shift to a genealogical concept of spatiality and its corresponding characteristic of immediacy--so important in the postmodern theories mentioned above--came to characterize an ideological denial of any theory of ideology, any historical or temporal referent, and any possibility of discursive formations as having historical subjects. Finally, it may be argued that this spatiality comes not out of poststructuralist or postmodern theory itself, but rather that the theory is a product of its lived context, characterized more and more by the immediacy of experience that life takes on with CNN (and tv/video in general), the fax, etc.

It is out of this problem of spatiality and immediacy, that those concerned with historicist or specifically Marxist interpretations of contemporary culture had to turn to some concept of mapping. I believe that Gayatri Spivak's famous essay, "*Can The Subaltern Speak?*" (1988b) provides a useful solution, by drawing upon her deconstructivist techniques to critique Foucault (as well as Deleuze) and, through Subaltern Studies perspectives, to develop and extend Jameson's own approach to questions of postmodern location and points of resistance. Indeed, my interests in Spivak's work have taken on a significant role in the development of this essay--first, the way in which Spivak deals with the question of ideology and the role of the intellectual; second, the usefulness of her specific blend of Marxism and deconstructionism as it relates to cognitive mapping with respect to the third world seen as the final frontier of capitalization and, most specifically, to the multinational corporate scene of late capitalism and the global division of labor; third, and most important to this paper, the way in which her theories relate to the need for both micro-theoretical work to complement the global, and the way in which this feeds back into mapping.

As Colin McCabe has noted, "Deconstruction for Spivak is neither a conservative aesthetic nor a radical politics but an intellectual ethic which enjoins a constant attention to the multiplicity of determination" (1988: xii). In order to give adequate specificity to Jameson's theory, it is also necessary, for my purposes, to bring the "multiplicity of determination" to bear in a critical fashion within the context of his theoretical system. Above all, I believe that Jameson's assertion of postmodernism as a cultural dominant and manifestation of late capitalism, has to be examined (or tested) according to the means by which that dominant articulates itself in relation to given specificities--cultures, social formations, peoples, places, and historical conjunctures etc. The "third world" and the subaltern therein come to central stage in this conception.

2.

The relationship between Jameson's cultural dominant and Spivak's "multiplicity of determination" may be indicated through an understanding of Spivak's unique blend of Derridean and Marxist analysis in relation to Marx's two terms of representation of the subject in *The Eighteenth Brummaire--Vertretung* and *Darstellung*. These terms can be shown, in turn, as congruent yet disjunctive figurations for coordinates that themselves represent overlapping macro and micro subject-positions in the world.

In my own effort at theoretical synthesis, the totalizing concept of late capitalism must be applied or related to the specific problematic totality of the figure of "the third world"--this in contrast with that other totality which we call the "first world." Both "first" and "third world" are totalities in their own right up to the moment before their "slippage" into the discourse of late capitalism as the global conceptualization of totality itself. A good point or entry here is to consider one major aspect of the criticism Aijaz Ahmad makes of Jameson's effort to characterize and indeed privilege "third world narratives" as constituting of "national allegories" in a postmodern context of lost macro-narratives and national identifications (cf. Jameson 1987a). In his rejoinder to this view, Ahmad (1987) questions the tenability of Jameson's "binary opposition of a first and a third world," and therefore, questions whether or not it is possible to accurately conceive of such a notion as "third world literature" and, what's more, homogenize narratives from various parts, or even in a given part, of the world under a single rubric or description. Ahmad also calls into question the political categorization which is supposed to follow logically from the terms of the "experience of colonialism and imperialism" (ibid. 5). Basically, Ahmad points towards the postmodernist theoretical theme of the obliteration of difference and underlines the gross generalizations needed to homogenize the multiplicity of literary or even narrative procedures from varying parts of Asia, Africa, and (an area he only mentions in passing) Latin America. However, while criticisms like Ahmad's should well be taken into account, I concur with Jameson when, in his "Brief Response," he states:

> The methodological problem is that such differences can only be established within some larger identity: if there is nothing in common between two cultural situations, then clearly the establishment of difference is both pointless and given in advance. [1987b: 26]

The point made here, as to the need for the establishment of an identity out of which differences articulate themselves, is more elaborately developed in the Gayatri Spivak essay to which I have already alluded (1988b) and brings us to the key points in the conception of third world phenomena as subjects of critical analysis. Spivak's essay is helpful in relating and applying Jameson's general theory to the third world, by providing us with a way for us to think of and "cognitively map" subjects which may be identified as belonging to the third world, while still accounting for differences, and at the same time avoiding old, static and deterministic modes of thought. Spivak's views most clearly correspond to Jameson's reply to Ahmad when she draws on Marxist perspectives to theorize the subject's problematic positioning between desire and interest, to finally come to the conceptualization of a non-unified subject in relation to micro- and macro- political spheres. Thus, she says:

We might consolidate our critique in the following way: the relationship between global capitalism (exploitation in economics) and nation-state alliances (domination in geopolitics) is so macrological that it cannot account for the micrological texture of power. To move toward such an accounting one must move toward theories of ideology--of subject formations that micrologically and often erratically operate the interests that congeal the macrologies. Such theories cannot afford to overlook the category of representation in its two senses. They must note how the staging of the world in representation--its scene in writing, its *Darstellung*--dissimulates the choice of and need for "heroes," paternal proxies, agents of power-- *Vertretung*. [Spivak 279]

While the whole of the above statement is important to any argument which tries to deal with a conception of the third world, and will require a great deal of unpacking, I would like to concentrate first on Spivak's sense of macrological and micrological *concepts*, *textures*, and relations, and to relate them, in turn, to the way in which I have come to understand Jameson's concept of cognitive mapping.

In thinking the difference between the concept of a macrological "idea" about the world (albeit an idea with very real consequences) and the "experience" of the micrological texture of the world, I am reminded of the way in which many students of dialectics understand the relation between Hegelian and Marxist versions. For Norman and Sayer, for example, "what makes [a conceptual Hegelian] statement true" is not that it exists in some realm independent from the real, or that it is statement "about a separate realm of concepts," but rather that it is "a statement ... about actual ... things in the real world" (1980: 352).

To make their point more understandable, Norman and Sayer add:

[To argue] that Hegel's dialectic is a conceptual dialectic ... [is not to say] that it is about concepts as distinct from being about things in the material world.... [This] ... would be a regression to a Platonic dualism... However ... the traditional philosophical distinction between conceptual and empirical truths [still holds]. Consider a standard philosophical example of a conceptual truth[: ...] One and the same thing cannot at one and the same time be both red all over and green all over. This ... is not an empirical truth. It is true in virtue of the connections between concepts [,] ... the way we use color concepts, ... [or] the language of colors.... The statement is not a truth

73

about a separate realm of concepts, but about actual colored things in the real world. Hegel's 'conceptual dialectic' consists of conceptual truths in this sense. [His] claim that all particulars are also universals is not ... to be discovered empirically. It is true in virtue of the relations between the concept 'particular' and the 'concept universal'. But it is a truth about all particular things in the real world[;] ... it asserts ... that they are also known as universals. And to say that it is true in virtue of the relations between concepts is to say that it is true in virtue of the way in which the relevant terms are used in the language (that is, used by humans engaged in the physical activities of speaking and writing). Thus the recognition of such conceptual truths is not incompatible with materialism. [ibid.]

To relate this perspective to the concept of micro and macro: could we not argue that the various "textures" in the micro-realms of Asia, Africa, and, of course, Latin America provide the phenomena necessary to construct some macro-"situational" concept so as to make possible the discussion of the subject of the third world? So, in his foreword to Roberto Fernández Retamar's collection of translated essays *(1989),* Jameson writes that the Cuban critic's "internationalism of the national situations"

neither reduces the "Third World" to some homogeneous Other of the West, nor does it vacuously celebrate the "astonishing" pluralism of human cultures: rather, by isolating the common *situation* (capitalism, imperialism, colonialism) shared by very different kinds of societies, it allows their differences to be measured against each other [and] ourselves. [xii]

Conversely, isn't such an imaging useful in conceiving of a "first world" to which the "third world" sometimes speaks, and vice-versa? Additionally, we should recognize the added necessity of thinking both a unity and a difference in considering Spivak's two "macro" terms--"global capitalism", and "nation-state alliances"--within the conceptual realm, and their relation to the very real textures they dominate. This recognition would entail assigning different quantitative and qualitative values to each of the two conceptual terms in order to construct asymmetrical, dynamic, and ever-changing relationships especially when both terms and relations are involved in the specificities of particular "textu[r]al" situations. It is here that attention must turn directly to the question of Jameson's cognitive mapping, which will also lead to resurrecting the skepticisms over the possibility of thinking the third world.

3.

In "Cognitive Mapping," Jameson points to "the moment of the multinational network known as late capitalism...in [which] lived experience makes itself felt by the so-called death of the subject, or, more exactly, the fragmented schizophrenic decentering and dispersion" which alienates the subject in a "perceptual barrage of immediacy" (1988: 351). It is out of this sensation of the lived context that Latin Americanists such as George Yúdice conclude that

> Rather than speak of a postmodernism, ... which runs the risk of identifying the style of one group as emblematic of a condition (Lyotard) or a "cultural dominant" (Jameson), it is preferable to theorize postmodernity as a series of conditions variously holding in different social formations that elicit multiple ways in which modernization has been attempted in them. [1992: 7]

Here, Yúdice's statement fails to integrate the question of domination which he along with fellow editors Jean Franco, and Juan Flores confirm as a common thread in Latin American experience. In the introduction to *On Edge* (1992), where Yúdice's above-cited essay appears, the editors present a veritable catalogue of terms used to signify totalizing modes of ideological and material domination--the "Monroe Doctrine", "Pan-Americanism," "the Good Neighbor Policy," "the Caribbean Basin Initiative," "the Brady Plan," the "new world order," etc.--as so many examples which constitute "just a jazzed up remake of an old standard" (1992: vii.). Postmodern theory negates totality on one level only to assert it on another. And this contradiction hearkens back to Spivak's comments on the dialogue between Foucault and Deleuze in "Can the Subaltern Speak?" in which a "failure...to consider the relations between desire, power, and subjectivity renders these major French thinkers [and by inference here, Yúdice] incapable of articulating a theory of interests" (Spivak 1988: 273)--above all, interests rooted in questions of class. This limitation, she tells us, is the result of a non-recognition of the role of ideology, which I would here identify with ideational and conceptual constructs producing and produced by the "cultural logic of late capitalism" in its inter-connections with the power of the multinationals and their control of the all pervasive high-technology of the mass media in a more-than-ever world system. Indeed, much of the concern with immediacy in theories such as those found in the work of Foucault, Deleuze and Guattari, and Baudrillard can be identified as symptoms of the late capitalist role of the marriage of high-technology and the media in the form of television–the war in the Persian Gulf, and role of the military and media "high tech" come immediately to mind (cf. Baudrillard 1991; Norris 1992; and for Latin American Sarlo 1994 and 1995).

Spivak's approach enables her to overcome the problems she finds in Foulcault, Deleuze, and other poststructuralist thinkers. By thinking of contemporary ideology and the articulation of subject positions in relation to their corresponding cultural dominant, she is able to conceive of a "representation" which exists in the "complicity of Marx's *Vertreten* and *Darstellen* in their identity-in-difference as the place practice" or "scene of their double-play" (Spivak: 277). This orientation enables Spivak to give specificity to Jameson's search for a method of cognitive mappings for postmodern positions and configurations of power and resistance, above all because Spivak's concern with subaltern third world representation mediates, modifies and extends Jameson's view of Marxist representation as a virtual "synonym of figuration" infinitely complicated by capitalist dynamics of production, consumption and signification (1988: 348).

To fail to identify the logic of a cultural dominant, to restrict inquiry only to terms of specific, independently held moments in a post-marxist scene of power containment is to be complicit in face of "positivist empiricism–the justifying foundation of advanced capitalist neocolonialism" (Spivak: 275). It is to take sides in third world disputes while failing to consider on the one hand the interests of significant subaltern sectors who are supposedly the subjects of struggle (but are they? to what extent? to what degree are they represented by the state or organized revolutionary groups? to what degree are they really a "they" or any singular, united subject?) and on the other hand the global scene of debt and economic domination which has made given disputes possible, and seeks to impose the terms for their continued postmodern reconfiguration. It is to accept the condemnation of "third world terrorism" while, at best, taking a stance of mystification in the face of advanced capitalist terrorist acts--including recent atrocities which are marked by such high levels of efficiency, technological verve and even aesthetic effect so that contemporary terrorism becomes virtually a representation of postmodern sublimity. A failure to specify cultural dominants in relation to third world contexts negates the primacy of the history of disempowerment, domination as the motivation behind "terrorism"; it leads to a view of terrorism as a reified subject, as an *instrumentalization* which provides a support mechanism for the ideology of the government and mass media--in other words, as the ideological arm of multinational corporate structuration.

Perhaps one way of thinking the difference between a first world and a third world country would be not solely in terms of stages in economic development, etc. (as in Ahmad's questioning of the use of the term), but also the level of ideological penetration and hence the more prolific existence in third world countries of more traditional overt forms of resistance than in a country such as the United States. However, such a view will probably require continual modification as racial and other forms of urban "disturbances," riots and the like emerge in relation to the vicissitudes of capitalist development and their effects on different groups; and as the third world penetrates the first, with late capitalism continuing to become a global reality.

Ahmad's description of working conditions in factories in India (1987: 7) provides an example of a residual or earlier form of capitalism which prompts a valuable representation of a third world subject--as in Jameson's example of Brecht (1988: 348). All this confirms Jameson's persistence in affirming the importance of representation in spite of postmodern disclaimers and complications, and his effort to posit the representational study of cityscapes and literary forms as crucial to cognitive mapping in relation to global totalizations and local specificities.

This overall emphasis on representation would seem to support the at least partial viability of Jameson's proposal for a national allegorical reading of texts; though such a reading must remain problematic and be subject to the test of the specificities of its application. Nevertheless, an allegorical reading of discourse or literature from countries or areas that h ave not undergone the complete experience of late capitalism is a valid procedure-- although Ahmad is undoubtedly right that other readings need to be developed as well.

The question of third world representation is precisely where I believe Spivak helps by her bifurcation of representational theory in Marx. Having given a rough example of my conception of what it is to map cognitively on a global scale, I wish now to turn from the "broad concept of representation"--*Vertreten*--to the concrete "economic" specificities of representation--*Darstellen*--and the scene of writing in late capitalism (Spivak 278-279). Failure to make the distinction between the general and the specific is to ignore "the international division of labor," to be

> incapable of dealing with global capitalism: the subject-production of worker and unemployed within nation-state ideologies in its Center; the increasing subtraction of the working class in the Periphery from the realization of surplus value ...; and the large-scale presence of paracapitalist labor as well as the heterogeneous structural status of agriculture in the periphery. [Spivak 272]

To paraphrase Jameson's point with which this essay starts: to lose the concept of specificity is to lose our entire purpose for thinking a totality as well. If we think in terms of actual cartography, our cognitive map serves very much in the same sense as one of those maps in which the spherical shape of the globe has been sectioned and flattened so as to be able to see, albeit distortedly, the world in its entirety at a glance--and, indeed, ultimately geography and cartography may have much to do with cognitive mapping (cf. Soja 1990). To continue, as we look at our map we can see that much of the integrity of the contour has been sacrificed with the advantage of being able to see the whole picture at once; and the relationships of specifics within a concept of a liquid whole. However, as we zero in on specific places, our map becomes entirely useless and, hence, the need for more localized and specific *terrain* maps to show us the "text[ure]" of the specific subject. Here we move towards theories of "ideology of subject formations that micrologically and erratically operate the interests that congeal the macrologies" (Spivak 279).

4.

What I have tried to express here is that, within the current framework of late capitalism, there can be only questions with tentative answers. With regards to Latin America alone the questions are endless--for example in the multiple and complicated problems that arise out of the "Indian question" in the case of the highland Mayans of Guatemala, and how these problems relate to both micro- and macrological concerns. How do we view the relationship of the various insurgent organizations to the indigenous populations during the period of guerrilla warfare and indigenous mobilization extending from the 1970s through the recent peace accords? Under what circumstances has the relationship "constellate" more along the lines of Marx/Spivak's term of *Vertreten,* or that of *Darstellen*; and what has been the overall role of representation in one formulation or the other?

Similar questions apply to the question of the evangelical movement in the highlands. During the counterinsurgency campaigns, the military permitted free movement to evangelical clergy while openly murdering more radical clerical and congregational elements of the Catholic church. At the same time, the California-based Church of the Word, an organization strongly involved with the New Right movement in the United States, was able to gain many converts among the indigenous population. In one sense the evangelicals were "filling a void" in the lives of the Mayas and providing an identity for them to relate to in post-holocaust Guatemala. To what extent was and is the evangelical movement tied to the reasons for this void in the first place?

In the most obvious sense, the evangelicals, with their New Right ties, appear as *Vertretung* ("agents" and "proxies") in their relation to the Mayans. Yet, on the other hand, matters are complicated by the fact that the majority of the upper levels of the military have, for religious and other reasons, come into conflict with the evangelical movement. This conflict is highlighted by the ouster of born-again General Efraín Ríos Montt in 1983, presumably by traditional, entrenched, Catholic elements of the army. Is the evangelical movement, then, a more direct attempt at ideological control by the U.S., which by-passes the Guatemalan military? The question remains, Who is representing who, and why?

In *Geopolitics and Geoculture (1991),* Wallerstein argues that the struggles of third world peoples since the 60s has resulted in a more favorable political positioning (via accommodation by the U.S.) for many subaltern groups, while failing to improve their material conditions of existence. However, this political accommodation, Wallerstein suggests, provides the *potentiality* needed for material change in the future. How does this potentiality figure in terms of the discussion in this paper of representation and interest? How does the integration of the post-counterinsurgency Mayan population into society as a whole relate to this potentiality, and their ability to identify with their interests, given their altered terms of representation?

A very specific series of questions that open out toward the work of García Canclini and others with respect to cultural hybridization and globalization might include asking whether the large-scale introduction of Mayan craftwork into the U.S. market raises Mayan cultural and political awareness and unity among the Maya. Does cultural representation through the crafts help with regard to political empowerment, as in Guatemala's new social movements? Or are handicraft production and representation nothing more than a matter of commodification without any significant benefit? Is it possible that it can be both--that there can be some positive relation between tendencies toward global commodification and heighten consciousness and resistance? Or, in other words, to what extent do our coordinates of *Vertreten* and *Darstellen* overlap? Finally, what ramifications do these question have for the analysis of indigenous testimonial and other written forms in relation to political discourse and literature and the overall mapping of (and involved in) cultural forms in recent years and today?

As this essay goes to press, it is worth noting how, in the wake of the Cold War Period, and the struggles of individuals like Rigoberta Menchú, Jennifer Harbury, Rosalina Tuyuc as well as new social movements and organizations (including indigenous-based ones), the U.S. had begun exerting pressure against CIA and military human rights abuses and controls. Ríos Montt's candidate almost won the national elections in 1996; but the peace process went ahead after the elections and came to a resolution by the end of 1996. In this respect, global and local, socio-economic and political problems came together in a way which spelled a new historical phase (cf. Smith 184 and 1990) and perhaps a new structural context for the two modes of representation discussed herein, in terms of both overall and literary cognitive mapping (cf. Zimmerman 1995 and Arias in this volume).

In closing, I have tried to show the meaninglessness of individual or peripheral types of interpretation without some larger frame of reference to give them meaning in the context of an ever more dominant global context. Making these types of broad connections is one of the most crucial tasks of comparatist analysis today, although the connections should always be open to criticism with respect to the specificities they draw upon. Conversely, critics in a given specific field should not be so quick to appropriate the rhetoric of the obliteration of difference. Such is the case with Ahmad when he scornfully cites Jameson saying that the criticisms of his theory of third world literature "do not strike [him] as relevant," but fails to include the second part of the statement--"to the argument I am making"--which is key to Jameson's overall argument. That argument, it should be noted, is in turn one geared towards a perception of the world from a unique position in the multinational sphere--a world in which external domination is not a given, as is more commonly the case with third world positions--whether such positions are, as they are more likely to be found, in Pakistan or Peru, in Guatemala or in the ghettos and barrios of Los Angeles.

FIN DE SIGLO: REFLECTIONS
FROM THE PERIPHERY[1]

Hugo Achugar
Translated by Robert Scott Curry

One needs an immense dose of disillusionment in order to live without utopia, and the idea of progress is the modern version of utopia par excellence. This includes those who deny belief in it but adhere to it, nevertheless, unconsciously. --E. M. Cioran, *Trapped in the Future.*

General lamentation over the disappearance of utopia is understandable. In all its forms, lamentation lightly clouds the vision of he who laments. The frequently heard affirmation that it is impossible to live without utopia, is in the best of cases, only a fourth of the truth. --Hans Magnus Enzensberger, *"An Appendix to Utopia."*

David and Goliath demands utopias as well as aforementioned qualities of social action. We know that this world is killing itself without any warning signs, men are needed who will return to mankind the natural and magic "dogma" of faith and life. --Fernando Calderón, "América Latina."

This essay is a reflection, from the standpoint of literary and cultural studies, on the problematic presented by notions such as modernity, postmodernity and avant garde in relation to the subject of enunciation in a peripheral situation. Furthermore, it is a reflection in light of a present that at once accompanies both the *fin de siecle* as well as the end of a series of social projects. This reflection does not adhere to the proposition that we are at the end of history; on the contrary, I believe that today's ideological debate has to do with a situation of change, which is eminently fluid, in which the rules of the game aren't clear or, in the best of cases, in which the position of the participants in the game have been profoundly altered.

---

[1]This is an edited (and abridged) translation of Achugar 1994.

1. The Position from Which One Speaks

To specify the position from which one speaks does not imply an exclusively geographical/cultural determination; to specify the place is to determine the position of the subject and its mode of enunciation. Rorty proposes conversation as a model for reflection, pretending by this means to eliminate the tyranny of authoritarian reason (cf. Harstock 1987). Others propose different models.

From where and how do we speak, then? We speak from a space configured by utopia, in an attempt at dialogue, but above all else from the precariousness of a situation that, with more intensity than ever before (the emphasis perhaps is determined to be my/our present), is postulated or known provisionally and destined to future derision. We speak from the Latin American periphery; from humanism's periphery where we have been placed by the neoliberalism of post-Keynesian society; we speak from the periphery of those of us who bet on utopia; and we speak from Latin American discursivity which is another form of periphery.

We speak therefore from a contaminated space because we know that any aspiration towards neutrality is yet another utopia--a false one. It seems possible to speak of Borges's ultraistic metaphors, of Vallejo's synecdochal constructions or even of the paratactical structures in Huidobro's poems from a space that is self-understood as aseptic and neutral. Furthermore, it is necessary and perhaps profitable to do so for all.... But no sooner do we move beyond what is rigidly technical or rhetorical (in the worst and most myopic sense of what we can understand as an assumption of rhetoric) than we find that the point of enunciation ceases to be neutral.

Our place is other. To reflect from the periphery, nevertheless, poses some problems, beginning with the very notion of periphery. What is the periphery? And who are we who are supposedly in the periphery? Periphery, a silenced subaltern: these are still valid categories but ones needing more specification and discussion (cf. Spivak 1988; Harstock 1987). The center is not homogeneous; and above all, as Nelly Richard has argued in a different, but not entirely opposed perspective (1988), the center also has its peripheries.

It is possible to find hegemonic and subaltern groups and center-periphery relations in the center. This implies, not only that the categories be revised, as Garcia Canclini suggests with respect to Gramsci's formulations (1991), but also the idea that, at a symbolic and discursive level, the center is itself traversed today by categories which, besides the socio-economic, include those of race, gender, and sexual orientation which require rethinking all hierarchical power relations and the nature of the categories themselves.

Furthermore, it is clear that in these regards one cannot continue speaking in relation to the periphery or to those silenced from a "we" that implies a totalizing universalization and homogenization. There are also peripheries within the periphery. We the *other* are plural, heterogeneous and, in a certain sense, traversed by conflict which, although not identical to those in the center, are similar.

It has also been proposed that "our" (Latin American) identities in their multiple spaces and times are various identities, to such a degree that it is possible to encounter various profound "I's" within us (cf. Calderón 1987). The risk of looking at this very multiplicity and heterogeneity is that we can lose sight of the fact that these characteristics are common to the center. Nevertheless, to fail to make a distinction is to be complicit in an inanity of analysis and reflection, while the exacerbation of distinction can lead to the confirmation of the same point everywhere.

The postulation of a universal identity of the individual which abolishes cultural, national, gender and ethnic differences, etc., can be as much a form of homogenization typical to the center's discourse, as is the canceling effect of the idea which recognizes the obvious: that we are all human beings (cf. Fernando Saveter's position in numerous published essays and presentations). And to recognize that we are all human beings can enable us to confront racist fascism from the perspective of liberal humanism, but it does not promote a real knowledge of individuals.

Passing on to another level, we find still another class of problems. On the one hand, there are the problems of those who attempt to reflect on cultural and symbolic production in the periphery. Given the rules of the game and the power positions within the academy, *they/we feel obliged* to be conscious or knowledgeable of some, if not all, of the problems discussed in the North or in the first world.

This obligation is a result of professional and academic demands as much as demands from the institutions controlling the legitimating power of intellectual discourse. And there is no doubt that a large part of their/our work consists in refuting perspectives sustained by the center or in elaborating a counter-discourse as an alternative to the hegemonic one.

On the other hand, some critics start with the premise that first world knowledge and problematics have a development or a sophistication that conjoins technological development and cultural reflection in a way that threatens to trivialize or "set back" the discussion of our problematics in the periphery. It is further argued that the theoretical agenda formulated in the center, is done so in ignorance and in a total devalorization of our problematics, with the pretension that it is possible to discuss and reflect on periphery and center as if they were equivalences. It is finally worth noting that these possibilities don't exhaust the suppositions or stereotypes with and on which one reflects from the periphery.

Reflection from the periphery, then, is traversed by these various assumptions and stereotypes, and generates varied sorts of attitudes. For example, Venturi (1991) and others have argued that modernity and postmodernity are phenomena unto themselves of realities other than our own, that the terms are not pertinent and should not have been considered. Another way of arguing, one that is traditional among critics and intellectuals, is to mechanically translate the center's problematics and insert them, passing them through a Procrustean bed, into our realities or, the other way around, to read our problems with glasses bought or imported from the center.

Another posture, that is closer to the one I wish to defend here, seeks to reflect on contemporary reality from the periphery while being aware of other discussions, but without this leading to translation and distortion. Looking from the outside is useful; looking from the inside is as well. What is not useful is to look only from the outside or only from the provincial villages. From Martí's point of view, one would say that the village-dweller shouldn't believe that his village is the entire world and nor should the metropolitan megalomaniac (or in effect the metropolitanized village-dweller) deny that the village and the margin exist. If the village-dweller runs a great risk by thinking of his or her micro-space as the center of the universe, the metropolitan runs the same or greater risk by ignoring the margin or by treating the Other as the etymologist who dissects the insect in his laboratory. The vision of the metropolitan can lead to, and has certainly too often led to, postulates of the Other or the Other's symbolic reality as a phenomenon fit for the zoo. The Other often, although not always, enters into metropolitan reflection as an exercise or as an occasion to verify that that which has been determined in the center's laboratory is the periphery's truth.

Among many things, a bet on the future of utopia today must involve assuming our similar and plural condition in multiple stages. This theme refers to the present attempts at what Fernando Calderón has called the "dead child dream" of regional integration (1987); the dream would obviously require a much better development in some collective enterprise.

Retrospective glances are not the issue then, nor are uneasy ones. To reflect on the writing and the imaginary of our time, especially from our time's new consciousness of its plural, modern, premodern and postmodern rhythms, cannot be accomplished without the insistence that one describe the place from which one speaks or reflects, without failing to inscribe the place from which one speaks within that which one speaks.

2. The Avant Garde's Utopia and Contemporary Utopia.

Jean Franco's introductory note to a special edition of *Studies in 20th Century Literature* provides a valuable point of entry:

> The essays published in this issue reflect the dark mood of much contemporary Latin American literature and criticism in the eighties. While, on one hand, non-canonical genres such as testimonial and the chronicle testify to the emergence of new social actors--women, subaltern classes, the indigenous--for most writers and intellectuals the end of the Twentieth Century seems to evoke anxiety rather than hope, backward glances towards the past rather than projects for the future. Even the debates surrounding postmodernism, again and again seem to develop into discussions of history and the failed, incomplete or authoritarian modernization of the past. The redemptive and totalizing visions of progress, of national emancipation, which were closely allied to certain concepts of originality, authorship and agency, now seem anachronistic. [Franco 1990: 5]

The blow history has dealt in these last few years to many of the conceptions that are important to Latin American intellectuals during past decades would seem to support Franco's observation. We could, perhaps, agree that the redemptive and totalizing visions of progress ... today appear anachronistic"; however we still believe that utopia has not been canceled.

86

What utopia? This we shall see further on. But there are other questions that come first. For example, where do we place the avant garde historically? Is the avant garde a part of modernity or its negation and thus at the same time the beginning of postmodernity? I think that the answer to these questions has something to do with the characterization of utopia in the discourse of the avant garde.

The history of utopia or rather of utopian thought in our America is old. With the utopias of the XIX Century now realized and/or degraded in our century during the twenties, Latin American *vanguardism* was flooded by the utopian spirit. Utopia--much present in those so-called "pure writers" who participated in Cordoba's university reform--was universal but also American.

National emancipation, as utopia on a continental level, the "*magna patria*" of those days, may now seem anachronistic or reformulated on a regional level; but, Henríquez Ureña's formula (1976: 6), "We will strive to achieve social justice and true liberty; we will advance, at last, towards our utopia"[2] seems to continue to have validity. However, today's reading of such texts is carried out in another key. The confusion of the present upon reading the past is worsened for not knowing where to place the dream.

But how do we read these verses from Huidobro's *Altazor*: "And tomorrow what will we put in this empty place?/ Will it be dawn or twilight/ And is it perhaps necessary to put something?"[3] or the verses that end the same author's *Ecuatorial*: "The child with naked wings/ Will come with the clarion between his fingers/ The still fresh clarion which proclaims/ The end of the universe."[4]

Is the *avant garde*'s disillusionment with the modernists accompanied by a utopian gamble as well? Inasmuch as one always reads from the perspective of history, or the narrating of history; the task of reading the disillusionment or the utopian impulse is part of the drama that the reader constructs.

---

[2]"Esforcémonos por acercarnos a la justicia social y a la libertad verdadera; avancemos, en fin, hacia nuestra utopía."

[3]"Y m áñana qué pondremos en el sitio vacio? Pondremos un alba o un crepúsculo? Y hay que poner algo acaso?"

[4]"El niño de las alas desnudas/ Vendrá con el clarín entre los dedos/ El clarín aun fresco que anuncia el fin del Universo."

The history or drama I propose tends towards the view which holds that the avant garde[s] were essentially utopian; and that, like so many other utopias, ended up in the garbage heap of history--museums and academic studies. To reclaim the utopia of the avant gardes, to exercise the right to a utopia is not to be anachronistic and involves a gamble on the future.

The avant garde's utopia wasn't only a criticism of modernity; after all, modernity had already seen distinct utopias and had put its faith in indefinite progress, in universal social justice, in scientific knowledge. Following Matei Calinescu's formula for modernity, I believe that bourgeois modernity (rationalist, competitive, technological and geared toward progress) is dismantled from the position of a culturally self critical modernity that gambles on being able to demystify the authoritarianism of the other modernity.

But it does so through a rationality that holds the belief that with the fulfillment of the bourgeois Enlightenment project came the destruction, oppression and barbaric irrationalism to which the lower classes were submitted. In a certain sense, an example of postmodernity like testimonio could be considered as a record of barbarous acts committed in the name of progress, a type of writing which belongs to modernity, that at the same time, inscribes a utopian vision within what for Habermas is the incomplete project of the Enlightenment by virtue of its gamble on the indefinite moral and material transcendence of humankind (cf. Calinescu 1987--especially the new chapter, "On Postmodernity 1986").

The avant garde's questioning of rationalist modernity takes us back to some of the themes which provide a cultural critique of modernity, but in other respects the avant garde continues some of modernity's definitive characteristics relating to modernity ambivalently, since it bases itself on some of modernity's qualities in order to deconstruct or break with other aspects. It is for this reason that the avant garde can take the form of the apocalyptic conspiracies of Roberto Arlt, the revolutionary socialism of Diego Rivera, the Afro-Cubanism of Nicolás Guillén, or the technological and populist fascination with the University Reform of Parra del Riego.

Nevertheless, the utopias of the various modernities and of the avant garde are not those of today; they could not be so even when one tries to recover them, by claiming (as do Habermas [1983] and his followers) that modernity is an unfinished project. It will be said that today's utopia is limited or in other words "socially democratized"; but I have no great problems with the qualifiers. The labels and qualifiers were a central preoccupation in other times, but and today we are moving in a different universe.

Skepticism, even Rorty's thoroughly postmodern relativism, can also be a sign of anachronism, another way of exercising nostalgia by looking at the world from a baroque hill of disillusionment. The right to a utopia can never be or have its basis in the utopia of the original avant garde nor in the painful memories of the totalizing utopian vision of the avant garde of the sixties. This latter utopia with its redemptive aspirations had as its central discursive image an "assault on heaven." Almost everything that didn't converge towards this celestial attack was silenced or degraded; the old saying "we can accomplish anything" continued to be valid, only now with a particularly messianic weight to it.

Today in the historic antipodes of that particularly American utopian hour found in *Altazor* or the work of Henríquez Ureña; in the valley in which the failure of the sixties has left us, gorged with electronic "gadgets," eating kiwis and contemplating the simulcast of the strategies in the Gulf War and Dubrovnik, and of the pollution in Santiago and Mexico City, the utopian king continues to preside over us as if, as Enzenberg says, "The frequently heard affirmation, that it is impossible to live without utopia, is in the best of cases, only a fourth of the truth"; this is our fragmented, contemporaneous, postmodern fourth. Is utopia modern or postmodern? What relation and difference exist between current ideas of utopia and the sublime and those that today sound anachronistic? What does the postmodern utopia consist of? There is no one single postmodernity as there was never one single modernity.

The disillusioned baroque awakening of Sor Juana Inés de la Cruz admitting the failure of rationality and celebrating divine illumination, synthesized in the well known final verse: "The world lit up and I awoke," can not be considered as a mode or image of postmodern utopia, but rather as an anachronism of today's disillusionment which today is the other face of postmodernity. Disillusionment's postmodernity dialogues wearing the face of modernity; utopia's postmodernity dialogues wearing the face of the avant garde--in particular, with that paradoxical, ambivalent and utopian *élan* which, like alpha and omega, freshly trumpets the end of the Universe.

3. The Faces of the Hydra: Modernity
and Postmodernity in the Periphery

Angel Rama has suggested that one should speak of "the three eruptions of modernity," or of various modernisms, suggesting that all three have to do with one single, general historical process (1989: especially 129-136). In a broad sense, this process of modernity corresponds with Latin American society's successive attempts at modernization and presupposes the existence of facts and lines of development which are not always hegemonic but which complete the panorama. After all, the notion of modernity as the opposite of contemporaneity is not necessarily identical to the notion of it as the opposite of postmodernity. On the other hand, whether or not the avant garde is included in a conceptualization of modernity affects the degree to which the boundaries between modernity and postmodernity become blurred (cf. Lethen 1986: 233-238).

This conceptual instability in relation to the academic drama of the protagonistic personalities of modernity and postmodernity--in which the multiple personalities of the avant garde play a central role--is basically due to the fact that it has to do with critical constructs whose existence depends not so much on empirical reality as on the narratives and periodizations that individual and social subjects make of history (cf. Bertens 1986: 10). In this sense, conceptual multiplicity and instability have much or more to do with the debate over daily social life and with the position of the subject of enunciation in this debate than it does with cultural phenomena considered in themselves and in isolation.

Along these lines, the Hydra could be considered as a way of representing the problem of modernity and postmodernity in our countries. This could be so in two instances: one, in relation to the multi-headed monster that Hercules destroyed; and another, in function of the location that the Hydra constellation has in relation to our southern region.

Another way of presenting this problem would be in terms of a kaleidoscope, or, to stay with mythic images, a sort of Proteus. It isn't only through the multiplicity of aspects and forms of the problematic of modernity and postmodernity in our countries that I have arrived at these images--after all, some thinkers of the North also refer to this changing and inaccessible condition of postmodernity--but also through the unstable diorama of the very notions involved.

The Hydra in Lake Lerna or the old chameleon-like Proteus are images of multiplicity and transformation; but also, in a certain sense, they represent the absence of the original, of incessant multiplication, of a kind of unlimited semiosis. However, freezing the Hydra in the southern sky leads to an appropriation of precise symbolic enunciation and production. The multiplying kaleidoscope has in its multiplicity a limited repertory, a position that determines which beautiful images can be observed (kaleidoscope comes from the Greek words for beauty, image and the act of observation).

Modernity and postmodernity, understood as codes or symbolic imaginaries, enter into our countries as resemantisized imports or as names for already existing personal experiences. I am not playing the old song of Latin American syncreticism, although in some ways its tones and strains are included in my project. Rather I wish to underline that the periphery's modernity is of the periphery's own making. It is glaringly evident that the entry and production of the imaginary and symbolic modes and motives is never pure, total, or absolute. Furthermore, it can sometimes happen that what enters are forms of production or central significations that, upon coming into contact with an institutionally diverse or heterogeneous community, undergo fundamental mutations and transformations that cannot be assimilated to forms and significations generated in other regions. Or it can happen too that an alternative form or signification enters along with what is hegemonically central to cultural processes or identities. In a certain sense what happens is that Latin Americans, as Fernando Calderón has shown, "live a cultural life that is a truncated and mixed pre-modernity, modernity, and postmodernity" (1987: 19). But if this truncated and mixed condition of cultural life is deafeningly evident in the periphery, it also doesn't cease to be present in the center.

Finally, it is possible to argue that the modernity of the center, in its planetary geography, has also anticipated the place of the periphery; but this argument fails to account for real processes occurring in the periphery-- among other reasons because it ignores the fact that the modernity of the center always already contained its own periphery.

On the other hand, it can be that the entry of certain symbolic systems supposes the restoration of processes and phenomena that have their origin in the periphery but which the center has interpreted and assimilated in function of its own imaginary and with a particular agenda that they nevertheless offer to the planet as a universal value. The center's reading of García Márquez or Borges as central figures of postmodernity--integrating them in series with Grass, Fowles, Rushdie, Doctorow, etc. (cf. Hutcheon 1988: 5)--is carried out with an ordering of the planet that paradoxically proposes decentralization, but from the position of the prison warden in the Panopticon--that is, from a Eurocentric position of classificatory ordering. In these cases it often happens that the mirror or landscape which the center offers us about ourselves, or about partial aspects of ourselves, ends by resemantisizing our own image or, as we will see, by constructing simulacra.

What we wish to describe is an unequal exchange or dialogue that is today part of a telecommunications society wherein the local is dissolved by an image which a triumphal transnational imaginary offers to the planet in an attempt at homogenization that is tantamount to sovereignty. The dialogue, in this line of argument, would be a product of the new conversation that the planet has managed to establish. But, dialogue or monologue, the problem is rooted in the theme of representation. Representation with the double meaning of delegation and mimesis.

The problematic of modernity, of the avant garde and postmodernity also involves the theme of representation, especially in relation to the question of the transfer or internationalization of cultural models that are independent of their socio-economic origins. The argument that postmodernity and modernity aren't Latin American phenomena carries with it implicitly--in its absolute logic--the notion that the Magical Realism or *real maravilloso* or the *garciamarquezismo* that has invaded the writing of the northern hemisphere is not possible. Or in any case that in order for the northern hemisphere to have produced magical realism the area should have in addition imported the poverty, underdevelopment and illiteracy that belongs to greater part of Our America.

But what's more, the processes aren't even uniformly hybrid or syncretic. There are, for example in the case of architecture, postmodern productions that are the very physical copies of realizations carried out in other spaces. And there are above all simulacra--simulacra of modernity or postmodernity. Sometimes in taking exterior or decorative or merely stylistic characteristics and by losing the original signification in the transfer, what is obtained are simulacra--and those forms of simulacra, of parody or, as we shall see, of hyperbole, that are precisely the ones proper to the periphery through which modern and postmodern works are constructed.

Also, the hyperbolization of models and codes almost carries us to other realities. The technological fury that invades the poetry of Alfredo Mario Ferreiro during the avant garde decade of the twenties in Uruguay is more realist than the futurist kings of Italy. As always happens, the periphery ends by constructing a discourse which, upon exacerbating the traits or traces of metropolitan discourse, erects a discourse of its own. The Argentine comic strip "Patoruzú" is the form with which Argentine modernity reworks the North American comic strip genre. But in a sense "Patoruzú" is also and above all else a nationalistic discourse which deconstructs first world modernity by counterpoising the civilized modernity of the center with the barbaric cunning of the periphery. After all, Isidoro, the good unproductive child of the bourgeoisie always ready to surrender everything around him for his own private gain is juxtaposed to Patoruzú whose task is the populist defense of the nation by attempting to synthesize modernity with nationalism, European civilization with local barbarity.

4. Modernity and Postmodernity.
Representativity and Representation

Modernity and postmodernity, as before with the avant garde and neo-avant garde, in the periphery have been understood on many occasions as stylistic currents, movements and codes and not as postures or ways of symbolizing or, better yet, as structures of thought and feeling in the face of contemporary life. At this point in my reflection, it is obvious, I believe, that I am not interested within this context in a technical repertory of the instruments and discursive means of modernity or postmodernity. On the contrary, what is important to me is, starting from the premise that we are concerned with two structures of thought and feeling of human beings, to see how these are formulated in the periphery.

I don't, nor do I want to, enter here, into a discussion regarding the difference or the periodization of the symbolic modes of production called modernity and postmodernity. In the Latin American periphery, the two modes have been dominant structures of thought and feeling in the hegemonic intellectual centers of our countries. To speak of a hegemonic character in this case doesn't imply a relation to dominant economic or social

93

sectors, given that in some countries the hegemonic intellectual sectors haven't necessarily had anything to do with the social and economic elites. Quite possibly because they were in contact with growing universalized and "simultaneized" information, these intellectual sectors understood that the gamble was in synchronizing the watches of our societies with the universal, or specifically western, watch. Besides, they attributed the backwardness of our countries to the lingering of flaws in the structures of thought that had configured the present they were actively producing. This was true as much for the moderns as the postmoderns, since in both cases bringing our societies up to date was and is confused with rejecting the institutional. That the rejection of the institutional in modernity is different from its rejection in the postmodern world deserves another discussion that is impossible here. But what interests me now is precisely to show that both modern and postmodern discourse in the periphery share, at an implicit level if you will, a common rejection of all that is institutionally based and which is responsible for the respective deteriorated present.

On the one hand an Oswaldo or a Mario de Andrade or a Vicente Huidobro or a Frida Khalo or a Pedro Figari or a Diego Rivera or a Macedonio Fernández or a Felisberto Hernández; or furthermore the youth of the 1918 University Reform or the César Vallejos, the Joaquín Torres, the Borges, the Carpentiers, and the Onettis could represent the modern discourse of our Latin America. However, picking names to represent postmodernity isn't so easy; and it sets off major polemics and doubts. Who are the postmodern writers and artists? Also, which postmodernity are we talking about? That of Néstor Perlongher, Armando Rojas Guardia, Yolanda Patín, Cristina Peri Rossi, Fabio Morabito, Nélida Piñón, Rosario Ferré, Raúl Zurita, Ricardo Piglia, Ignacio de Loyola Brandao, Mario Levrero, Leo Masliah? That of Borges, García Márquez, Cortázar, Donoso, or Fuentes? Or that of Rigoberta Menchú, Eduardo Galeano or Elena Poniatowska?

The problem is complicated if we throw other names out on the table: do we assume that Carlos Gardel represents popular or populist modernity? What do the "Fabulous Cadillacs" from Argentina, or the Panamanian Rubén Blades, or the Uruguayan Jaime Roos represent? Are they modern or postmodern? Or by chance have I committed the horrible error of opening the door of poetic genres not validated by the tradition of belles lettres. Couldn't it be that the phenomena of postmodernity and modernity are missed in this analysis--missed because of an alteration in the rules or conceptual conventions by which we think of artistic or aesthetic problems? The academic institutionalization of the avant garde has reached its climax, and our time needs to hang the portraits of its ancestors in order to recognize its geneology and effect. We still have no examples (or at least not frequent ones) of Batman, Agustín Lara, Mafalda, Isabelita Sarli and He-Man in our museums. And this is so although we now can see Carlos Gardel, Marylin Monroe and cans of Campbell's soup in frames, poems and the ritual memory of our present imaginary. This reference to our contemporary Parnassus is meant to date the enunciative situation of all attempts today at describing notions of the avant garde, modernization, modernism, modernity, postmodernity, postmodernism and contemporaneity. It isn't the same to describe the avant garde within the context of its historical moment as it is to describe it today. The difference implies a discussion, a struggle for periodization and also for an interpretation and its significance. Both debates are precisely central in the present (postmodern?) hour of our societies, peripheral or not.

Although the European modernity of a Marinetti, of a Duchamp, of Dadaism, broke with the fine arts at an earlier time, it didn't necessarily open the door to non-cannonical discursive formations. Modernity's break achieved its own basis for notions of art and beauty. But, at the same time, its flirtation with popular or "low" culture made possible a dialogue, not a comparison. Latin America's peripheral modernity, in some cases, integrated or assimilated itself into European modes--in this sense Huidobro but also Torres García are notable examples; but in other cases it radicalized the popular or the populist wager, as we can see in the cases of Rivera and Vallejo (although I'm not going to discuss this aspect of the theme here).

Postmodernity, on the other hand, as much in the center as in the periphery, appears to open the doors to the mixing, contamination and dehierarchalization of the multiple and heterogeneous. In modernity, heterogeneity was introduced through the exotic; but it kept the accent that its assimilation to the hegemonic conferred upon it even in its almost anthropologically-based points of difference. In postmodernity there is a sort of more democratic or chaotic coexistence--listeners/readers select the qualifiers--that facilitates an unedited anterior valorization. Television, with its scarcely selective offering of all kinds of discourse is no stranger to this dehierarchalized coexistence, since its interrupted and fragmentary syntax allows virtually no coherent relationship to the crisis of macro-unities or uniqueness.

In any case--and in a sense different from what is indicated at the beginning of this work--neither is the periphery homogeneous. Postmodern production isn't the same in highly dynamic societies as in stagnant societies, or ones where social mobility is highly improbable. In countries where social dynamism is greater, the possibility of the coexistence of multiple projects is much more important than in those countries, like my own Uruguay, where stagnation permits the hegemonic systems of value and valuation nursed on the aesthetics of modernities to censure and depreciate all attempts to postulate symbolic productions that do not convey dominant values.

Finally, I should point out something central to the discussion about modernity and postmodernity in relation to the theme of representation and to the fragmentation and constitution of the subject (cf. Achugar 1991), at least somewhat in the terms Gayatri Spivak (1988a and b) has set forth. This problematic isn't new to the Latin American periphery, nor does it make its appearance with postmodernity: it has been with us for a long time. Its emphasis might have changed and perhaps the difference in degree might have made for a qualitative transformation, but it's not unprecedented.

We may note with respect to Spivak that she is a woman from the third world who, paradoxically, occupies a central position as a voice from the periphery in the discourse of the first world. As she has observed in the case of India, with special reference to the condition of women during colonial society, the voices silenced by the central subject have another history to tell, a different story opposed to the official one of the metropolitan center and its empire. Or, to put it another way, the position of the subject of the enunciation of the colonial subject suffers a substantial change during this century and at the same time its participation in the public sphere is changed (Spivak 1988b). The discursive space of the public sphere--at the global level or of the first world of the periphery--has changed into a shared space where an attempt at the construction of or search for a new identity takes place. That new identity is not the homogenizing one imposed by the monologue of imperial discourse, but rather a heterogeneous one, achieved by being differenced and plural, perhaps more democratic and respectful of other identities.

The history of the erosion of the monologic discourse of the central subject (European, white, masculine, heterosexual and literate) which was of such significance for modernity resonates today in postmodernity. The process unleashed during the brutal transformation of everyday life during the industrial revolution (and which involved a series of experiences not only in the hegemonic sectors, but among those who lived the revolution from the margins) doesn't appear to have ended. The present technological revolution is also changing daily life. It is possible that the mirage of democratization that introduces technology is only this: a false splendor of computer chips. It is also possible that technology diversifies information channels and that the sacred spaces of modernity become contaminated by the postmodern vanguard. It is possible, finally, that the utopian impulse multiplies, the Hydra combines with the Phoenix bird, and that the fragmentation that some lament today will be the expression of a less centralized and programmed life in the future.

To conclude, I should also point out that the artist, man or woman, of the periphery always writes or paints or makes music from the periphery, and this mark of his/her enunciation problematically crosses his/her discourse in ways that do not happen in the discourse of the metropolitan artist. This is to say that although the discourse of the metropolitan artist is marked, in his or her case, the place of enunciation isn't problematic. After all, for the metropolitan artist there is no space other than his/her own, there exists no world other than his/her own.

The central subject in a sovereign or imperial act narrates his/her history as his/her story. In the periphery, the narrating subject recognizes his/her marginal situation; and if in some cases he/she "forgets" this situation and (between notorious quotations) assumes a central voice, the effect is one of parody or simulacrum. The marginal voice cross dressing as if it were a central one is also a realization of its own situation.

To paraphrase Cioran (a figure at the same time central and marginal in more than one sense), one needs an immense dose of disillusionment in order to live in the periphery without utopia; and the idea of a redefinition of the periphery as a space of utopian skepticism could be the contemporary utopia. In this formulation, the periphery is a privileged place from which to think the world, all the while knowing that it will be a long time before we are inhabited by the greater gods of the contemporary Parnassus. The end of the century/millennium in the Latin American periphery doesn't have to be reduced to the point where our imaginary should merely be an immense cornucopia with a McDonald's logo on it, blessed by presidents and bishops. The end of the century/millennium of the Latin American periphery is connected to the planet's satellites; but although "I am blind and know nothing[,] ... I forsee/ that there are more ways." And this blind seeing of Borges--wrong, ultraist, modern and postmodern--looks out from our utopian place.

II. Specifying South

Alicia Haber, *Museo Virtual de Artes del país*, 1996.
Reproduction courtesy of the artist.

A STAR IS BORN: ACTION GROUPS AND POWER, THE INDUSTRIALES AND THE DI TELLA INSTITUTE IN ARGENTINE MODERNIZATION [1]

Nora Bonnin

1. Power and Action Groups: A Theoretical Frame

Conflicts and resolutions constantly result from the interaction among different groups within a given society. Creative solutions to historical conflicts, particularly when brought about by previously marginalized action groups, mainly result from an efficient use of power. Insight into the spheres of power is crucial to understanding as well as implementing change.

In Latin America, the struggle to move out of spheres of marginality is not only crucial for whole countries and areas within an international context, but it is also so for large sectors within each historically constituted national configuration, the examination of action groups and their ability to use, extend or empower given cultural and social spheres is crucial for any study focused on questions of political change.

This study attempts to provide a logical means to explain the emergence of "new" action groups within decision-making and negotiating spheres in Argentina. To ask how groups achieve access to the arena of those who have a predominant influence is to ask how those groups may attain active power from positions of relative weakness. However, some effort should be made to define what is to be understood by "power."

---

[1]In addition to the general indebtedness of this essay to Beatriz Sarlo (1988) and other writers cited (above all King 1985 and García Canclini 1988 on Di Tella), I wish to acknowledge my interviews with Narcisa Hirsh, Osvaldo Giesso, Alberto Heredia and Leda Schiavo (1994). The first three figures were and are active in the cultural life of Buenos Aires; the fourth visits the city with some frequency. Hirsh is a cultural activist, film maker, feminist and ecologist. Giesso, director of the Cultural Center of the city of Buenos Aires, is a *Maecenas*, art collector and theater producer. Heredia is one of the best Argentine contemporary sculptors. Schiavo is a professor of Spanish and Latin American literature at the University of Illinois at Chicago. None of these people has been directly involved with the Di Tella Institute. Standing outside the Di Tella, they helped me look a bit inside.

Many have committed the ontological error of objectifying the concept. Power does not exist in isolation. Rather it is best understood as a conceptually bound phenomenon which becomes a concrete occurrence exclusively when and as circumstances allow; it is a phenomenon born of the social realities encompassing individuals and groups--or what Randall Collins (1992) refers to as "the de-reization of social creations." One might say that power in fact is a collective illusion in constant flux, as in the Borges story, "La mancha del tigre." This perspective leads to two ontological interpretations of the concept of power as we know them in contemporary social science theory. The first may be defined as real, specifically *active*, power--the sort of power we can easily recognize in our day-to-day struggles within society. The second interpretation views power as a *strategy* or reckoning--that is, one produced by action groups evaluating areas of power in their social environment. The link between both concepts is constituted by what Nelly Richard (1990) labels "interstices of power" ("intersticios de poder"), and which I would prefer to call "power gaps" (PGs).

The notion of such gaps greatly clarifies the conceptualization of systems. Pgs exist in all human social systems; they can be located and characterized through lucid systems analysis. This is possible if we base our assumptions on the idea that currently all social systems are structures of political negotiation. Acceding to power becomes possible when previous active decision-making fails to function at maximum efficiency levels and fails to reach all possible spheres of implementation. Accession to power is almost always difficult, but always possible, for power is never unique or permanent. It can be created anew, and there can be "shifts of power," involving the constant "play of subject positions" posited in post-structuralist and postmodern discourse. In this sense, PGs constitute the best means for conceptualizing and actually moving to the acquisition of active power.

The achievement of active power on the part of innovative groups is a direct consequence of transitions and transformations within society. All action groups emerging within a given society have given roles to play. Those roles, and the social commitment they entail, are what empowers any given group within a social context. Whatever power a group might claim, legitimize, or actually have assumed can only be based on the strength of the role it has been assigned or taken on. The restructuring of action groups is often the result of given political, economic or religious changes. In short, it is the redefinition of the common interest and of the role of groups in relation to the common interest that produces new action groups or new relative powers among existing groups. Realignments favoring a common cause are one way to resolve conflicts. The need to protect a new common interest leads to decisions which, in turn, provoke new conflicts and bring on new consequences. A zone of power is delimited by the decisions of a group and by the consequences of these decisions on the given configurations they influenced. To define an action group is, therefore, to designate the scope of its influence. Consequently, the definition of any power group must be based on the effects of the decisions it makes. Accordingly, diverging groups within a social system must be identified with their respective spheres of influence. This is so whether one wishes to trace the position of a given group within the system, or observe the group's area of influence in order to define its orientation and preferences, as well as the tendencies and sub-group configurations which constitute it and differentiate it from others. Tendencies will be marked by a certain manner or style, or by the group's support of certain schools of thought and sensibility. The way in which this support is given, denied or withheld, the trends an individual action group wishes to embrace, its motivating factors, enthusiasms and concerns, as well as the matters it ignores or censures, its possibilities for broader affiliations for participation and hegemony in a multi-group process or the formation of a more powerful social bloc, can be unravelled and scrutinized. One possible reading of a given action group's code is offered by the way in which the group declares its preferences. Some groups declare those preferences openly, others less so; some will have to exhibit more inventiveness than others. These matters should be kept in mind as we briefly consider the emergence and rise of the Argentina's *industriales* and the Di Tella group.

2. Argentina, 1950-60: The industriales

During the fifties, the traditional Latin American trio formed by Argentina, Brazil and Mexico embarked on a new relationship in response to the new world order emerging in the post-World War II era. For Peter

Evans, the world's leading economies initiated a new phase so that what had formerly been considered a wealthy periphery now became semi-peripheral (1979: 290-313). Evans detects a pattern common to all the emergent semi-peripheral countries. With respect to the Latin American trio countries, we may begin with the fact that they are large and rich, with considerable consumer markets among their Latin American neighbors. Inevitably each of these countries could be defined by social groups resulting from the relationship between capitalist-style production and a certain industrial infrastructure. Nevertheless there is considerable variation from one country to the other, especially since each one has its own cultural configurations and its own particular relationships with and among its rural sectors and its regional neighbors.

Capitalist industrialization implies not only owners and workers, but also the development of technology and education, matters which require an appropriate ideological and cultural ambience. The process of industrialization is lengthy; it both requires and produces changes in social relations which are particularly dramatic and visible in Latin America's agricultural societies. These changes generate circumstances which lead individual owner and worker groups to react in order to safeguard or improve their positions within their respective societies. It would be wrong to designate these groups as "new"; rather they are pre-existing groups now re-articulated and articulating new interests, which up to the moment have been characterized by few public interventions.

In Argentina, the *industriales* group matured slowly but consistently up until the middle of this century. From then on, they became the legitimizers of the Argentineans' social code. The most representative of their institutional sectors was the Di Tella.

In 1918, the Argentine Industrial Union (UIA), a group of fairly powerful industrialists in Buenos Aires, Rosario and Córdoba, attempted to impose its interests on the government's economic policy. UIA activism had begun as early as the crisis of 1890, when the organization mounted "information campaigns" to persuade public opinion as to the economic benefits of protecting the national industrial base through import restrictions (De Imaz 1970: 163).

In spite of this early start, it should be noted that the UIA's firm and perhaps unparalleled protectionist stance did not begin to take hold until the public perception of the importance of industrial production to the national economy began to take root. And this perception was only consolidated when industrial production had already surpassed the agricultural sector's contributions to the GNP, and most crucially, when the producers themselves became government policy makers.

Some scholars (above all Cornblit 1967) attribute the UIA's long-term marginality from the spheres of power to the immigrant origin of the *"industriales."* Indeed, given the enormous number of immigrants entering the country at the time, as well as the numbers of those who returned to their homeland, it is easy to conclude that the immigrants lacked any nationalist motivation and did not feel committed to the country's political life until long after 1914, when only 1.4% of all foreigners had sought naturalization.

The virtual absence of industrialists in decision-making processes for many years after industry had become crucial to the national economy had clear consequences for government structures and policies. Finally, the *industriales* came to occupy a place within society that was proportionate to their objective importance and would finally promote their decision-making power. But it would take years for this to happen; and the process by which a modernizing industrial-based hegemony would develop was very slow and profoundly mediated by the long-standing and lingering influence of the rural sector.

With a level of socio-economic and political power that was only eclipsed by mid-twentieth century, the rural sector remained the social legitimizer of Argentine cultural life for more than a century after nominal independence. Without doubt, it was the group that, for its history, its experience and its long-standing relations with Argentina's political, ecclesiastic and military powers, was the most influential over the entire society.

Vertically and horizontally, the country was bred and fed by rural sector codes. What Argentineans drank, ate, danced and wore was somehow inspired or approved by the rural group. Whether we like it or not, it is undeniable that in the long period before industrial hegemony, the image of Argentina was based on the gauchos and the pampas; indeed the image persists even today. The literature, the paintings, the architecture, and even the academic models were brought, inspired or supervised by the rural sector. This was the heyday of Victoria Ocampo, the perfect ambassador of Argentina's pampa-based national image. In these circumstances, the *industriales* could not compete with the rural sector, unless they could create

105

their own economic niche and establish their own social role. This was to be their project for several decades in this century.

The industrialists did not achieve the status as a full-fledged pressure group with a common objective until 1918 when they launched what at that time was their most extended protectionist campaign. The campaign marked the beginning of a new time for them since it led to the first protectionist law, signed by President Irigoyen, favoring Argentine industry through the restriction of imports and the application of high customs fees (Cornblit: 25).

The two World Wars marked phases when the UIA advanced with the drop in imports of European manufactured goods and the subsequent improvement in the indices of industrial production. After the First World War, the government lifted its protectionist measures, and only brought back new ones around 1930 in tandem with the world-wide economic crisis. Beginning around 1933, and in the lapse of merely five years, Latin American exports dropped 60% due to drastically diminished foreign buying power precipitated by the economic crisis (Keen and Wasserman 1988: 321).

The Great Depression of the thirties marked a new stage in Argentina involving the economic practices of import substitution. Those years were decisive ones for the country. From 1900 to 1914 the manufacturing sector employed 22.06% of the work force. From 1925 through 1929 it employed 26% of the work force; between 1940 and 1944 the percentage increased again to 26.36%, reaching 27% between 1945 and 1949. In 1955 the numbers dropped once more to 26% of the total work force. In the years ranging from 1900 to 1955, the manufacturing industry grew by 3.94%, rating second in growth only to that of the government sector which had increased its employees by 8 per cent. Commerce and the service industries came in third with an expansion of 2 per cent. The most stunning statistics, however, were those of agricultural production marked by a reduction of 14 per cent.

Two causes can explain agriculture's surprising decline: lack of demand for agricultural products on the international market and an overall or at least relative decrease in productivity of the sector as a whole. But whatever the reasons, it is the contribution of each sector to the overall national economy that is of interest here. The fall of the agricultural sector coincides then with increased industrialization. The industrial sector absorbed the excess labor force released by the rural quarter and its demographic growth.

Yet this expanding strength did not prompt its access to the realm of government policy-making. If one compares the production of industrial and rural sectors and then contrasts it to the percentage of individuals within industry who are active in government teams, one might be surprised by the results found in De Imaz. By 1918 the industrial sector contributed with 20.4% of the GNP while the rural sector contributed with 24.3 per cent. Meanwhile the percentage of *industriales* in the government teams was only 14 per cent. Between 1910-45 the industrialists' contribution to the GNP was at 24.7% compared to the rural sector's 21%; but they were only 5% of the government team. What is surprising is that by 1945-49 only 1.25% of the government is of industrial origin while their contribution to the GNP is 23.5% versus 18% from the rural sector. Even lower is the 16.6% rural sector GNP contribution during 1950-55, while the industrial contribution was 22.7%. During this period of time, there is no one individual from the industrial sector in the government team (171-72).

The industrial sector played an important role as an employer. During 1900-1914 the manufactures employed 22.06% of the population. From 1925 to 1929 they employed 23% of the population; during 1940-44, 26.36%, and from 1945 to 1949, 27%; in 1955, 26 per cent. The manufacturing sector grew 3.94% from 1950 to 1955, the second in growth as employer after the State which grew 8% in this respect. Commerce and services grew 2 per cent. But the most significant variation was the 14% diminution in rural production.

According to De Imaz, the industrialists made up 28% of the governing force in 1955, and 32% in 1966 (172). How may we account for their integration into government and other spheres previously unfamiliar to them such as academic or ranch-owning circles? One obvious explanation is that the industrialists as a group were quickly becoming an elite. The wish to expand their scope of interests beyond their own economic niche demonstrates growth and an attempt to become socially and ideologically integrated. That process explains, in part, how the new elite developed.

Even though they were taking roles beyond their original niche, still they had to conquer the decision-making arena; and in order to achieve this, they needed a PG. The PG space was articulated by the economic and political spheres on international and national levels. The World Wars and Peronism were the essential points for their emergence. Above all, the post-World

War economic situation created the space in Peronist nationalist and specifically developmentalist policies which favored the industrial sector. But the industrial group's emergence as hegemonic happened only after the coup d'etat removed Peronism from the Government. It happened in the social vacuum generated by the Peronist absence and the rural sector's inability to run the country.

In 1955, a military coup removed Perón from the government after nine consecutive years of Peronist power. The Army assumed command, banned the Peronist party, and even the names of Perón and his wife, and soon after called for elections.

More than forty candidates formally participated in the subsequent presidential race; one of them, Arturo Frondizi, received the votes from the large pro-Peronist bloc and won the elections. The situation was clearly one of political break-up and leadership void. Many of those who celebrated Perón's fall imagined things would return to what they had once been. But this transition was a crucial one for the *industriales* and the entire country.

Perón's departure had marked the end of one Argentina and the beginning of another. When he had first come to power in 1946, several aspects of social relations such as speech manners, style and taste in art, as well as Argentina's "pace with the rest of the world" were all determined by the landed bourgeoisie. Their influence, however, both politically and socially, was profoundly eroded by the global post-war economy as well as by the actions of the Peronist government. Argentina's role as the world's "bread-basket" had reached its limit. Simultaneous with this economic change, the hegemony of the nation's those artistic circles somehow representing a quasi-Frenchified version of bourgeois culture, was coming to an end; and artistic producers became increasingly experimental and controversial.

None of the changes in the mid-nineteen fifties were led by the landed bourgeoisie. Perhaps this explains why they were unable to form a unified front after Perón's fall from power. World-wide economic factors, as well as the Peronist experience itself, were termed a case of "zoological encroachment"--i.e., something foreign and external which had somehow intervened in the previously worked out logic of national evolution.

The significance of what had happened remained totally misunderstood. Twenty years later, the change had been consolidated and identified; it had become the Argentine middle class. Perón's government had provided laws and institutions that opened the way to the legal configuration of the work force. Other strategies of that government's push to protect industry were nationalizing the exploitation of the country's energy sources, expanding roadway networks and imposing strict regulations on foreign imports.

Strangely enough, it is commonly believed that Perón and the industrialist movement did not get along. The fact is, however, that Argentine industry had never before received such strong backing as it did under Perón's government. This point should be stressed because the changes advanced by that government gave way to a tacit agreement with the industrial sector, very much like the trends developed in Brazil and Mexico where the Triple Alliance was the open agreement among the government, national industry, and foreign capital. Perón's government was the first which openly protected national industry, establishing patterns that deeply affected the country's subsequent development.

Perón's support also privileged blue collar workers, an item perhaps missing from the elite's checklist of policies for the country. Perón's government did not of course invent the work force; however, it gave shape to it within the modernization process affecting Argentina's socio-political system. What is evident is that the Peronist government was very much skewed toward the industrial sector, and that this sector--including the workers as a key segment of the *industriales*' world--was the one most favored by its policies.

3. The Di Tella Foundation Institute

The Di Tella Foundation was inaugurated on the 22nd of July, 1959 in memory of Torcuato Di Tella, founder of the Siam Di Tella industrial complex, a privately funded cultural project. Ten per cent of Siam Di Tella's stock provided capital for the Foundation, which also received the family's art collection. Di Tella's sons, Guido and Torcuato, who created the Foundation ten years after their father's death, implemented a U.S. model of corporate financing, thus effecting a transfer from traditional structures to ones of contemporary business management. In this transfer, private funds were to be channelled toward intellectual and cultural activities.

In taped interviews with John King (1985), the Di Tella brothers explained how they had hoped that the Foundation would set an example to be emulated and that U.S. private and government entities would be willing to contribute funds to Latin American projects of similar structure and function (King 49-70). Initially they supported research projects in the areas of sociology and economics in which they were personally interested. Another facet of their activity revolved around the Di Tella's art collection which was to be exhibited to the public. During the sixties, more important and elaborate Argentine projects and whole research centers were initiated and developed thanks to the innovative efforts of the Foundation and a funding base which drew upon various sources.

The Di Tella family and some smaller Argentine sponsors contributed domestic funds for the plastic arts, especially painting and sculpture; they also helped to promote artists and intellectuals beyond the circle of the Institute itself. The Ford Foundation, the Rockefeller Foundation and the Alliance for Progress itself provided international support for the more ambitious, extensive and expensive projects and centers. Not coincidentally, the larger enterprises emerged just as Alliance for Progress activity and funding were in full sway. In this context, the Foundation's activities would grow and diversify, giving way to the Instituto Torcuato Di Tella; to the promotion of various forms of advanced studies in music, art, audiovisual experiments including theater and dance; and to the establishment of Di Tella's important Center for Social Studies in Belgrano housing sociologists, economists, semiologists and members of other associated academic disciplines (King: 49-70).

Most of the artists, as well as the viewing public of these presentations, belonged to the middle class. According to King, Regina Gibaja published a study of the attendance of the first public exhibit housed in the Museum of Art (59). Although I have found no additional attendance studies in King, García Canclini or elsewhere, Narcisa Hirsh, Osvaldo Giesso and Leda Schiavo (see note 1 above) corroborate the predominantly middle class public attendance at Di Tella events. Attendance, of course, was not universal; and there were many who considered the Foundation's work a sterile undertaking which failed to bring about any relevant change in social and artistic traditions. Others were simply shocked by what they considered the moral and aesthetic affronts posed by the Di Tella's artistic and cultural orientations.

Indeed, as King argued in his book, the Di Tella's proposition was the New York aesthetic code in Argentine garb. Within the U.S., this code was counter-cultural, libertarian and at times leftist-chic. But outside of the U.S., this same artistic proposal was delivered from the owner of the world's most powerful economy, and from World War II's victorious army--that is to say, from the mid-century's big winner. All of this makes sense when we think that the down-on-the-land bourgeoisie was classically allied with Europe, and saw itself as a weak version of Europe in a tentative process of reconstruction; and meanwhile the new dominant group of Argentina was more sympathetic toward New York-based propositions as an alternative development model. The Di Tella group did not create a situation which was much more complex than what any single group could expect to handle; but it legitimized and institutionalized the new proposals which the changing times brought to the table; it legitimized the propositions, the producers, the sponsors and the spaces created by Argentina's internal changes and its evolving global role.

Along with Garcia Canclini, Marta Traba, Damián Bayón, Oscar Massota, *Revista Sur* and the media in general were critical of the group, pointing to the Di Tella as an agent of U.S. cultural penetration. It is also true that those who backed the Di Tella were not the majority; however, they were of the utmost importance when it came to measuring the changes that were taking place in the country.

Of course, economic and political variations are not always equally significant, even though they were just that in those areas where the population was the largest and most densely concentrated--namely in cities such as Buenos Aires, Rosario and Córdoba. Support also came from other areas, but to a far lesser degree. The Foundation did not echo the needs of first generation Argentines nor of native peoples from more sparsely inhabited regions whose system of production differed from the one found in coastal regions. But the Foundation came from and indeed represented the new urban middle sectors emerging in many areas--and above all in the three most industrial and densely populated cities of the country.

The Di Tella Institute became the legitimizer of the changes of the post-Perón era. Most Argentineans knew what it meant to be middle class; they believed in development, a rising standard of living, access to education, overall social mobility, and progress. Above all, they believed in modernity, and they believed they were experiencing it. To be modern also implies to seem so. Therefore people painted, consumed, talked, danced, dressed, read and thought in a modern version, as they might in New York--or at least as they might imagine themselves in their own Buenos Aires vision of New

111

York--mediated by given Argentine cities and cultural currents. The Di Tella was part of the process of legitimization of a modernity people believed they were touching with their hands; and to certain extent it was true, even though the result was not perhaps quite what they imagined it to be. The Di Tella operated as an agent of a tacit agreement between the people and the modernity message. This is what the Institute's directors, intellectuals and operatives championed; but it is also what, consciously or not, the broader population was actually experiencing and wanting.

The Di Tella Institute fed a public passion which it helped to promote and then articulate. The institute met the conditions as a center for the organic intellectuals of a broader group; and it did this by presenting, and having the wherewithal to deliver, a new cultural model consonant with the emerging group propositions and aspirations. For the *industriales*, the Di Tella represented the transition from *calculated* to *active* power. The industrial background of the Institute may be the key point in understanding why the Di Tella could help the *industriales* achieve one of their most important goals: to become the major producers, employers, and social legitimizers of their society. The Institute supported and proposed a kind of creativity which represented a rupture with a past hegemony; but as a modernizing legitimizer, it was not as revolutionary as people sometimes claimed or liked to believe.

As a mediator between the earlier Paris-inflected, semi-aristocratic modernity of the rural titans and a more contemporary New York-based middle sector version that was seen to correlate with the new industrial hegemony, the Di Tella simply introduced new images to the already known. But revolutionary or reformist, resistive or affirmative, it produced an array of tendencies and forms which generated possibilities that are not conscribed by their original intentionalities or genetic origins.

That the New York model, with Jackson Pollack, John Cage, Andy Warhol and countless others, stood on the verge of an artistic transformation that would lead to the arts of simulacra what we today call "the postmodern," that that development would become internal to Buenos Aires contemporaneity as articulated in the work of Beatriz Sarlo (1995) is a partial consequence of a broad transition in which the Di Tella cultural model had a significant part.

4. Summary and Final Conclusions

The example of the Di Tella Foundation and Institute makes possible the clarification of three aspects of social change: the emergence of a new group, the cultural consequences of such an emergence, and the process of group power-acquisition. But in the Di Tella's case, these aspects emerged in relation to the group's concrete accomplishments.

In sum, the end of the fifties witnessed the emergence of the *industriales*, as the growingly hegemonic group in the social arena. Over the years, the group expanded in function to become the producer of a new social ambience, mainly expressed by intellectual and cultural activity. Their emergence was the result of their interaction with a strong agricultural sector in a downward period. With the landowners receding from the cultural and social arena, and with an efficient process of economic insertion, the *industriales* became the legitimizers of new social codes. In its research as well as its artistic activities, the Di Tella was the most direct representative of these changes. Di Tella representatives made their particular mark by their strong support for the social sciences, by their confrontation with the artistic establishment, and the sense of openness their artistic center provided.

As representative of the *industriales*, the Di Tella did not come to the stage to preserve the traditional "sciences" and "beaux arts," but to propose critical analysis, questioning, and experiment either in the social sciences, psychology, or in the arts, where their own *New York*-style artistic proposals helped transform Argentine cultural life in the fifties and sixties.

The new cultural proposals did not become the only voice of the artistic expressions, but they did throw fresh light on the previous situation. The Foundation's role was as a generator of discussions. The responses produced by its role became new efforts toward the modernity of social relations. Perhaps because the Foundation was initiated by an industrial group of immigrant origins, it could generate new perspectives, subject positions and cultural processes that gave it special relevance as a force of Argentina's contradictory and retroactively detained modernization.

The processes by which groups accede to new positions and levels of power, how these processes affect the group's immediate social context and the overall effect of the transformed context in a more area-wide or global network, and how at least a major dimension of the question of power shifts in relation to power PGs is a question of the formation of preferences, or what Pierre Bourdieu (1984) has theorized as "distinctions," are matters important to understanding Latin America's recent history. This has been the focus of this brief portrayal of the De Tella Institute. But it should be noted that, given Argentina's "semi-peripheral status," and its relative hegemony in the formation of cultural styles and indeed taste and reception within the Southern Cone and Latin America as a whole, the case of the Di Tella is not only significant as a possible developmental model for other Latin American countries, but directly important to the understanding of what Neil Larsen (1995), among others, has attacked as a "culturalist fetishization" of social and political theory in recent Latin American studies.

That an early Di Tella watcher like García Canclini is so important in social as well as specifically cultural theorizing today (in reaction against as well as conformity with, such entities as FLACSO) is testimony to the growing cultural position achieved by the Di Tella since the 1950s and now especially since the fall of the military dictatorship in Argentina. Even if we see Argentina's key postmodernist critics as questioning the metropolitan cultural model implicit in Di Tella activities, still few would doubt the group's role in providing a base or counter for mediation in Argentina's recent history beyond the "guerra sucia" and the night of the generals. What role the Di Tella might play in Argentina's future hegemonic and oppositional developments, as the country enters more fully into the age of globalization, is a matter for future study.

MODERNIZATION AND AUTHORITARIAN CULTURE IN CHILE

Patricio Navia

From the beginning of Pinochet's dictatorship, Chilean social scientists recognized the profound overall changes the military government was generating. First seen as results of an *authoritarian culture*, they seemed to be ephemeral phenomena that would eventually disappear, with the country able to re-acquire non-authoritarian traditional cultural values. However, it was feared that some transformations would be internalized by society and would survive, although under continuous transformations into the post-dictatorship Chile.

When the dictatorship finally ended, it was clear that many authoritarian-induced changes were going to remain in place. Leading scholars, especially those grouped around Santiago's Facultad Latinoamericana de Ciencias Sociales (FLACSO) suggested that not all transformations resulted from the authoritarian cultural model; and instead that a number of other reasons explained these changes--among them, international politics, economic development and the country's own social and cultural development.

In 1988, FLACSO scholars Brunner, Barrios and Catalán argued that several cultural transformations resulted from the arrival of *modernity* and, thus, were permanent and independent of the dictatorship (21-25). Although their study analyzes mainly the interaction between authoritarianism and modernity, the framework they proposed can be used to analyze political, social and economic transformations as well. According to this study, Chile's *incorporación a la modernidad* was a process which began in the 1920s. The *authoritarian culture* began with the military dictatorship in 1973 and affected arrival of modernity hindering some transformations and fostering others.

This paper will discuss *authoritarian culture* and *modernity*, as well as the interaction that exists between the two conditions. Is one subjected to the other? Which changes are the result of the arrival of modernity and which of Pinochet's authoritarian culture? Will authoritarian changes survive the recent democratization processes? The differentiation is important to

115

determine how the dictatorship transformed, or attempted to transform, Chilean society. Distinguishing between authoritarian and modernity-induced transformations will explain the role of the dictatorship in changing society.

If some changes resulted from the arrival of modernity, then they would have taken place regardless of the government in power. On the other hand, if some changes were solely the result of military actions, then their survival was to be severely threatened when the military no longer held power. These transformations might have been only dictatorial policies that would fail to have a lasting effect. It follows that the survival of these transformations into the new democratic process would tend to support the argument that Chile's democracy was similar to Central America's *facade democracies*, or as Agustín Cueva puts it, *democracias restringidas*--or controlled democracies (1988). At another level, the differentiation needs to be qualified in terms of the interaction that exists between government policies and the country's journey to modernity. One needs to account for whatever role the dictatorship had in expediting or obstructing the arrival of modernity--a process which would have probably been different if the Popular Unity government had stayed in power until 1976 or if, instead of a coup, Congress had impeached President Allende and a new Christian Democratic government had taken power.

These are considerations at stake when I suggest that since 1973, Chile has experienced a dual phenomenon of *incorporación a la modernidad* and the forceful establishment of an *authoritarian culture.* In order to sort out an explanation of this dual phenomenon, I will analyze four specific aspects of Chile's journey to modernity and the nation's experience with authoritarianism. In part I, I will discuss the origins of the arrival of modernity. In the second part, I will analyze the role that the governments of Frei (1964-70) and Allende (1970-73) had in the arrival of modernity and the immediate effects of the coup. Third, the changes made by the dictatorship at the cultural, social, educational and economic level will be analyzed in relation to the arrival of modernity giving special consideration to the ways the dictatorship manipulated, obstructed and expedited many transformations already ongoing at the time of the coup. Finally, the transformations taking place during the post-dictatorial period will be analyzed to underscore the current struggle that exists between modernity and authoritarianism. A final consideration of the argument over a possible postmodern condition in Chile will serve to indicate the direction arguments of authoritarianism and modernity are currently taking. In all of this FLACSO's studies of popular culture and authoritarianism, military rule, military spending and the re-emergence of democracy--matters which have been at the forefront of the discussion of modernity in Chile and Latin America in general--and much criticized, I might add, by James Petras (1990) and others--will be placed in relief in this essay.

1. The Arrival of Modernity

According to Brunner, Barrios and Catalán, modernity arrives in Chile in the 1920s (1989: 23). Although these scholars do not specify the reasons for placing its arrival then, historical accounts tell us that at that time the number of people participating in socio-political life increased significantly as urban sectors grew and an industrial class, related primarily to mining, also started to develop. Among the events Brunner and his associates think about is the presidential election of Arturo Alesandri. A populist leader of the northern nitrate workers and urban poor, Alesandri was elected president in 1920. He was forced to resign in 1924 when Colonel Ibañez took over power, and was finally brought back to power in 1925 and re-elected president in 1932. In 1925, he led the drafting of a new constitution that became the basis for what was to be a period of almost uninterrupted democratic life in the country, the beginning of modernity (Aylwin 1985).

However, the growth of the politically active population did not bring about a change in Chile's highly hierarchical and clientelistic political life and government. Even within the anti-establishment parties associated with the political left, clientelism and populism were very much present. Contrary to the views of Furci (1984), Pollack and Rosenkranz (1986) and Dinamarca (1987), who see the emergence of the two major leftist parties as a result of the formation of a large working class population in the nitrate area and Santiago, Drake (1978) argues that the Socialists' success in politics, compared primarily to the Communists, was due to the existence of a unifying voice within the party that could attract the masses, rather than an attainment of a level of consciousness among the people. This populist voice was Socialist Party founder, Marmaduque Grove. The Communists seemed to have more of a grass-roots organization, as Furci notes (1984); however, their electoral representation remained rather low as their support was only significant in the mining region.

This populist tendency within the left, as well as certain populist approaches of center and rightist candidates (Alessandri and Carlos Ibañez primarily) lead one to question the level of political stability reached in Chilean politics in the thirties and during the decades to come. Chile went through a a short-lived *socialist republic* led by Grove (1932); it endured a strong comeback on the part of Ibañez, who had held power from 1927 to 1931, unsuccessfully running for the presidency in unique alliances with the left, right and/or center until he was re-elected in 1952; it experienced the continuous presence of Jorge Alessandri, who was president from 1932 to 1938 and then maintained a populist discourse as he moved to the political right in the decades which followed. A somewhat stable political climate only prevailed during the three continuous Popular Front governments led by centrist Radicals and supported at different times by Socialists, Communists, *falangistas* (Christian Democrats), liberals and conservatives. Nonetheless, even the three administrations went through some instability. While Radical presidents Aguirre (1938-42) and Ríos (1942-46) died in office, president González Videla enacted a law in 1949 that outlawed his former Communist allies and led him to an alliance with the right to form his cabinet (cf. Drake 1978; Furci 1984; Pollack and Rosenkranz 1986; Moulián and Torres 1987; Dinamarca 1987; and Urzua 1987). The prosecution of Communists and the reduction of civil liberties caused the breakdown of the Popular Front administration and the rise of Ibañez. Ibañez's populist government cleared the way for the triumph of the conservative Alessandri in 1958.

This history indicates that by placing the beginning of the modernization process in the 1920s, one overlooks a number of very concrete elements of premodernity in Chile's post-1925 political life. However, DeShazo (1983) shows that the growth of the urban working class and the establishment of a permanent population of miners in the north provided the basis for consistent political participation and the formation of groups which did not respond to the interest of traditional political forces. In the social and cultural spheres, Bernardo Subercaseaux (1985a) shows the tremendous growth in the publication of books and magazines. Others have pointed to improvements in the educational, health and social services (Aylwin 1985; Ponce 1986).

However, Subercaseaux's work on the presidency of Balmaceda (1886-91) provides an alternative look at the arrival of Chilean modernity which implies that Balmaceda's politics and his strategies for creating a strong

118

central government with active mass participation were signals of emergent modernity. The president's death in 1891 and the subsequent defeat of his reformist policies and ideas resulted in a temporary setback in the country's adoption of a modern condition.

According to Brunner, Barrios and Catalán, with Frei's rise to power in 1964, Christian Democratic "reformist policies . . . induced social change" and eliminated "the conditions of preservation and reproduction of the cultural institutions and modes of interaction identified with traditional culture" (1988: 24). For these researchers, Frei's government marks the turning point in the arrival of modernity. Whereas before Frei modernity arrived subtly and limitedly, with him modernity entered through the main door and was promoted as well as sometimes actually adopted. Yet, one must be aware that Frei's ascension to power needs to be directly linked to the growing power of the left (cf. Roxborough, O'Brien and Roddick 1977). The Frei phenomenon can also be understood as a center-right attempt to prevent the left from electing a president. In fact, I will argue that Brunner and associates overestimate the influence of the Frei government in the arrival of modernity to the country.

Another important aspect of modernity is the level of political participation. Women gained the right to vote in Chile in 1949 and first voted in a presidential election in 1952 (Caffarena 1952, Klimpel 1962, Vergara 1974, Covarrubias 1978, and Kirkwood 1986). Literacy requirements were totally lifted by 1970 and the voting age was set at 18 the same year. But in this general trend toward modernization in voting as well as other processes, we should underline contradictions opposing any simplistic, progressive, and linear explanations. Urzua, for example, points to the problems the Radical Party governments had in pushing forth the legislation that would grant women voting rights. Popular Front candidates dragged their feet on the issue for fear, Uzua argues, that women would support conservative policies, and out of a concern with "more urgent matters" which precluded Popular Front candidates from pushing the legislation.

In brief, the arrival of modernity in Chile is not a clear-cut process identified by or with one specific event, trend or period. The subsistence of traditional, pre-modern forms of government, politics and mass movements considerably undermined the changes that are characterized as evidencing modernity. It is clear, however, that when Salvador Allende was elected president, Chile was well immersed in its *incorporación a la modernidad.*

The coup against Allende and the dictatorship that followed were the ultimate attempts to undo and counteract the growing influence and power of the left. The repression against leftist parties, the 1980 constitution and its *leyes de amarre* (deadlock laws) are part of a wide ranging plan to prevent future leftist regimes from attempting to carry on any sort of reformist policies--such as Allende's and even some of Frei's.

Clearly the objectives of the dictatorship were not limited to preventing the left from holding power again; they had to do with a new conception of Chilean society and political life, which, as I have argued, altered the process of modernity's arrival. The attempts seem to have paid off. After the dictatorship was over, the leftist parties no longer had the electoral support they once enjoyed and were forced to align in a coalition with Christian Democrats. Certainly the disappearance of the Soviet Union and the worldwide adoption of capitalism also played a role in the decline of the left, but contrary to more optimistic possibilities leftist parties still enjoy elsewhere (even in Latin America), the Chilean left has diminishing opportunities for major political and electoral gains and their only plausible strategy is to be the minority partner in a government coalition dominated by Christian Democrats (Bitar 1980; Arrate 1986; and Vodanovic 1988). The continuous struggle in Chile has been the challenge to the hegemonic power of the right posed by the left and to a lesser extent by the Christian Democrats. In the political arena, Chile's incorporación a la modernidad has been characterized by an interaction between traditional forces in power and new emerging leftist forces.

Brunner, Barrios and Catalán note that the arrival of modernity was also characterized by several cultural changes: a differentiated system of cultural production for mass audiences, a shift in the center of culture from the private to the public sphere, a disappearance of national culture, the emergence of mass everyday culture, and a growing internationalization of culture (1988: 25-38). The process of mass consumption of culture in Chile has been extensively analyzed by Subercaseaux (1984, 1985a, and 1985b) and others (Catalán and Munizaga 1986; Catalán, Guillasasi, and Munziaga 1987). However, these analysts have tended to overemphasize the dictatorial effort to eliminate all forms of *cultura contestataria* (culture of resistance and counter-response), as much because of their active political commitments and beliefs as because of their scholarly interests. Moreover, although concerns about the long term effects of these transformations appear in the work of Subercaseaux and Catalán, their main objective was not to identify traces of modernity as it was to find links between new forms of cultural expression and consumption and the dictatorship's conception of Chilean society.

2. *The Role of Frei and Allende*

Before discussing the effects of the dictatorship and its authoritarian culture, we must turn to the roles of the Frei and Allende governments in helping, or preventing, the arrival of modernity. Frei, founder and leader of the Christian Democratic Party was elected president with an impressive majority in 1964. With the unofficial, yet evident and effective, support of the right, Frei defeated leftist coalition candidate Salvador Allende. Allende had come very close to winning the presidential bid in 1958 when he was defeated by conservative Jorge Alessandri. Indeed, the sum of all votes obtained by leftist candidates (Allende from the FRAP alliance, Luis Bossay from the Radical Party and the independent candidate Zamorano) constituted more than 55% of the total (Tupper 1987: appendix) in the 1958 elections. It was no longer feasible for the right to expect to win an election where they faced a unified left. Moulián and Torres (1987) suggest that since the 1936 presidential election, it was no longer feasible for the right to win an election without a political alliance. The election of Ibañez in 1952 was the result of an alliance of the right with the center and center-left; and as noted Allessandri's victory in 1958 was due to a major split in the left.

Drawing upon Peeler's concept of *accommodation among elites* (1985), we could well see Frei's election as the right's acceptance of their decreased electoral power and their willingness to compromise in function of a reformist, not revolutionary, program. However, it can also be argued that the Chilean elites' accommodation was rather a short-lived tactical manoeuver. It was over before Frei's period was completed.

If Frei's Revolution in Liberty program reflected concerns with the growth of the left, so did the already-launched United States Alliance for Progress program of which Chile was a major beneficiary (Lowenthal 1991). U.S. interests and those of multinational corporations were to prevent the Marxist left from democratically reaching office. They all sought to undermine the widespread support enjoyed by leftist parties when they offered their support to Frei. It was in this framework that the Christian Democratic government carried on an Agrarian Reform, developed the television industry and mass media, launched an ambitious program to rebuild and create new roads and other major construction projects, led a campaign to modernize the educational and health care system, and provided access for lower sectors to improved public housing. Public universities underwent a radical process of democratization and modernization. A great deal of effort was put on improving industrial productivity as well. Finally, Frei's government nationalized copper mines, the leading source of revenues for the country (Aylwin 1985; Fleet 1985).

Frei believed that popular unrest and discontent, and thus the possibility of a revolution, could only be eliminated with real progress and opportunities. His Revolution in Liberty program represents the informal compromise of traditional oligarchical sectors, the growing middle class and foreign interests to prevent the breakdown of democracy and secure a capitalist economy. The results were not very successful.

While Molina (1986) offers a positive analysis of Christian Democratic efforts, Fleet postulates that the inability of the Frei government to live up to its intent represented a defeat for growing Christian Democrat influence and power. Whatever the interpretation, the fact is that by 1970, the center-right coalition had broken apart. The right no longer supported Frei and had their own presidential candidate. Socialist Allende was elected president as he narrowly defeated conservative Alessandri and Christian Democratic Radomiro Tomic. The Christian Democratic electoral support was both disappointing and strong. It was disappointing because it showed the dissatisfaction with Christian Democratic reformist policies (Tomic obtained little more than half the vote Frei had obtained six years earlier). However, it was also strong in the sense that Tomic's discourse was more reformist than Frei's; in fact Tomic was closer to Allende than to Alessandri. The left and Tomic together had obtained around 60% of the vote (Tupper 1987).

When Allende came to power, many of Frei's reforms had failed; yet there were a few very important ones that had succeeded and helped Allende carry on his more revolutionary program. The limited success of the Agrarian Reform, the nationalization of the copper industry and the increased participation of the state in social welfare provided Allende with an important base for his reforms. The outspoken dissent of the right and the ambiguous position of Christian Democrats, which shifted from constructive to furious opposition, along with Allende's decision to push his reforms against all odds, led the country into political and civil confrontation that ended with the 1973 military coup (Roxborough et al 1977; Garretón 1983).

However, a number of Frei's and Allende's reforms had resulted in the effective involvement of traditionally marginal sectors in the government and economic life of the country. The image of a *compañero presidente* who heard the people and whose government actually represented those who had no voice was very powerful in bringing forth the concept of the state encompassing all sectors of society and particularly reflecting the needs of the marginal ones. In this regard, it can be said that the periphery visited the center and, thus, effectively acknowledged the center as its own, thus validating the legitimacy of the state as the social and political entity that represented the entire nation.

In general, the almost three years of the Allende government brought radical economic and social change. The state actively participated in providing health, education and housing to the poor sectors; through nationalization and price controls, it attempted to undermine the power of the economic elite. Frei's agrarian reform was widened, and more land was expropriated from big landowners. Protectionist economic policies that had once benefitted the private industrial sector, were further implemented to protect the production on newly nationalized industries.

All these measures caused an outbreak of protest and opposition from the economic and agricultural sector represented by the political right, and from the middle class and the Catholic Church largely represented by the Christian Democrats. With the support of multi-national corporations, the rightist National Party and the Christian Democrats effectively opposed Allende's reforms in the Parliament and the streets. The Supreme Court also opposed Allende's measures and called many of his proposed reforms unconstitutional. Soon after his inauguration, Allende was fighting a broad coalition of international and oligarchic economic interests, political groups and important sectors of the population.

The heterogeneous group that supported Allende was more preoccupied with pushing forth their specific priorities than with unifying behind Allende's program. With inflation and political instability on the rise, confrontation was imminent. Allende continued implementing reforms; and eventually, with the enthusiastic support of the right and the consent of Christian Democrats (not to mention any extra-national actors), the military overthrew Allende and put an end to the Chilean Road to Socialism.

However, the short life of the Allende government did not prevent it from launching major social, economic and cultural transformations that were embodied in an overall discourse of modernization through active state and workers' participation. Although many of these programs were never fully implemented, the expectations of modernization and the self-assigned role of the government to bring about modernity were deeply rooted in society and remained long after the Chilean Road to Socialism had vanished.

Thus, whereas Frei's main contribution to modernity was a structural one, Allende's also represented the first real interaction among all the sectors that conform the nation. With Allende, the periphery came to the center and confronted the traditionally established patterns of power. The result was the breakdown of democracy in favor of the traditional powers, yet the process of modernization could not be reversed. With the initial consent of Christian Democrats, the outspoken support of the right and a weak official stand of the U.S. and other foreign governments, the military launched a plan to undo many of the reforms brought about by Frei and Allende.

Indeed, the institutional image of Chile's dictatorship partially responds to the level of political modernity attained in Chile during the previous Frei and Allende governments. Despite Pinochet's personalistic and arrogant approach to politics and his struggle to become the leader of the Junta, Chile's military regime was not based, nor was it dependent, upon the figure of Pinochet. The higher corps of the Army, Navy and Air Force had planned the coup in advance, and it was their political and economic ideology that constituted the basis for the program implemented.

Although Genaro Arriagada (1988) has shown how Pinochet maneuvered to become the leader of the government and struggled to maintain his position throughout, testimonies of other military officials and coup plotters indicate that Pinochet only joined the coup plotters a couple of days before it was to take place. Pinochet has stated (1979) that he participated in the planning of the coup and he has suggested he himself led the group that overthrew Allende. However, Correa, Sierra and Subercaseaux (1983), Harrington and González (1987), Marras (1988), and Ahumada et al. (1989) have shown that Pinochet only joined the coup plotters upon realizing that Allende's government was to be overthrown regardless of his own stand. Furthermore, Marras (1988) and Correa et al (1983) suggest that Pinochet's controversial economic team, *the Chicago Boys*, was brought in by the Navy, not the Army. The Army, on the other hand, has been widely associated with the horrifying violations of human rights more than any other branch of the military (cf. Nunn 1977; O'Brien 1983; Valenzuela 1986; Falcoff 1989). The military regime in Chile cannot, then, be compared to traditional dictatorships. Asturias's *El señor presidente* and García Márquez's *El otoño del patriarca* just do not portray Chile's military dictatorship, which, like those in Brazil, Uruguay and Argentina, was institutionally and not individually based. Guillermo O'Donnell has called such dictatorships "Bureaucratic Authoritarian regimes" (1988). Augusto Varas has pointed to the difference between well organized, clearly structured and highly hierarchical, professional armed forces, such as Chile's, and others that have yet not abandoned ideas such as *caudillismo* and loyalty to big landowners (1985, 1989a, and 1989b).

A country that was well emerged in the process of entering modernity necessarily had to count on a highly professional, apolitical armed forces. Salvador Allende's speech to the United Nations in 1971 reflects the idea of a highly independent Armed Forces, loyal to the constitution and the democratically elected authorities (Allende 1975). In fact, several researchers have studied the struggle that existed within the Armed Forces between the *constitucionalistas* who wanted to remain loyal to the government and the *golpistas* who wanted to plot a coup.

Among the constitutionalists was the army chief general, Carlos Prats. He fought to maintain political stability within the constitutional framework until political pressures forced him to resign a month before the coup. In general, the decision to carry out a coup has been characterized by both supporters and opponents as a very difficult one. The whole process of planning and preparation took a long time, and the final decision was finally made not without posterior regrets (Ahumada et al 1989). The original affinity of the Armed Forces and the oligarchic sector did not prevent the military from enacting changes even in the composition of the oligarchy. Strong opponents of Allende's economic plan, the traditional large landowners and industrial producers faced an increasingly competing market as the neoliberal economic plan was adopted. Many new entrepreneurs emerged and the composition of the oligarchy changed from traditional land owners to a variety of economic groups formed by or grouping around young aggressive entrepreneurs (Vergara 1985; Zeitlin and Ratcliff 1988).

The uncontrolled growth of the military apparatus (Arriagada 1988), the inability of agricultural producers to prevent economic reforms that favored newly emerging sectors--namely services and foreign-owned commercial enterprises--and the growing influence of young economists and bureaucrats in the government resulted in the definitive shift of power within the oligarchy. Capitalist and bankers replaced landlords as the most economic influential people in the nation (Vergara 1985).

Zeitlin and Ratcliff have recently shown that family ties allowed traditional oligarchic landlords to maintain their presence among these new entrepreneur sectors. But the change from agricultural-based wealth to industrialist-made fortunes signified a change in the political platform of the right (1988). And whatever the precise socio-economic and political interests in the new order, there is no doubt that for the private economic sectors, the benefits obtained by overthrowing Allende were more than the previously described losses. On the other hand, military regime survival beyond that of the *Marxist threat* itself was no longer advantageous to many of the old and new elite sectors. Among them, the upper middle class, traditionally grouped in the Christian Democratic, Radical and Liberal parties, first broke away from the Junta. Other sectors were to follow.

Without extending the empirical narrative at this point, I would suggest that a game theory approach would simplify the characterization of in changes in interest alignments and political allegiances involved as functions of one key shift in the equilibrium point from "supporting the dictatorship" to "opposing the dictatorship." From this point of view, the addition of upper middle class sectors to the opposition was the major cause of the shift (Fleet 1985; Arriagada, ed. 1986). When these sectors joined the left in the opposition against the military government and in favor of democracy, putting aside past differences and confrontations, the dictatorship came close to falling. Although the protests of 1983 and 1984 failed to bring down the government, they secured the way to the 1988 plebiscite.[1]

3. Transformations under Pinochet

The transformations and changes during Pinochet's regime occurred at all levels of society. However, in order to advance a methodological analysis, they will be divided into four major areas: political, economic, social and cultural.

The political transformations related to constitutional matters, popular participation, representative democracy and the institutionalization of military power. Economic changes were mainly characterized by a drastic

---

[1]Arriagada (1988) discusses the underlaying reasons that prevented an alliance with the Communist Party; Fleet (1985) focuses on the opposite: the strategic move made by Christian Democrats to the left to oppose the dictatorship. However, Christian Democrats were never aligned withCommunists (De la Maza and Garces 1985; Hales 1986 and Aylwin 1988; Garretón 1984 and 1987, and Moulián 1988.

reduction of state ownership of public enterprises and industries, a rapid shift towards a market economy and, in general, the reduction of the state apparatus at all levels, except the military. The social transformations were characterized by a drastic reduction in government programs for health, retirement, unemployment and education. There was also a curtailing of the possibilities of traditional social organizations such as labor unions, student federations, neighborhood organizations and church-related groups. The country underwent a privatization of all services which brought about drastic differences in accessibility. Cultural transformations included censorship, government ownership and/or control of the means of communication (TV, newspapers, magazines, radio stations); the persecution, prosecution, torture, incarceration, exile and death of dissenting intellectuals, cultural actors and political opponents; and, overall, the imposition of a single discourse.

Clearly, at every level, some changes responded primarily (if not solely) to the needs of modernization. They were caused by the arrival of modernity. Also, many transformations were almost exclusively the result of the authoritarian model. Most changes, however, resulted from a complicated mixture of authoritarianism and modernity.

At the political level, the greatest changes were caused by the imposition of authoritarianism; and few political changes can be attributed to the *incorporación a la modernidad*. The economic and social transformations resulted from an interesting mixture: while most transformations were caused by the arrival of modernity, the economic and political connotation the military gave to them were evident attempts to further strengthen the authoritarian model; nevertheless limitations placed on group modernization processes could not totally eliminate the processes and their originating groups, which were to prove crucial to the success of the 1983-1984 protests. Finally, the transformations at the cultural level were sometimes caused by modernity and others by the authoritarian cultural model. However, the dictatorship hindered, fostered or attempted to modify modernity-led cultural transformations in order to fit the needs of its authoritarian cultural model.

A. Political Transformations.

Political transformations began immediately after the coup. Congress was absolved; the Junta undertook control of the legislative, executive and part of the judicial powers; it permanently suspended constitutional rights. The Junta first governed with *bandos militares* (military decrees) and then with laws that modified the 1925 constitution until the enactment of the 1980 Constitution when the country was still under state of siege and civil liberties were severely curtailed.

With the 1980 Constitution, there continued to be three independent powers in the government. However, the military had now a constitutionally mandated role in each of the three. In the executive branch, the armed forces played a crucial role in the National Security Council. In the legislative, there was a constitutional provision for the appointment of 9 senators, six to be chosen by the National Security Council and three by the Supreme Court. Since the number of popularly elected senators was 38, roughly 20% of the senate was to be appointed by the outgoing military government. In the Judicial branch, military courts were charged to judge all terrorist activities and all cases where military personnel was involved.

In sum, the Constitution remained highly authoritarian, responding to the needs of an immature political society that required guidance. This guidance was provided by the regulatory role of the military through measures such as the national security council, military courts and appointed senators. The excessive power of the military and the difficulties to bring about much needed political reforms are the most important legacy of the authoritarian model.

The national plebiscite that approved the 1980 Constitution was repeatedly denounced as fraudulent. The prohibition to campaign against the proposed constitution, the nonexistent access to mass media by the opposition and, above all, the lack of constitutional guarantees for the voters profoundly questioned the legitimacy of the entire process.

The reforms negotiated in 1989 after Pinochet's defeat in the 1988 plebiscite failed to alter the document's authoritarian thrust. Subsequent efforts to modify the Constitution (including the successful negotiations to democratically elect majors and aldermen) have progressed extremely slowly and have caused some political unrest. In this regard, modernity has yet arrived in Chilean politics; and dictatorial practices need to disappear if the country is to be regarded as modern in its political institutions and practices (Aldunate, Flisfish and Moulián 1985; Maira 1988).

In general, the transformations in the political sphere experienced during the Pinochet years respond almost exclusively to the authoritarian culture rather than modernity and their subsistence well beyond the years of the military justify, and in fact, make it necessary to continue referring to an authoritarian political culture.

B. *Economic Transformations*

It is perhaps at the economic level where the transformations carried on by the military have received most attention. The economic program of the military rested upon a liberal economic approach set forth by a group of economists trained at the University of Chicago in the 50s and 60s, known as Chicago Boys. According to Valdés (1989), the Chicago Boys sought to follow liberal economic ideas aimed at reducing the role of the state in economic activities. The state should not interfere with the development of the private sector. It was not the role of the state to own and operate the means of production. Health, education, retirement and other social services should be provided also by the private sector in order to maximize accessibility and minimize costs. All economic activities should be left to the market. The Chicago Boys anticipated a process of economic shock that would result in the disappearance of all unproductive industries and the development of many new productive ones that would be competitive at national and international markets.

The result would be a country whose engine of development was the private sector with social problems being solved through sustained economic growth. Industries that had previously been owned by foreign investors and had been nationalized by previous governments were returned to foreign ownership. Many traditionally state-owned companies were also privatized. A number of important financial groups developed within the country in a short period of time.

Vergara (1985) has studied the "rise and fall" of the Chicago Boys and their monetarist policies--their relations with new entrepreneur groups, political sectors and the military, their struggles with rival economic theory schools and their supporters, the controversies between political hard liners identified with the secret police, and soft liners identified with political opening. The Chicago Boys' economic program was adopted with the endorsement of the Navy rather than Pinochet's army. At first, the top economic posts were held by formed Christian Democrats and retired military generals, but as time passed a number of technocrats and advisors who previously had lower posts rose to take control of the economic program (Fontaine 1988).

The 1982 economic crisis temporarily ended the reign of the Chicago Boys; but by the end of the Pinochet years, the Chicago Boys had once again gained control of the economic policy making sector. In part, their 1982 downfall was a product of the liberalization of the market and the negative effect that had for many unproductive and inefficient private and public industries.

However, the world recession also hit Chile hard. The Chicago Boys' economic plan caused many inefficient and unproductive industries to go bankrupt as they were unable to compete with foreign products imported to Chile. As many factories closed, government revenues went down and unemployment increased, the political effects of the crisis forced Pinochet to move away from Chicago-style liberal economic policies and adopt a more interventionist approach to lead the country out of the economic crisis.

When the country began to recover, the Chicago Boys regained control of the economic area; thus using the financial structure built before the crisis, they further developed the free market approach rather successfully. Vergara suggests that free market economics caused the crisis. However, it was a result of the international recession, the structural errors of the economic team and, in general, the cost of moving from a developmentalist to a free market economy (Edwards and Edwards 1991). Many industries that were not ready to compete in a free market went bankrupt causing unemployment and leading to the social crisis. Certainly, the inexperience and irresponsible behavior of many young and newly-converted Chilean capitalists also worsened the crisis. But the government's strict fiscal policy with its high social costs started to produce sustained growth in the mid 80s.

By 1988, the economic system of the Chicago Boys was regarded as a success (Lavín 1987). Pinochet campaigned on economic issues to win the plebiscite, but the center-left opposition also compromised behind the economic program (although they used the term socially oriented free market) and was successful in focusing the campaign in human rights issues and political liberties. The 1989 presidential election was characterized by similar issues. The center-left coalition stressed their social orientation in the economic program, but fully supported the continuation of a liberal market approach.

The political ideology of the Chicago Boys was contingent on their economic ideology. Contrary to other sectors that supported the coup, the Chicago Boys did not get involved in human rights violations, exile and political repression. While there were some who greatly identified with

Pinochet and his political views, most were pro-free market rather than pro-military. The new democratic government has maintained the economic program of the Chicago Boys, but has also increased social expenditures. Chicago Boys economists have complained that the new government has stolen their economic policies. But, as Patricio Silva correctly notes (1991), the new government's economic policies were led by what he calls The CIEPLAN monks. The Corporación de Intestigaciones económicas para América Latina (Center for Latin American Economic Planing) was closely associated with the Christian Democrats (hence the designation as monks); the Center proposed the concept of social market economy in which the state was to benefit the dispossessed and pursue greater social justice. The fact is, however, that the CIEPLAN focus on reducing poverty and improving social services and labor laws has been conditional on not modifying the economic program.

In the economic arena, the transformations towards a free market economy represented the arrival of modernity in Chile. The military government drastically speeded the process by repressing the political unrest that the "shock economic plan" would have caused had it been implemented in a democracy. Currently, Chile prides itself in being the leading Latin American nation in adopting a free market economy; however without the military government, Chile would not be enjoying such a lead today.

C. Social Transformations

Closely linked to the economic transformations were social changes related to education, health, housing and labor relations. Pinochet's economic team developed new policies and laws that drastically changed the structure and provision of social services and thus altered Chile's overall social relations. In general, following the economic trend, the state drastically reduced its participation in providing social services and allowed for the private sector to own and administer them. From organizing basic education instruction to handling retirement funds, the private sector was offered new areas for their entrepreneurial spirit (Garretón 1989).

The military government transferred the control of elementary and secondary school to municipalities; it maintained strong controls over public universities, subsidizing their operations but violating their autonomy. While still providing subsidies for elementary and secondary education, the military attempted to restrict the role of the state, allowing the private sector to administer educational services with the goal of increasing competition among schools and improving the quality of education (Brunner and Barrios 1987). Parents were now free to decide where to send the students and each municipality was free to determine their priorities for education. Logically, higher income and better educated families took advantage of the new system, while low income families and poor municipalities lost the benefits they had enjoyed in the old system. Upward social mobility became more difficult. Access to quality, equal education, which is a necessary element of modernity, was restricted as the profit-making entrepreneurial spirit gained access to educational services. Whether education should be in the hands of the state or the private sector is a matter of heated debates in modern societies. The intensity of such debates in Chile is a mark of modernization scenarios.

As noted, the transformations n higher education were also profound. However, the national University of Chile, which had campuses in all major cities, was restructured; and regional universities were established, thereby creating potential benefits for the provinces where new universities were established. The traditional centralized university system was ended at a great cost to the power and influence of the University of Chile and higher education in general. Also, there were provisions made for the existence of private universities. However, while encouraging private initiative, the government still controlled the major national and regional universities. Only those students accepted into the highly competitive public universities could apply for fiscal financing. The cost of private universities remained unaffordable for low income people. Access to public institutions was solely based on academic performance, thus allowing some social upward mobility. However, since higher income students could opt to attend private universities, high income clearly guaranteed the access to higher education.

In sum, military induced transformations were authoritarian as they related to university autonomy and unclear with regard to the role of the state in providing education. The direction higher education transformations are taking in the new democratic government is still unclear. So far, universities have reacquired their autonomy. High university officials are no longer appointed by the president, but are elected by the faculty. Private universities have acquired strength and many enjoy good reputations, but fiscal credits for students are still available only for public universities. Brunner led a government committee to restructure the educational system.

The committee put an end to the most clearly authoritarian practices that existed in universities during the dictatorship; and faculty members who had been expelled due to their political ideas were rehired. Sociology and political science departments closed by the military were reopened. In general, traces of authoritarianism in public universities were removed and university autonomy was restored.

Transformations in housing policies followed suit with those in education. While the state continued to subsidize low income housing, the middle class had to pay a larger share of the burden when buying a house. Former generous government subsidies were now market bonds known as Unidades de Fomento. The rapid increase in the price of these Unidades de Fomento was a great incentive for developers to build new housing units and sell them to the public which in turn could also opt for a small government subsidy to provide the down payment. As the price of the Unidades de Fomento increased, the monthly payment for the house increased accordingly. At times of economic crisis, high inflation and diminishing salaries, many families incurred high interest debt and renegotiated their escalating monthly payments. In reality, public subsidized housing for middle class families disappeared. The government undertook the task of providing housing for the most needy; yet as the number of people in extreme poverty rose, the government became unable to satisfy their urgent housing needs (Vergara 1990).

With regard to health provisions, while the government still controlled and operated public hospitals, the development of private institutions was encouraged. The national health care system was honored at public institutions and a number of privately owned hospitals and clinics. The handling of health insurance also changed. While traditionally the government had administered the national health system, now private agencies could collect mandatory insurance contributions from employers and provide employees with health services or issue bonds for employees to obtain health services elsewhere.

Access to health came to be directly correlated with good employment. Lower income people both in urban and rural areas had no access to the best systems and were left to obtain health care in public hospitals. With the emergence of the private sector, the funding for public health decreased significantly. Programs to prevent child malnutrition, women's medical care and health benefits for workers and elderly were greatly curtailed. Many public hospitals incurred heavy debt; health care workers fled the public sector in search of better paid positions (Vergara 1990; Edwards and Edwards 1991).

The new government has attempted to improve the quality of public health. However, the sector was in very bad shape and lacked the minimum funds to attempt a recovery. People with access to a private health system certainly enjoyed the benefits of modernity, but those depending on public health care needed financial support that the government was not been able to provide. In October 1992, as the health situation worsened, the minister of Health, physician Jorge Jiménez, resigned his post and a new minister was appointed and charged with negotiating salaries and benefits for the public health workers well as developing a plan to rescue the public health sector. The crisis was deep; the problems remain to this day.

With regard to labor benefits and regulations, the policies of the military were aimed at reducing the power of organized labor and reducing the role of the state in protecting workers' rights and securing retirement plans. Several of the transformations pushed forth by the military were undone by the new democratic government in 1990. However, labor unions and collective bargaining have lost ground in relation to pre-Pinochet governments; and workers' benefits have significantly decreased as Chile's economy has moved towards a free market model. A major transformation was the handling of retirement funds. While previously Chile had a system similar to that of the U.S. social security system, the creation of the Asociaciones de Fondos de Pensiones (Pension Funds Associations, or AFPs) was a major shift towards a privatization of retirement funds. The privately owned AFPs could use the workers' retirement monies (paid directly to them by the employer) for private investments. While still guaranteeing those funds, the state no longer had the task of collecting, handling and controlling them. The state's role was now limited to establishing investment regulations and supervising the financial activities of profit-seeking AFPs (*ibid.*; also, Piñera 1991).

In synthesis, the government moved away from its previously active participation in all social services towards a *laissez faire* approach that reduced the role of the state to setting regulatory laws and intervening when crisis threatened the stability of the private service sector. However, political pressures coming particularly from the 1982-1985 protests forced the dictatorship to alter some policies. The military regime began sponsoring private-public partnerships which have been further increased by the current government. Also, the 1982 economic crisis forced the state to intervene and take control of most private banks and several financial institutions, assuming the debt but also incurring in ideology-violating measures to protect and stabilize the economy and satisfy social demands (Ponce Molina 1986; Vergara 1990; Cortázar and Muñoz 1990).

Although dictatorship supporters now claim that Chile was a leader in Latin America in implementing liberal economic policies and in reducing the size of the state by privatizing industries, the impulse given to these transformations did not bring about modernity per se. Furthermore, one can find clear traces of clientelism and authoritarianism in the promotion of these transformations. As argued, social conditions in Chile have worsened for an important part of the population, and modernity has clearly not arrived for them. Indeed, Vegara's study of social policies towards the poorest sectors under the dictatorship points to a sharp rise in real and proportional numbers of people living in poverty and the shrinkage of the middle class due to the elimination of government subsidies for health, education and housing, among other services. Furthermore, the secrecy that encompassed the privatizing of many public enterprises, along with the rapid wealth accumulated by individuals closely related to the military, raises questions about motivations and the equity of the process that accompanied social transformations. Many state-owned industries were sold at remarkably low prices which resulted in a net loss for the country (*Newsweek*, September 26, 1988).

D. Cultural Transformations

Transformations occurred in the production and distribution of the arts, literature and mass media--in television channels, radio, film, music and magazines. The transformations were mostly the result of the authoritarian culture, although a few resulted from the arrival of modernity. Authoritarian changes related to censorship and the promotion of the official military discourse. Technological changes and the introduction of new marketing mechanisms were clearly induced by modernity's arrival and advance. Some peripheral discourses that called into question the representativity of traditional Chilean culture also emerged and will be analyzed in the section on postmodernity. In this section, I will focus on changes that were directly caused by the military government.

Upon the success of the coup, the military attempted to depoliticize the nation by eliminating all vestiges of the previous government and by

135

launching a campaign against politicians and political institutions. They also put forth a new conception of culture and cultural production. The dictatorship declared war on cultural producers whose message had social implications and who were, correctly or incorrectly, perceived as supporters of Allende. Artists, singers, writers and people involved in media and mass culture were fired, arrested, tortured, exiled or killed. Those who survived and were allowed to stay in the country were deprived of access to television, radio stations, newspapers and magazines. The few that maintained their jobs in television, radio stations and other media usually recurred to self-censorship. The government maintained a strict control of all the media, especially television, making sure that only the official discourse had access to mass media. Intellectuals friendly to the regime enjoyed disproportionate attention in military-controlled television and rightist-owned newspapers. Among their first actions after the coup, the Junta closed down all leftist newspapers, radio-stations and publishing houses. The government-owned publishing house Quimantú, which had launched a campaign to increase the level of readership in the country and promoted leftist and liberal writers both foreign and national, was also eventually closed down (Subercaseaux 1985a).

Soon, the Junta had accumulated enough merits to be regarded as a totalitarian regime. The manner in which the government promoted its definition of culture, artistic production and consumption has been carefully studied. Subercaseaux (*ibid*.), Catalán (1986 1987) and Brunner himself (1981) have analyzed the government's actions and goals. In general, the leading strategy was to achieve total control wherever possible and to effectively create an environment of self-censorship elsewhere. Yet, a culture of resistance arose and grew stronger and more popular. Soon, different sectors developed their forms of "cultura contestataria" and began promoting alternative cultural discourses often expressing outright dissent from the military. These efforts were limited in scope as they never enjoyed access to television or the press. A reduced number of radio stations were the only media access to these groups. The church, universities, neighborhood and non-government organizations, and even independent research institutions became centers of reunion, promotion and resources for people who opposed the national discourse by advancing an alternative one. Among the best known centers, CIEPLAN and FLACSO (see above), but also ILET (the Latin American Institute of Transnational Studies), AHC (the Christian Humanist Academy), CESOC (the Contemporary Society

Studies Center), SUR (the Agency for Education, Documentation and Investigation) and CENECA (the Center of Communication and Cultural Development) carried on important academic research and provided the space for intellectuals to organize. Eventually, these centers became think tanks for the democratic opposition to the Pinochet government.

By the late 1970s, a few independent weekly magazines associated with the Christian Democrats and the moderate left made their way into the market. Their outspoken opposition resulted in repression against their editors and staff. Several journalists were killed and many more sent to prison. These magazines, along with a few radio stations, won the effective support of international organizations and of the Catholic Church, and became the leading voices of cultural dissent. Poets, writers, art critics, singers and cultural producers in general used these means to regain access to the media and the broader public. During the protest period, a number of more radical leftist newspapers and magazines were also allowed to circulate thus effectively undermining the government's ability to censor written press.

However, most of this culture of resistance occurred at the level of small groups. Networking became a crucial element in the formation of broader cultural alliances against the regimes. Indeed, the grassroots nature of this opposition may explain the relative success it had in perpetuating cultural values fiercely fought against by the military. The 1982-1985 period of protests brought about an opening in the official means of communication; and alternative cultural voices received more press and television coverage. The magnitude of the protests gave these groups an implicit mandate for representing of popular discontent.

In my visit to Chile in August 1992, I was amazed at the resurgence of images of the Allende years and before. Pablo Neruda, Victor Jara, Violeta Parra, Miguel Enríquez, Allende himself and many others are widely known and admired by a youth that bore no memory of the Popular Unity government. Cultural values of the early 70s had been recovered by a youth that 20 years later reshaped them by introducing elements of their own authoritarian-based cultural experiences (cf. Boyle 1992). This is because the images of these men and women were mythically construed by a youth that had no easy access to accounts of that period and whose information was often gathered in semi-clandestine meetings, protests, church-sponsored activities and even limited radio and magazine coverage. There was a whole generation of youth that at least once expressed their resistance by tuning in the Moscow Radio program "Escucha Chile."

The military had sought to stop modernity from arriving at the sphere of cultural consumption in order to help perpetuate its regime; it had kept a tight control over the means of communication and cultural distribution in order to fit dictatorial objectives and thus prevent Chileans from enjoying the benefits of modernity in the process of cultural consumption (Sunkel 1983). The country was prepared for more liberal regulatory laws of cultural consumption and distribution before the 1988 plebiscite; but the Pinochet regime's authoritarian objective of self-perpetuation prevented the arrival of modernity. The military feared the propagation of alternative cultural discourses rather than the effects of a modern structure of cultural production, distribution and consumption and thus opted for its tight and restrictive policies.

Soon after Pinochet's defeat in the 1988 plebiscite, the military government changed the laws that regulated TV stations ownership. While before only the government and public universities could own and operate television channels, the new legislation allowed private ownership of television stations. The arrival of cable TV also made regulatory laws more difficult. Similarly, the laws which regulated newspaper, radio and magazine ownership were loosened. In fact, of course, cultural production did not stop during the Pinochet years. Alternative cultural models developed despite the difficulties of accessing mass media. Also, the repression that existed against cultural producers at the low and high cultural level did not prevent the active production level that existed throughout the Pinochet years. More than in any other area, the policies with regard to cultural consumption were a total failure, since the "unofficial culture" was more popular than "the official culture" and in fact survived the repression and the official isolation.

Modernity-induced transformations were mostly in the area of technology and distribution. Television became the leading mode of mass culture consumption. The traditional isolation of the provinces from Santiago decreased as the nation became unified by better roads, more accessible transportation and television itself. Regional differences diminished and awareness of national and international situations increased. Those elements also affected cultural production and consumption in ways that were not related to the military regime.

4. Modernity and Postmodernity.

The fourth objective of this paper is to present the post-Pinochet debates that exist with regard to Chile's journey through modernity towards a possible stage identified as postmodernity. Although the debate is relatively new and has been developed more in the arts than in the social sciences, it has been acquiring greater attention among scholars as the remaining traces of authoritarian culture are removed from Chilean society. Nelly Richard published *La estratificación de los márgenes* in 1988 when Pinochet was still in power. Her work offers important insights about future arguments over modernity, authoritarianism and postmodernity.

Richard focuses primarily on the marginalized sectors of society and their relationship to the *center*. She argues that modernity, characterized by "the illuminating fundament of its philosophical and historic enterprise," may be defined as a project of realization in and by which society implements a design of making efficiency and technique the basis of "functional rationality." Linked to "a developmentalist mode of industrial progress," modernity involves the fusion of "its progressive and liberating ideals into a globalizing and integrating conception of the subject of history and society" (1988: 39).

Clearly, the objective of modernity is to level different social groups by improving access to services, decreasing income inequality, etc. "Any unbalance in level" is perceived as an obstacle to modernity's prescribing dynamic. Thus, from the perspective of modernity's "international centers," the provinces are conceived as zones of a "disphase" to be absorbed and surpassed by the expansive rhythm of the rationality of the metropolis" (40). For Richard, Latin America is among these provinces, which she also refers to as "*marginal and peripheral cultures*" (1988: 43). And, she argues, it is, on this basis, possible to embrace the concepts of postmodernity and apply them to Latin America. True, Richard offers intrinsic modifications to postmodern postulates when she makes her application. Within Latin America, certain sectors are periphery within the periphery. The arrival of modernity to the Latin American periphery did not mean arrival to what were the most geographically local and economically marginalized sectors within peripheral countries, which offer new sets of interactions and responses to and within postmodern culture and which may be pointing to new modes of articulation and resistance.

Richard attempts to open the boundaries of the resistance to the Pinochet government by including peripheral protests as part of a widely shared believed that the dictatorship must come to an end. Under her interpretation of peripheral resistance, most forms of shantytown discontent, youth rebellion and women's movement activities are intrinsically rooted in the overall discontent with the military regime. For instance, the traditional songs of the exile groups Inti-Illimani and Quilapayún and those of singers like Isabel Parra, Angel Parra, Patricio Manns and others are no more intrinsically anti-Pinochet than the non-directly political rock songs of Los Prisioneros. If the song that identified the youth of Allende's popular unity was *Venceremos*, then the song for the anti-Pinochet youth was Los Prisioneros' *"El baile de los que sobran"* (1986). Further, although *El baile* makes no direct political reference, its validity lies in its peripheral origin, just as that of the rock group.

Hernán Vidal (1992) has questioned Richard's views on several theoretical and practical grounds. By analyzing Richard's journal *Revista de Crítica Cultural*, Vidal has suggested that supposedly left critics like Richard actually promote more than analyze postmodernity in Chile. The *Revista de Crítica Cultural*, Vidal argues, is characterized by an idealism among its participants that is caused by two factors, the late adoption of the postmodernity debate by Latin American critics and the operational characteristics of the profession in the post-Cold War context.

Vidal argues that Richard's approach to postmodernity as presented in the *Revista de Crítica Cultural* proves to be little more than wishful thinking and an illusive use of already existing cultural characteristics to justify and explain links between aesthetics and politics in an era of "catastrophic social change." Richard's approach to political transformation occurring in Chile during the Pinochet decades and her attention to peripheral resistance expressed in non-traditional means are seen by Vidal as a way of "neglect[ing] the reality of violence to make peace with the power that caused the violence."

Whether or not Vidal is correct, Richard's approach to postmodernity, and the discussion that it will generate in times where the electoral possibilities of the left and the likelihood of social change are greatly reduced, will lead critics and supporters to focus on non-traditional means of resistance and popular expression in ways that have been underplayed in the past. Popular culture and most specifically the peripheral consumption of, and responses to, mass media culture produced in the center and

140

distributed to the periphery, will inevitably become more important in future sociological and socio-political studies.

Whether postmodernity is an actual stage and, further, whether it can be said that Chile is entering a phase of cultural, social and political development identifiable by characteristics of postmodernity is an issue about which magazines such as the *Revista de Crítica Cultural* will foster debate. Also, the continuing affiliations that exist between Chilean social and cultural critics and leading schools in Europe and the United States will probably result in the application of theories of postmodernity to different developments taking place in a country that has only in recent years has re-entered the path of modernity. The validity of such approaches, as Vidal argues, no doubt merits careful consideration; but he fears a focus on what he considers secondary matters will distract from other more crucial issues.

Nonetheless, Richard's contribution to the field of cultural resistance is a valid one insofar as it legitimizes the often disoriented but clearly independent forms of resistance that developed outside the traditional realms of political expression. As Garretón observes, peripheral resistance against an overwhelming dictatorship was often perceived as a failed political tactic that might even be damaging for a successful opposition strategy (1984, 1987).

The forms of resistance defended and validated by Richard were and still are constantly called into question by Vidal and others because they did not develop within the realm of organized opposition and thus, it is argued, did not serve the objective of destabilizing the regime. For some, resistance without a larger, organizing framework, is reactive and fragmentary and cannot serve any broader purpose. For Richard, non-coordinated resistance is valid in and of itself. Nonetheless, as Vidal argues, one must be careful in not assuming that these forms of resistance will necessarily evolve into organized action in the periphery aimed at increasing its influence in the center. The existence of Los Prisioneros, then, does not mean that Richard can suggest that the power and forced legitimacy of the dictatorship will be challenged. To do so, Vidal argues, would represent "wishful thinking."

5. *Conclusion*

The presidential elections of Frei (1964) and Allende (1970) resulted in modernity's definite arrival in Chile. But that modernity was characterized by the persistence of premodern social, economic, political and cultural conditions. The military coup of 1973 altered the arrival of modernity significantly, fostering some transformations, hindering others and developing a concept of authoritarian culture. The interaction between modernity and authoritarianism and the appropriation which the latter made of several elements of the first help to partially explain the support the Pinochet regime still has among some democratic sectors in the country.

In sum, at each level analyzed, the arrival of modernity was altered by the emergence of the authoritarian regime. At the economic level, the rapid arrival of modernity was accompanied by traces of authoritarianism. At the political level, modernity was obstructed by the authoritarian approach to political institutions and participation. At the social level, modernity was deeply intertwined with authoritarian policies and ideology. At the cultural level, modernity was prevented from arriving due to the military's strong interest in imposing its cultural discourse.

Placing the transformations in an increasing scale of authoritarianism, economic transformations would have fewer traces of authoritarianism while political changes would have the most elements of authoritarianism. Social transformations experienced advances and retreats in the arrival of modernity and cultural transformations hindered the arrival of modernity.

The above scale partially explains the approaches used by the military government and the democratic opposition in the 1988 plebiscite. While the government based its campaign on economic and social reforms and successes, the democratic opposition, while committing itself to the economic program, stressed the presence of authoritarianism in the political and cultural spheres. These factors explain the agenda of the democratic government and the criteria used to determine priorities. The Aylwin government first addressed urgent social problems, eliminating the authoritarian legacy in political institutions and government, encouraging independent cultural production and pushing minor alterations to the economic program in order to provide funds for increasing social expenditure.

As for a postmodern aspect to all this, the leading cultural analyst on the subject in Chile warns:

> Even in its contexts of origin, postmodernity has not finished the recognition of its trace in the midst of so much dispersed diversity and heterology. A significant part of Latin America has yet to complete its thoughts on the

unsolved aspects of its projects of modernity. Latin America has just begun to lay out its positions with regard to postmodernity. [Richard 1988: 50]

In the specific case at hand, Chile experiences the possible arrival of postmodernity just as it negotiates key dimensions of Western European-style modernity. While at the same time remaining part of the periphery, the country faces its possible emergence as a peripheral center with marginalized sectors that continue to be provinces of what is some ways still a province. All of this provides a variety of new fields to study and arguments to be made with respect to Chile's past and future.

POSTMODERNITY AND EVERYDAY LIFE
IN MONTEVIDEO

Marquesa Macadar
Translated with Marc Zimmerman

1. Introduction: Montevideo in the World

This paper is part of a long journey through the imaginary of Montevideo in 1992. "The imaginary" will be understood as the field composed by religion, mysticism, political activism, street theater, graffiti, carnival, drugs, and other activities or behaviors through which Montevideans organize and express their experience. Even though we speak about a Montevidean imaginary, it should be understood that there is no single Montevideo that is the basis for any monolithic imaginary. Although various groups coexist and share many of the same experiences in a city structured by the same institutions, nevertheless the ways of experiencing the socialization process are diverse. For one thing, class perspectives configure perceptions, values and everyday struggles. On the other hand, the Montevidean imaginary is not only the product of national and local forces, but global ones as well. Global issues dialogue with local concerns, generating a process in which new themes, directions, and imperatives arise and begin to elaborate their own forms and relations.

This paper will explore how global and local contexts interact and how their limits are kept intact or blurred. Even though interest here is specifically on the Montevidean imaginary of 1992, it is necessary to consider preceding years to elucidate "themes, directions and imperatives" (cf. Jackson 1994).

2. Getting into Montevideo: An Insider Point of View

February 1992. In Uruguay as in any other corner of the world, we can sense the *fin-de-siglo*, as well as the end of the millennium. Any change of centuries shakes up views and assumptions regarding the relationship of humanity and the immediate and broader world. If a change of year affects us, how much could a change of decade, of century, and moreover of millennium, impact our lives? Whether we state the issues directly, or carefully construct intellectual edifices to evade the issues, they remain present and active in our collective unconscious. Changes are occurring with vertiginous rapidity; the rate of change is accelerating. The syncronicity of events overwhelms us. The flow of information drugs us. It is almost impossible to synthesize all the information and knowledge that touch us in one way or another in just a couple of hours. We go to bed invaded with information which, by its very process, escapes our reach. Day breaks, and in a blink of the eye, the torrents of information and urban headaches display their scope, scene and stage, as if everything were taking place in the midst of a storm-driven whirlpool, where we frantically struggle against the current. Ordering the data and giving--or trying to create--an explanation for them becomes an exhausting, demanding and often futile task.

Some information is neglected, some is consumed. The selection process is arduous, and there is no time to do it properly. What's more, this process is sometimes left to inexpert hands. Contradictions batter our minds, everything becomes increasingly blank. It is essential to look for a scape-goat, a rear door, an out.

And then there is a specifically local history involving eleven years of dictatorship, eleven years where the information was selected and grossly distorted by rather unsavory people. Meanwhile the hegemonic world was modifying and reinventing its premises, as we kept living and nourishing ourselves with old recipes. The conditions we lived under were oppressive. The established powers didn't even have the hypocrisy to claim we had minimal rights, such as the right to difference--even in its most trivial senses. Almost all rights were unknown. Then the doors of democracy were opened, and a whole new world that had been closed for us now broke through.

The hegemonic prescription of Order, Morality, and Fatherland has been ruled out of order. Now we have to find our own prescriptions. And the fact is that we do not even know how to begin. During the dictatorship some strident, syndicalist and populist movements were gestating. In their midst were people who still remembered the old prescriptions of the sixties. But the world and Uruguay of that time were to experience great change. It was quite a blow when we went to the streets in 1985 and realized how different things were. Where were we to begin? The social movements dismembered themselves, and their discourses turned obsolete. The partizan proposals of the left did not answer to a changing reality in which we lived. The desertion of activists was massive. The few groups that survived this process are those that are more attached to popular sectors. Whatever the state of confusion and information bombardment, whatever rational elaborations and discursive modes mounted to account for the process, it is the terrible material conditions of people's lives and the anger those conditions have induced that are shaping and indeed determining their fate.

The upshot is that reality is atomized and dispersed; and we experience discouragement, emptiness, and ontological hollowness. We turn to other places for what past predicaments and explanations have not given, or have not seemed to give, to us. We survive by building "shelters" in which we protect ourselves from confusion and ugliness. There are three distinctive shelters: religion, drugs, and artistic-intellectual evasion. And then there's a fourth one, which deserves a prize for perseverance: abuse of power-- abuse perpetrated today in the shelter of shelters provided by Latin America's neo-liberal democratic polities. The Montevidean panorama is invaded on the streets and walls by new images unrecognizable in the 60s, 70s or even the early 80s. We are in a world of anomie and shelters. We start our trip through this world by looking at the walls.

3. Pintadas

It's not a matter of gang-symbolizing graffiti, but of fully articulated sentences that people paint on the walls to express given group or individual views on public concerns. Now, in '92, we immediately notice a vertiginous change in the pintadas. While in the eighties they addressed political or social issues, now the pintadas address questions of sexuality and personal identity. While before partisans or social activists were the ones who wrote on Montevidean walls, now the pintada writers are individuals driven by their personal anxiety.

The pintada, "I shit on the politics and religion of old people," is signed by "Absolute Monarchy"--apparently a group, but really an individual. Some of the new pintada authors, Masculine Liberation and Headeaters, are "unipersonal enterprises." The pintada, "In search of a phalocentric society," expresses Masculine Liberation's underlying mono-enterprise philosophy, but in a manner that is so ludic and elusive that most of the passersby will not understand it. And there are other enterprises which are more fleeting and in which the ideology is more hermetic. Examples abound in the phantasmagoric pintadas of Los Comecabezas (The Headeaters--or those who eat one's head): "Take care of your boyfriend"; or "Do you know where your boyfriend is right now?"

While the pintadas generally express individual representations of fragmentation in group identifications and imaginaries, there are nevertheless groups whose members do in fact write pintadas that somehow express a resistance to history and a high level of cohesion even as their pintadas place them "in the world." So, for example, there is no precedent for Jewish group expression in pintadas in the years prior to '92; but now Jewish writings appear on the walls. A well known one is "Long live Majón '91,"--referring to the group of Jewish young people set to visit Israel during the year in question.

The individual pintadas correspond to "le transitoire, le fugitif, le moité, le contingent..."--i.e., qualities which Baudelaire equates with "modernité", and which Habermas (1988) sees postmodern aesthetics as recasting. Meanwhile the group pintadas reflect the other, apparently "contradictory face" of Baudelaire's modernity, which he termed as "l'éternel, l'inmutable." It is in fact this dialectical integration of the transitory and the fixed in social life which creates what we would today define as a postmodern "structure of feeling."

Beginning in March, the Uruguayan Socialist Youth group (JSU) launched a campaign that, because of its optimism, could be considered that other face of the postmodern condition or spirit. Reflecting a joy and vitality which seemed to exist in spite of everything, the youths wrote different *pintadas.* "Because hard times are coming (la mano viene brava), we put passion into everything we do," or "Benny Hill died, but our joy will never die." Another very recent variant to appear on the walls is: "Let's do our thing: Youth Jobs First." What is striking here is that this is a pintada generated by the usually somber Democratic Socialist Party; and the informal, ludic turn of the words is emphasized by energetic graphics, smooth strokes, unjarring, comfortable and even joyful color combinations-- all features of postmodern aesthetics where lightness counters the aesthetics of the sixties. A final example of the pintada as a kind of wall cheerleader trying to revitalize flagging spirits is one that reads: "Don't get down, there's much more to get out of life."

147

4. Religion

One of the most striking features of Montevideo today is the continuous recycling and sacralization of social spaces. Theaters become pentecostal churches; beaches become sites for magical offerings. Different religious tendencies, Occidental or Oriental, bloom without pause.

Rafael Bayce (1992) identifies four religious tendencies existing in Montevideo, which in his view "answer to the triple challenge of postmodernity, postindustrial society and late capitalism." The first two tendencies emphasize the ultra-mundane; the other two emphasize the magical intra-mundane. The first ultramundane tendency draws on varying modes of oriental mysticism, which search out the imperfections of transcendental reason. The second tendency questions the causalities and situational manipulations as they are dealt with within classical instrumental reason and seeks meta-rational and esoteric knowledge sources (4).

Bayce presents the next two tendencies, Afro-Brazilian religions and Protestant Pentecostalism, as examples of what he terms as the "magical intra-mundane." Both of these tendencies are sensorial, cathartic, communal and participatory. The first focuses on forms of spiritual mysticism that are largely African, with Islamic touches and draw on "neo-magical" modes to affect everyday spiritual and material welfare. Afro-Brazilian religions, such as *Macumba, umbanda* and gauchos, have a normative ritual rather than an ethical one. On the other hand, Protestant Pentecostalism is a liturgical vesion of intra-mundane religion which stresses the content of ethical revelation.

Bayce offers two different possible explanations for Montevideo's overall religious explosion; he also seeks to understand the preference of Montevideans for Afro-Brazilian practices. The first explanation is articulated within the global context: the fall of Enlightenment thought, and the loss of faith in reason. The second explanation is framed within the particular post-dictatorship Uruguayan reality: the fall of the Democratic Guru. The living memory of a ruthless Dictatorship, with criminal leaders exalting Morality and imposing discipline, makes Uruguayans less credulous towards any supposedly unique and correct way of acting in the world--i.e., ethics.

Afro-Brazilian religions have more tolerance and fewer ethical strictures with regard to human doings. There is a closer affective and cultural proximity between the devotee and the religious hierarchy. The *mai* and *pai*

(Afro-Brazilian religious hierarchies) provide more refuge, shelter and support than what comes from a set line or creed; they satisfy needs rather than imposing a code of ethics; they allow catharsis rather than promoting constriction. Above all, they supply people with a sense of communal belonging that is more extensive than the family and smaller than the state.

All of these modes of interacting are radically opposed to what we had to face under the dictatorship. In those days, we were given classes in Morality. They intimidated us with the *Ought to Be*, our duty of defend the Homeland. We were taught not to trust a stranger, a foreigner, any *Other*. All sense of community was eradicated; the community was the state, the *Fatherland*--that totalizing abstract whole which was supposed to define our being and ways of being together. Our needs, our affectivities, our cultural worries were subversive and corrosive. On the other hand, our efforts to join together in a fight for a dignified life were buried under papers. We had to hear "this cannot be done, the Army might get angry!" The omnipotent power became more powerful than our intentions and desires. Then what was the sense of losing our already lost lives, of breaking up our already broken families? Men and women started to feel the need for pleasures, joy without the political and moral mediation that told them what they should be. That was when they began to choose their unconditional *pai* or *mai*, who was as much a sinner as they were--but who could help them psychically and materially, just by listening to them.

It is not clear whether these phenomena have anything to do with post-illuminism. There was a vacuum and we tried to fill it. But for these social actors the vacuum was not reason itself. Montevideans drowned in a general pool of uncertainty, of concrete, immediate, to-the-point questions which did not find concrete, immediate, to-the-point answers. But is this because of the crisis of reason, or is it due to the fact that reason's mechanical, standardized, schematized use cannot explain these kinds of paradoxical situations.

If we understand reason as a possibility for exchanging ideas, as a medium without which it would seem impossible to live in this world at the end of the century, could we not argue that this feeling of emptiness is the product of an irrational world which legitimates physical force in order to install order? Or could we not read as the consequence of the absurdity of people dying of hunger in a world which has the resources to feed all of us?

5. New Trends in Mass Consumption

We now take a longshot of the changes in the city's general appearance. The key question here is how much an image or concept can become incorporated in our "collective mentalities" and beyond the shared discourse and pretensions of "decision-power groups."

First there are the major impressions evoked by this Montevideo of 1992, in contrast with the Montevideo of a few years ago. From this perspective, we can notice some distinctive features that transfigure the face of Montevideo. First there are the cash stations; second, the blaring McDonald's street advertisements and, above all, the billboards; finally, there's the strong presence of bright colors (mainly pinks and purples) on the facades of private and commercial residences.

The cash stations reveal an increase in what Bell calls "distribution services" (31). For Bell, post-industrial society involves a shift from industrial labor and basic needs supply to administrative labor and services supply--i.e., a situation in which more labor force is concentrated in services. But this is not to say that Montevideo forms part of post-industrialism, for here the Baudrillardian "post" simulacrum-aesthetics serves a different function in Uruguay's particular peripheral social formation of what Trotsky, and now, in postmodernist terms, Yúdice (1992a) has termed "combined uneven development."

The appearance of McDonald's on the Uruguayan landscape is also a special case. The transnational hamburger appears in the country of cows-- and fat cats. The phenomenon can be considered as an instance of U.S. transnational insertion through persuasive advertizing, or as an instance of particularized Uruguayan appropriation, re-territorialization and re-functionalization. In the latter interpretaton, McDonald's loses its U.S. meaning (a quick and cheap way to eat), to become a form of presuming on the part of the economically (if not mentally) privileged classes in what can be seen as another symptom of reconversion of first world cultural capital in other world contexts.

The eateries, teahouses and fashion-boutiques, even the University's Sciences College, can be seen in the upwardly mobile Pocitos neighborhood paint their facades with light colors. The quick spread of these color preferences can be seen in the bright pink and purple setting for Channel 10's *Subrayado* news program--even *Subrayado* publicity is backed up with the same colors. Are these coincidences or products of an epidemic? Can this

150

sort of quick spreading so common in Uruguay today be interpreted as the internalization of the postmodern condition, or as an echo of a fashion framed in function of Baudrillard's simulacrum aesthetics that will soon pass (ibid.)

The McDonald's boom and the new gawkish consumption sites are installed in a context marked by other changes that have been part of the Montevidean scenario for a longer time, although they have been viewed as post-dictatorship phenomena. First is the greater array of bars, cars, and other night sites; second the overall spread of fast-food chains; finally the appearance of a new audience for foreign rock groups.

Clearly we imagine ourselves living in a lighter epoch. The preponderance of new bars can be related to the variable that Giddens calls "security and risk" (1990). Our "lightness of being" means that the bars no longer seem to need metal curtains protected from barricades or menacing stones. The cars give us mobility, speed, nomad-ness, a fugitive indeterminacy. The fast food chains have appeared, spread out and grown-- all very quickly. Is this an intent to satisfy the t.v. audience for foreign programs? Or is it related to the household reorganization required by more and more women working outside the home, creating the need to eat outside and quick? Whatever the reasons, Montevideans seem to submit to the elusive fallacy of progress, ever seeking to achieve the living status of the hegemonic metropolitan world.

The affinity of youth for foreign rock groups is clear post-dictatorship. Rock music was the animating element for the activist youth of the 82-86 period (cf. Verdesio 1987). With a clear and distinct profile, ex-activists regroup and re-encounter themselves around the "good music." The new sensibility draws its creative and cathartic energy from new, transnational objects--for example, video and publicity. Further on, this paper will focus on some of the objects that embody this sensibility.

If we were to take an intermediate camera shot of the city, we could capture such phenomena as the overall recycling of theaters and other sites, as well as activist desertion. Just as some theaters (the Princess and Radio City) became pentecostal churches, so too the Censa theater became an aesthetic center; the Cordon & Liberty theaters became discos; the California became a parking lot; the ABC, a video gameland. These are seven of the eight theaters recycled (the eighth will be mentioned below). The aesthetics centers are part of the ideological store of "postmodern lightness," along with the cigarettes, fast foods, and so much more.

The ABC's recycling as a war game video center points to the concepts that Baudrillard considers, however questionably, in function of "the war that never was", or "the war that will never be" (1991; see also Norris 1992). The war started on a manipulable screen; the war ludicalized itself, and lost its tragic connotations--especially among those of us for whom the heat of the bombardments was never part of our everyday life.

Light and vegetarian mania start to invade our senses through street signs and other kinds of advertising. National cigarette companies like Coronado and Nevada put light and moreover ultra light cigarettes on the market. Montevideo experienced a fashion burst of restaurants in all their variety. Vegetarian restaurants spread all over the city; so too "all you can eat", fast food, macrobiotic, and other specialty venues. Publicity suffered a clear shift towards postmodern easiness or lightness.

This last point is illustrated by the electoral campaign of the Frente Amplio, a coalition that joined different sectors of the parliamentary left. Using light colors and festive graphics, this campaign had a tone very different from the 1972 or 1984 elections. The most popular slogan was "Get with it, vote for the Frente Amplio."

Another important element was the candid, reliable image portrayed by the Frente's Mayoral candidate, Dr. Tabare Vázquez, a medical man whose image and charisma were part of the package offered to the voter. This campaign was a success, and many Uruguayans will agree that it contributed to the Frente Amplio's overall electoral triumph.

Not unrelated to the recycling of spaces and the overall production of lightness is the phenomenon of "activist desertion," which became frequent during the late 1980s and in turn produced further distinctive changes on the face of the city. The frequent university and street demonstrations suffered from a significant decrease of voices and overall participation. And why not consider the most popular and persistent activities?

6. *Moving towards the Streets: Carnival and murga*

Montevideo's carnival stresses European as opposed to African traditions. Instead of Brazilian-style parades, samba competitions and sexual flaunting, transvestitism, and the like, Uruguayan carnival generally involves theatrical competitions protagonized by *murga*s, or neighborhood performing groups that present vaudeville-like satirical skits (or números)

152

including several musical numbers based on known songs from traditional music, rock, etc., sung a capello and with original lyrics expressing the neighborhood's or group's feelings of the moment

"Falta y Resto" is not typical or paradigmatic of other *murgas*. It is distinguished by maintaining at least a facade of "political consciousness." Furthermore its audience is not based on neighborhood affiliation, but on other forms of relation and identification as they emerge in the present historical transition. *murga* costumes are generally colorful and exuberant; they are designed each year for participation in the costume contest. The traditional colors for la Falta are red and black. But during the Carnival in question, la Falta participated in the contest with a somber costume, a black suit from the twenties "gangster" era. The stage setting was a witty arrangement of mock mirrors and masks. These elements helped to make the message more effective. And the message was an insightful one:

He he he he he	The members of each
and you believed it...	*murga* that you saw are
he he he he he	yourselves... reflected
it was all a joke...	in a mirror!!!

These verses can be found in the last or "farewell" couplet, where song messages generally suggested in earlier stanzas are often "materialized," or denoted linguistically. In this *murga* an earlier excerpt reads:

When it goes away, Falta	from the silence
When carnival forgets it	to the future.
like a teenage remembrance	IT WILL RETURN

The idea expressed here is a diachronic one. We are told about a temporal prolongation (*desde*–from, *hasta*--to) creating a virtual narrative of continuity and even redemption. The message transmitted through the lyrics is clearly optimistic. It addresses teenagers explicitly:

An ideal trembled	what you should do
and for you,	and what you should think
teenager, they want	if you jump,
to impose	you're jumped

153

The emphasis now, is clearly on the addressee and the connotative function of *murga* language. In spite of the fact that there is a referential function implicit in the text's first line, it's the connotative function that is privileged. This emerges in the subsequent verses:

Don't let them   your anger
step over   or your tenderness.

Or, afterwards, imitating the treatment of the mothers towards their children, Falta sings:

You cannot   wait
form an opinion   you have to wait
you have to grow up   there's some one else
Freedom's something   ahead of you
you don't know how to use   step over him.

Such words call upon   teenage frustrations with traditionalist and institutional repressions, above all stemming from family and political conservativism; they often point to a more radical stance:

You have to succeed   be an activist and act
you have to be an activist   You have to obey Uruguay

The old dichotomy of the Uruguayan left gave way to a more complex reality.   Repression was no longer correlated only with "fascists", "conservatives," and "military types."   Now the reality has become more plural, and this is why it was harder to apprehend and articulate:

Oh mamma mia   don't get upset at us.
mamma mia   It's for your good
where will we go.   for mine
For your own good

Various exhortations in the penultimate stanzas of this song represent the *murga's* "*retirada*" (closing act or adieu) and operate in the same conotative manner. Some of the exhortations are:

Create	Keep singing your song
build	till we invent
even though	still another...carnival
it's turned out wrong.	And bring some joy
Don't quit fighting to be happy	to your heart.

The last lines are the refrain, another warning for the young:

And don't ever	disguise reality
let them	for you again.

The rhetorical image of disguise appears here again. This image has a duality, because the message of reality is told in the context of Carnival, the feast of dissembling. In these stanzas there are not many references to "social reality." Indeed an objectifiable context appears in few passages. Other than the "retirada," the only overtly referential passages are the ones quoted above--although in other couplets a few things are told, such as the following:

All together let's cry.	socialism's a bullet
I'll cry, and they'll cry	gone awry,
they've let the country die.	it's better to lie down
Uruguay's gone to pot,	and die.
liveable it's really not--	

This is followed by a "Buaaaa..."–a phrase which accomplishes a totally emotive function in keeping with the previous words.

Throughout its performance, Falta y Resto emphasizes its addressee, rather than the message itself or its context. Both message and context appear as accessories of the fundamental intention, which is to relieve teenagers, encourage them to be happy (even though they don't give them any clue about how to achieve that happiness), give them energy and hope, make them strong. Reality, happiness, hope are intersubjectivities whose meaning is never explicit but seems to be shared. There is no rational communication: the meanings are suggested and felt through allusions. The message is not transparent; it offers many readings, with parameters that are difficult, if not impossible, to establish at a rational level.

Falta's intention of motivating and germinating hopes (out of happiness or whatever--we have to figure it out for ourselves) was achieved to the limit. When it first performed its skit, the group's success was so huge, it won the Carnival contest by public vote; and it became a featured act at the El Galpón every weekend--an instance of Garcia Canclini's "cultural reconversion" (1995a).

A postmodernist sense of hopelessness and a loose feeling of defeatism are not the prevailing sensations in our Montevideo, at least not among the key *murga* performers. As Falta y Resto themselves sing, it seems to be

That old dream,
it's just been knocked down
and among its ruins
sprung forth
the new adolescent seed

that today
goes round the world
and returns
to start
the revolution

Whatever its contemporary meanings might be, the macro-sign of revolution (and all that produced, and is produced, by it) was not completely lost or forgotten. This sign was not only shaped by the *murga*, but also by its audience that followed Falta y Resto with great attention and energy. The group was the injection of hope for many people, especially for those most ignored: the adolescents. It seems that at least for such groups and their fans (Montevidean equivalents of Stanley Fish's "interpretative communities"), Lyotard's "death of the grand *récits*" (no matter how many and complex the discursive variations) was not the byword.

We can observe intents towards incorporating new ideological content, or breaking old left-right and other dichotomies. However the formal structure or discursive style in which the predominant connotative function involves using an imperative, "have-to-be" tone, expresses an axial principle that is ethical and which expresses a grand récit that seems to repeat or rearticulate forms that belong more properly to an ideological store and aesthetic rooted in the 1960s.

Here the effort is not to make assertions about how different and heterogeneous people live and feel; the effort is not to discuss reality, or "what is"; rather it is to achieve subjective interpretations, participant readings of what is explicitly denoted or implicitly connotated in recent songs produced and consumed, so we may grasp the sense of verisimilitude, "what seems to be" prevalent in Montevideo.

7. *Video*

Perhaps no arena provides a more significant and symptomatic gauge of majority sensibilities in Uruguay than the video produced in this country without a film industry. Video offers "channels of expression," that provide us with an independent experience of an art based on temporal as well as spatial dimensions. Montevideans have developed different video formats--documentaries, fictional documents, video-clips, video-art, and fiction.

We turn to a fictional documentary, "Mama era punk" ("Mama was Punk"--cf. Casanova 1988) because it provides telling insights in relation to our theme. The video is organized as a book into six segments that stand like structural compartments or spaces for emotions and attitudes. The Prologue introduces the main theme, in a simulacrum of the real that still photography can provide and that videos can give movement. Multi-sensorial images build up around a central space constituted by an entertainment park, Parque Rodó. In these images youths appear dancing to the beat of "Rock and samba," one of the amusement park rides. These audio-visual, taste and smell images of the park itself awaken Montevidean childhood memories of 'churros' and sweet corn. But anyone who has once gone to the park knows that those who dance close to the Mambo amusement park ride are marginal youths. By a process of association, the six segments of the video lead us to conjure up visual images related to terms such as: the homeless, people with painted faces, a young man with a trumpet, etc.--icons clearly correlated with cultural and/or socio-political marginalization--at least for the interpretative community to which the icons are directed.

In "Mama era punk," as Bayce tells it, "Emigration starts to elicit the happiness phantom that for two years democracy was in charge of eliminating" (1992: 10). The content of the song evoked negative opinions from critics espousing an "aesthetics of commitment." But what is certain here is that it is not necessary to present reality as it should be, but as it is perceived--as a plural and incommensurable phenomenon for which only our intuition can give a sense of totality. These videos present alternatively real and fictional testimonies. But the fictions are sincere, bother whomever they bother. The youths portrayed raise, and are still raising, flags against dullness; they are young people whose adrenaline circulated too quickly for a country in which life walks too slowly. In this video there is no definite judgement, but different voices (most of them formerly silenced) which find expression. If our presentday life incites a peripheral postmodern reality, then with videos such as this, we can say that we are confronting a postmodern aesthetic.

8. The "Retro" Wave, Neighborhood Agglutination and Youth Politics

They could silence those people who protest in the streets, but the voices that are in each house, in each neighborhood, can not be silenced—A teenager, in "Silbando bajito" [Whistling softly] a "Mama era punk" [Mama Was Punk] segment.

A. Recycling Everything

Just as theaters are recycled, so are houses, and even eyeglasses and shoes. The Mogador, the last of the recycled theaters, was converted into a striptease house, thus preserving one of the most common monument-icons of the fifties. Old town is in a process of reconstruction, as the colonial houses are bought by upper class fashion designers who redo and recycle the buildings according in a melange of juxtaposed styles.

Eyeglass frames are sold in popular outdoor markets of Piedras Blancas and Tristán Navaja, where the used, the stolen, and the antique go at low prices. These markets are located in poor neighborhoods, where bargain hunters, penniless readers, and alternative-style fashion-horses hang out. The eyeglass frames are recycled, and adapted for prescription lenses. The shoes go back to the sixties: platform shoes, shoes with high heels, thick soles, and enormous bows. All this leads us to question the religious and mystical presences in the city, and to focus on how popular political groups do what they do.

B. Popular Movements and the New Ethos

I identify neighborhood aglutination with those popular movements which come together around common preoccupations as well as basic and urgent needs--for example, fights for housing, educational access, jobs, working conditions, medical services, access to the familiar canasta; fights against police repression, inflation, and so on... These issues are felt and shared through the social bond among neighbors. The neighbors talk about the issues and assemble around them, doing community work, organizing around Christian communities and other existing organizational forms, or creating cooperatives and other new forms--including popular movements.

Popular movements are those social groupings which involve people joining together with a clear and practical objective (Echevarría, Regent, and Ruetalo 1987: 33). Examples of these are the "cacerolazos" (pot clangings) and anti-dictatorship black-outs that took place mainly during 1983 and 1984. Afterwards in 1986 the same methods were repeated to protest the amnesty law protecting military officials and agencies. This type of geographic or neighborhood community is not isolated from the whole society to which it belongs. Even though its preoccupations are local, it is immersed in a broader social structure that conditions and is conditioned by, its situation. Indeed, while "all urban experiences touch [every] sector of neighborhood life" (ibid.: 36); the localized, neighborhood experience also has the power to influence, just as it is influenced by, the overall urban context. In this way, more global social situations resound in the destiny of such organizations. The years of 1983 and '84 mark a "period of reconstruction and creation of the organized expressions of civil society, in the framework of the fight against the dictatorship" (34). And the period's overall social agitation now finds its correlations in contemporary neighborhood organizations, which complement the resurgence of predominantly non-geographically-based union movements.

The young people within this context see themselves involved in movements which were previously considered marginal (cf. García Canclini 1990: 10). The youths identify themselves with their generational and neighborhood situations. Their distinctive feature is what Martín Barbero (1987a and b) calls "sociality," understood as the process in which people (in this case the young) relate themselves to their environment of external, socialized entities such as family, educational, religious, army, political institutions, mass media, etc.

During 1984, when the elections approached, the youth organizations saw themselves mitigated by the number and quality of their representatives. People with partisan interests became involved in those organizations that were clearly popular and neighborhood oriented. This circumstance, plus the important loss of members to specifically electoral work, contributed to the slow dwindling of organization membership and participation.

159

In 1986, there were still some intents of "olla popular" or other popular youth group participation in urban struggles. But they had neither the force nor the adhesive power they had had in the wonder years of the popular, neighborhood and urban movement. Sporadically, some conflicts arose among families who became homeless. But hunger strikes, demonstrations, and solidarity marches (culminating with the Tres Cruces movement or "*movida*") ultimately disappointed the hopes of the youths who participated in them.

This same year saw the beginning of a popular theater movement involving youth from a different socio-economic sector but nevertheless sharing a common view of the political issues at stake in the city. In 1986 the "*Red de teatro barrial*" was created, and participated in a cycle of significant neighborhood and youth movement activities ("el arte en la lona" of 1987; the anti-razzia movement of 1988; "*la marcha de las antorchas*" of 1989), followed by "*La otra historia*" encounter held in the city of Libertad. This sequence established a particular niche for youths whose voice frequently resounded in legitimate spaces.

Meanwhile, the meeting of "lo culto" and "lo popular" was expressed in the "Mama era punk" video, where the oft-silenced, "other" voices of the non-establishment young involved commentaries that moved away from standard political demonizing and polarization. "Political parties don't do much more than write pintadas and slogans, but they don't feel the razzias... and later they just come to look for the vote." ["Lo de los partidos politicos queda en pintadas pero no sienten las razzias...y después vienen a buscar aquí el voto".] The teenage persona of these lines (again from "Silbando bajito" in "Mama era punk") enunciates a distance from right and left wing political parties and the generalized institutional disillusionment which characterizes youth "otherness."

The teenagers have neither an official nor unofficial social or political standing which authentically projects their concerns. They are doubly marginal--first by age; secondly by their status as social "pariah," "liberated" from conformist structure through their institutional abandonment. The great majority have no fixed or union-affiliated jobs; most are unemployed, or, in the best of the cases, subemployed; many have to work in the informal sector.

Since 1984, though each year to a lesser degree, the popular movements became related to popular political entities. Examples of these are Trotskyist and anarchist groups, movements such as the MRO, MPP or MLN which have almost always been marginalized from the parliamentary decision sectors. In the 1986-89 period of disenchantment, there was an anemic ebb in the groups organizing people around a social work process drawing on theoretical bases in Pauo Freire's popular education concepts, or the concepts introduced by Liberation Theology. Expressing the general ethos, one young rocker in a video clip pines, "I'm disappointed with every one. They go to receive the Pope, but they don't go to a rally for the public transportation fare. This tells you that there's something wrong,...or that the people are terrorized,...or that there are too many old people" (Casanova 1988). This ethos still permeates the times, and every aspect of cultural life in early 1990s.

9. *Final Comments and Other Moves toward Cloture*

This essay has presented illustrations of "lo popular", "lo masivo" and "lo culto" that seemed interesting to point out for the light they shed on the heterogeneity, limits and facades of Montevideo's "pluralistic society." The illustrations were selected according to the amount of attention or "noise" the examples have created in the general pool of emotional, sensual and intellectual images characterizing Montevideo 1992. Intellectuals and cultural producers have attempted to counter the obstacles posed to the light, heterogeneous world in which our illustrations interact. And all the hybridizations and reconversions theorized or realized cannot prevent the emergence of some clearly distinct voices and their referents.

Even though everyone seems to be touched by postmodern strains, the question remains whether or not the music is internalized and reaches the deepest structures of our being; or whether the notes only make untranscendental retouches on our most superficial being structures, to which we transfer our desires and needs, disguising their supposed meaning. Following Yúdice's Latin Americanist reading of the Baudrillardian simulacrum, we can't know to what extent each element is imposed or authentically felt (1992). But we can see that the "modernist ideal" did not collapse, at least among certain people for whom particular variants of the ideal still live as part of a Montevidean imagined and interpretative community. Moreover these elements are not generally absorbed in the forms imagined and sought after by the powers that be. Face-to-face sociability plays an important role in our socialization process; many of us still see humanity as modifier if not maker. But these matters can only be understood in relation to ourselves and our relational antennae. We cannot frame such relations, or reduce them lucidly; we can only intuit them. Creating a world where difference is respected doesn't just mean that there's respect for divergent political positions, but also for varied ways or choices of being-in-the-world. For some people these ways of being-in-the-world are part of a mutilated memory; they are pre-modern options that have been virtually uprooted from popular memory, but the roots are still there, however mangled. What we can do? The times pressure us to accede to hegemonic ideology, and this produces a clash between group memory and the historical revisionism of command sectors. Can we resist hegemony?

For those of us who can pass as mainstream, it is easy enough to adapt to new inputs and impacts, to take on fashionable explanations. But for those who live their everyday life in a permanent ambiguity between institutional discourse and their experienced world, there is too much noise which cannot be organized in any easy harmonic whole or final score.

This work has been an effort towards deconstructing the concepts of Postmodern condition, Postmodernity, and Postmodernism in a peripheral social formation. It was my intention to see these concepts as things in the world to be experienced rather than as theoretical and epistemological constructs; I have sought to observe them interplaying in everyday life with different social actors. My effort was driven by what Jackson has defined as a kind of spirit for placing practical and social imperatives ahead of scholastic rules and abstract understanding. To paraphrase Jackson's wording, I may say that I have given ontological priority to social existence and its forms of disclosure, as a way of doing justice to the subaltern.

I wanted to call for what Rorty has described as an "open-ended conversation" (1979: 365-394) with Montevideo, its streets, its people, its needs, the theories circulating its world, their resistance and their complicity.

I am as colonized as are those people whose voice I tried to echo, and my interpretation is as far from the truth as any other interpretation; but it is a voice that I considered imperative to be heard. I am a participant in Montevidean history-making, but I am not--and can't be--a participant in Montevidean *murga*s, since I don't belong to that mode of sociality. In spite of the fact that I have studied *murga*s, it would be a romantic idealism to think that I could ever be at one with them. This is why, even though they were present and in communication with my "everyday lifeworld," my language games and discourse, their logic and imperatives were, and are, different from mine. I can have a sense of them, but there is no way I can live their struggle, suffer their everyday fight against hunger and social deprivations, be under their skin, internalize language games, and react as they do.

What I have tried to convey is their voices, plasticized in their chants in which they "describe and share experiences ..., through which they show [the way] ... they work together ... to create coherent scenarios that articulate shared meanings" (Jackson: 10).

In my work I wanted to see how the collectivity "finds the raw material for its social bond not only in the meaning of the narratives it recounts, but also in the act of reciting them" (ibid.). For my own sake, this narrative, this journey through Montevideo's streets and imaginary, was intended to let me know and to act towards the rest of the collectivity; it was "an instrumentality, ... a way of accomplishing things rather than a way of possessing reality"; it was a way of sharing the differences, of appreciating others and doing them justice, rather than "representing truth." My intent was to appreciate "everyday goals, practical problems, and social existence," to be part of a Montevidean version of "the gritty and obscure drama of everyday life" (ibid.: 11), but also a narrative of my city's everyday richness and colors, its light and lightness of being.

INSCRIPTIONS IN THE WAR ZONE

Excerpts from an installation by
Silvia A. Malagrino

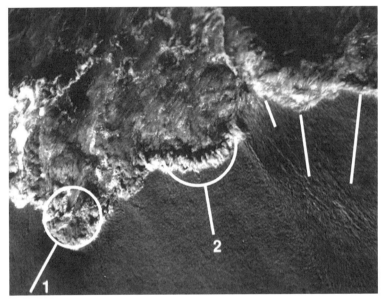

Inscription
Detail from installation. Silverprint, 8" x 10", 1993

Dream

I am standing in the middle of a wind and water eroded depression which seems to be a crater. The landscape is spectacular - colored rocks, red sand, volcanic ashes. The location is not precise - it could be somewhere in the Andes or the Himalayas. The time of the day is not defined: dawn or sunset. The wind begins to blow turning to a dust storm that hurts my body and it becomes impossible to see. I notice that I am not alone. A dark figure appears walking towards me. As the figure reaches me, I realize it is a nomad. I ask for help. The nomad takes my hand, gives me a small stone and says that it will help me to find my way. On the stone there is a word written: *REMEMBER*

"First, we will kill all the subversives, then we will kill their collaborators, then...their sympathizers, then...those who remain indifferent, and finally we will kill the timid."

General Ibérico Saint Jean,
Police Chief, Buenos Aires, Argentina, 1970's

The Hunt
Detail from installation. Silverprint, 20" x 16", 1993

EPILOGUE

Point of Departure
text by Mónica Flores Correa
translated by Esther Parada

I see your womb as an elongated line. My hand glides over your round belly, conjuring luck. Barely touching my forehead with my fingertips, I see each rite of initiation, each passage, as if it were today, January 1993, as if everything were about to begin, as if, at the dawn of the world, dew was about to fall on the black flower, and over my mouth.

The strange thing about every story is that it is circular. In general, no one recognizes this, because no one knows the point of departure. It could be a mother's womb or a brothers cry for help, a sister's terror. It could be a birth, a death, an embrace, the day one abandoned forever one's native country or one's hope - or both.

The circle closes when, without intending, perhaps upon awakening some morning, one returns to the mother's womb or the embrace, to that plaza, or - more precisely- to the fire tree in that plaza in one's native land; and one discovers that the old people who sat there on the bench are different but are the same.

A poet writes about "the slow migrations of humanity." He talks about each one of us, about our journeys, and the spiritual pilgrimages of each man and each woman. That is, of every sorrow, every miracle of endurance, every surrender, or defiance of destiny; in other words, each revelation to which we always blindly return.

The South/Missing
Detail from installation. Silverprint, 60" x 40", 1993

Michael Piazza, *Method*, 1997.
Photo courtesy of the artist.

III. Specifying Textualities, Transfixions and Appropriations

Raúl Quintanilla, *Tripping con Colón.*
Home page from *Artefacto* website. Managua, Nicaragua, 1997.
Courtesy of the artist.

DE-COLONIZING KNOWLEDGE, REFORMULATING TEXTUALITY: RETHINKING THE ROLE OF CENTRAL AMERICAN NARRATIVE

Arturo Arias

1. Introduction

The 1990s point to the beginning of a new period in Central American history. This new period can be dated from the electoral defeat of the Sandinistas in February of 1990. The end of the guerrilla cycle and of the utopian dream of revolution changed the symbolic framework of the Central American subject, and it redefined priorities, identities and cultural projects. Common sense indicates that this should have also changed this region's literary narrative. After all, if we agree that narrative texts are symbolic systems of representation that generate "truth effects" through their discursive practices, it is evident that they register these subjective changes in the perception of beingness; and their study should enable us to explore transitions in identity as well as in ideology.

We can define discourses as areas of knowledge organized and ordered in such a manner so as to suggest specific ways of appropriating truth and power. Discourses are formed by linguistic utterances. Language does not reveal knowledge as such, but captures it within itself so to speak, generating its own "truth effect" that is symbolically expressed through the medium of literature. And literary changes frequently bespeak some measure or parallel of changes in human history and life.

Traditionally, period changes in Central America have always been marked by stylistic changes in which the challenge is that of redefining the writer/reader relationship through transformations in reading practices. In that process, old-fashioned representations of reality are substituted by new verbal signs that evoke or allude to a new imaginary concept of "the social".

The end of the 20th century is a fluid moment, in which the very identity of being Central American, of being from the Third World, and of being a postcolonial subject, can get lost in the strong winds charged with acculturating connotations. As García Canclini puts it:

> For the first time in history, in the second half of the Twentieth Century, the greater part of all goods and communications received in each nation

173

have not been produced in their own territory, they do not emerge from their own particular relations of production, nor do they carry signs that link them exclusively to a national community. Rather, they have other bearings that indicate their belonging to a deterritorialized system. [1992]

Given these parameters, we are forced to ask ourselves: is this scenario what changes Central American literature? Or is it the critical gaze over Central American literature itself? After all, part of the First World's insertion in Central America implies a reflection about the nature of the critical instruments themselves. The adoption of postcolonial or postmodern conceptual tools force the critic to embrace a broader definition of literary studies, more or less along the lines already invoked by Terry Eagleton:

> My own view is that it is most useful to see "literature" as a name which people give from time to time for different reasons to certain kinds of writing within a whole field of what Michel Foucault has called "discursive practices," and that if anything is to be an object of study it is this whole field of practices rather than just those sometimes rather obscurely labelled "literature." [Eagleton 1983: 205].

To this one has to add the problematic of a Central America that, with the signing of the peace accords in El Salvador, the electoral defeat of the Sandinistas, and the recent signing of peace terms in Guatemala, has "exited from history." That is, it has stopped being a source of conflict -- and by extension, it has disappeared from the news -- in the First World.

It has been said for a long time that the Central American drama is precisely that it concerns absolutely no one when it does not disturb the sleep of any super power. "Repression in Guatemala is worse than elsewhere," wrote Nobel-prize winner Gabriel García Márquez in 1976, "not so much because of its unquenchable intensity, nor because of its heartless ferociousness nor because of its prehistoric duration, but rather because there is almost nobody left in the world who still remembers it" (1986).

Between 1978 and 1990 Central America managed, at a very high cost, to capture the world's attention. But in the nineties, it would seem as if we had returned to the previous situation. Central America has a Nobel-Prize winner who is also a tireless Mayan fighter for human rights--Rigoberta Menchú-- but, even so, it still matters very little, and to very few, in the cultural sphere.

174

However, the cultural heritage that the Central American crisis left us is enormous and its recognition is only beginning. What is more, many of the traits celebrated in the First World as postmodern were already present in Central American cultural production since at least the 1970s. However, an absence of critical recognition of this postmodern presence combined with a singularly poor regional critical tradition has prevented the acknowledgment of these facts.

Nonetheless, as with the narrative of the seventies and eighties, the starting point for its critical recognition is the revolutionary experience lived in the region during these years. An entire group of young First World academics became interested in Central American issues when the region first surfaced in the news due to the Sandinista triumph and to the Salvadoran and Guatemalan civil wars. Beginning with an explicitly political commitment, a general curiosity in the region's cultural production soon followed, and with the passing of time, the emergence of Central American critics, the intertextual relations between both sets of critics and the transculturation of intellectual tools, it has gradually become an actual critical evaluation.

In this article I will *not* do an inventory of Central American literary production during the present decade. There are still very few texts worthy of note. By way of contrast, the seventies and eighties were marked not only by revolutionary explosions, but also by literary ones. Up until now, the nineties are just as forgettable for their literary production as they are for their transitions to democracy. When we observe the overall picture we only come across the rise of Rodrigo Rey Rosa from Guatemala, the last novel by Honduran Julio Escoto, *King of Sunrise: Dawn* (*Rey del albor: Madrugada*) and the gradual emergence of little-known Rosario Aguilar from Nicaragua. We could add Sergio Ramírez's last collection of short stories, and maybe another text or two. But the fact remains that after the prior explosion, we seem to have been left only with the hangover and the heartburn.

After all, the texts with which the very scarce Central American criticism delights itself at this moment--the fictional works by Sergio Ramírez, Gioconda Belli, Claribel Alegría, or Carmen Naranjo, or else testimonial narrative in which Rigoberta Menchú's stands out--were all produced in the previous decade. We keep waiting for "the great Mayan novel," "the great Afrocaribbean novel," etc.; and perhaps they will never arrive as novels but as something else: testimonial, popular theater (the case

175

of the Garifuna theatrical piece *Louvabagu* in Honduras)--perhaps even some other form of a hybrid genre that arrives unexpectedly.

Furthermore, I should add that my assertion of the absence of a Central American critical tradition does not deny the fact that at this very moment a new crop of first-rate critics is emerging from within Central America. For the most part, they are people who have been trained in Europe. Their names include Ligia Bolaños, Magda Zavala, Helen Umaña, Lucrecia Méndez de Penedo, Manuel Salinas among others.[1]

2. *Rethinking the Role of Central American Narrative*

The critical reflection to which we have made reference forces us to interrogate ourselves, once more, about the present situation of Central American narrative. This interrogation yields a minimum of problems to be confronted. Simply as examples, we can name the following: For whom does the Central American novelist write? Do readers exist for such texts?

If we mention these questions, it is precisely because in the Central American context, textuality emerges from within the margins of marginality. In this particular region of the world, discourse is not only marginal in relation to centers of world power, but it is even marginal in relation to the smaller centers of peripheral power: Mexico, Buenos Aires, Sao Paulo. For example, to be Guatemalan is to not even be Chiapanecan, it is to come from somewhere further away, a Mexican "under erasure" as deconstructionists might say, or else an OTM (Other Than Mexican) as the U.S. Border Patrol classifies us.

From within this marginality of marginality, the Central American writer is forced to choose which discourse he/she is going to reappropriate, and how he/she is going to try to instrumentalize it as an emancipatory

---

[1] The "new" criticism of U.S. based Central Americanists and Central American researchers has already found an institutionalized outlet in the annual international conferences of Central American literature that have taken place in Central America since 1993. Organized by Jorge Román-Lagunas, a Chilean now teaching at Purdue University at Calumet in Indiana, the conferences were co-sponsored by Central American cultural and educational institutions, along with the host nation's writers organizations, and with private and at times governmental financing. It is in relation to this changed literary/cultural context, as well as to the broader context of Central American postmodernity and globalization trends, that I would wish to consider certain important texts and tendencies in Guatemalan narrative literature.

project. It is, besides, a process done blindly, feeling one's way, since in the majority of cases it is not the result of a conscious reflection, a conceptualization of the problem, but rather an intuitive and creative reaction. As a result, there is the risk of making mistakes. There is the risk of choosing those inappropriate discursive practices, so that it works backwards. Instead of emancipating, it ratifies the metropolitan power.

However, the alternative to not speaking, to not making mistakes, is silence and invisibility. The silence of the subaltern. The silence of the peons who only speak to say "yes, master," "as you order, master," while they lower their heads and salute with their hats.

Risking mistakes, the contemporary Central American intellectual chooses to self-represent him/herself as a marginal subject, finding ways to establish a dialogical relationship with the metropolitan center. Forced to speak, the contemporary Central American intellectual has to learn how to use the dominant Western discourse and has to assume the risk of complicity with the hegemonic centers of cultural domination, and with the non-hegemonic sub-centers that monopolize the power of the marginal validated from the center (Mexico, Argentina, Brazil), as the price to pay in order to find their own voice.

As a result, their discourses are complicated. They are processes that are simultaneously conflictive and transformative; they are processes that simultaneously accept and refuse the cultural imaginary horizon that emanates from the metropolitan centers. They do their duty but they do not obey. It is the mime that imitates but simultaneously makes fun of what is being imitated, as Homi Bhabha would possibly say. Like colonial discourse, colonized discourse speaks with a double voice. On the one hand, it imitates dominant discourse in its aspiration to become empowered, thus appropriating, cannibalizing dominant discourse. On the other hand, it strips--it carnivalizes--that same discourse, emptying it of any power and rendering it useless (cf. Bhabha 1989, 234-241).

In other words, the fundamental contradiction is the following: how can a person who comes from the margins of periphery participate in the relationships of power of cultural production and still be able to manufacture weapons for resistance without yielding to the dominant power (the one that buys or rejects manuscripts, the one that guarantees the production, circulation and consumption of the products one manufactures given that we lack a market to be able to do it from within our own sphere of interests)?

177

That is why the contemporary Central American intellectual mimes discourses, speaks with a rolled tongue, with a spicy parodic, ironic tongue, waiting for the right moment in order to be able to sneak in through the cracks in hegemonic discourse before being called to order, before being caught in the act. Here we have the classic principle of sabotage at work. It presupposes that you pretend to be whom you know you are not, in order to sneak through the lines to the place where you are going to plant your terrorist bomb. Discursively speaking, this is the moment of the irrational terrorist revenge for the abject destiny that we were forced to live in our forsaken part of the world.

We know from experience that from time to time the Central American intellectuals have to reexamine themselves, go through self-criticism. They always have to examine if they have not gone astray from the established route, have not lost the steps indicated by the concrete needs of their own communities. Thus, the constant reexamination, the constant underlining of one's identity. Because certainly Central American intellectuals are tempted to join the hegemonic metropolises. That is why they also convert to the respective faiths of those at the center: Yesterday, Marxists, Leninists, Stalinists, Maoists; today Bakhtinians, Foucauldians, Habermasians or Deconstructionists. But, watch out. Always carnivalizing, always ironizing, because there is a consciousness that one is a different type of animal, a different subject appropriating hegemonic discourse, seeking to transform it according to one's own subversive interests.

Often placed in a plurality of hegemonic centers because of turns of fate that often have to do with unexpected displacements from the periphery (exiles, scholarships, marriages), they raise their voices as a means of empowerment. They speak and they name themselves, knowing that they are building themselves as objects of knowledge, and that they are displaying knowledge that will be circumscribed by the act of their own descriptive construction, of their poor discourse, which is not the same as "bad literature."

Are these intentions without consequences? Erroneously or not, are they not only speaking of and for themselves? Even if nobody will publish or read them? They do it, chameleon-like, as transvestites in a perpetual strip-tease, as an object of seduction that teases the eye but never becomes completely naked. Subjugated knowledge? Not for them. Maybe for the First World reader that globalizes and essentializes all those "exotic" discursive practices of the so-called "Third World" under the wrinkled

178

concept of "magical realism." But, again, who reads the Central American writers? If they are inaccessible, it is because they don't have anyone who will answer the message they placed inside a bottle they threw to the sea long ago. Without a dialogical response, discourse does not exist. Without a critical response, literature does not exist. Where is the critic that talks to the Central American writer? They are not characters in search of an author. They are writers in search of a critic (and, more often than not, of an editor). But they are represented in their words. Even if it is only as a wish, a desire, but it is the word that builds the worlds of dreams that procreate their own fairy tales in order to keep the author alive despite his death foretold, they are his/her Scheherezade.

3. What's Happening? What's Happening is that the Band's Drunk

Re-thinking, then, textuality and the role of contemporary Central American narrative, we can see in its most recent examples how the drunkenness with revolution has given way to a heavy hangover. This paves the way for a literary intensity that generated libidinal effects. I am not the first one to point out how certain political practices can liberate desire and create new flows and intensities (cf. Lyotard 1984). Until here we could picaresquely suggest that the previous effect is nothing but "war fatigue." The problem is that many of the texts that lean in this direction had already been published even before the wars came about. So, how to explain it?

It is my belief, then, that what is happening in Central America goes beyond "war fatigue" or at least beyond the fatigue of militant writers who felt the need to write about something else in order to preserve their sanity, as both Gioconda Belli and Sergio Ramírez said at some point in time.[2] In the recent past, "formal literature" (poetry, the novel) attempted to create a national cultural identity as a means of problematizing the nature of the nation-state. It attempted to create a nationalist discourse that would produce ideological consensus among vast sectors of society. At present, this is being done by the testimonial genre, while so-called "formal" literature has displaced itself towards the libidinal space, towards the space of desire,

---

[2] Personal communication with Gioconda Belli; plus an affirmation by Sergio Ramí-rez during the question-and-answer period of the panel on his own work during the XVI LASA Congress. Los Angeles, September 1992.

where it articulates discourses that reoccupy subjectivity but without a totalizing effort, nor a consensual one either.

We can verify this tendency when we observe that in the present context, nationalist discourse is found in testimonial documents such as those of Rigoberta Menchú, Mario Payeras, Nidia Díaz, Elvia Alvarado, Ana María Castillo Rivas, Omar Cabezas, Víctor Montejo, etc., while writers that during the late 1970s were still trying to build a nationalist consensual cultural identity such as Sergio Ramírez, Gioconda Belli, Ernesto Cardenal, Lizandro Chávez Alfaro, Gloria Guardia, etc., have displaced their discourse towards a literature that talks of crime stories, baseball, provincial gender issues, cosmic mysticism, erotism, etc.

Of course, when presented this way, the emphasis unjustly falls on the contents of those texts. And, after all, part of what is happening with the displacement indicated above is that the transformation taking place is fundamentally a linguistic transformation. Let us see some concrete cases.

Maybe the most complex novel published in recent times in Central America is *A Performance With Mobiles and Stick Puppets* (Una función con móbiles y tentetiesos) by Marcos Carías. In this text there is a constant shift of point of view that breaks continually with the narrative flow, the work's "legibility" in the traditional sense, so that from this deliberate conceptualization might emerge another way of pondering a reality that cannot be separated from its discursive practices. Linguistic signs self-represent themselves as brief futile illusions since, though they pretend to be references of another reality--voices of people who do not appear on the stage, so to speak--in reality they only represent themselves. The sense to which these utterances allude almost like annunciations is forever differed. The reader is ultimately left only with a collage of voices that are nothing other than themselves, though they pretend to be symbols of ulterior and posterior truths to the text.

What the linguistic and formal game does is to clone passion and desire with precision and intensity. It is as if the will to affirm the need to be a Honduran could only be framed in experimentation and fractured discourses. It is also an anarchic and revolutionary will that denies existing forms and searches to undermine conventional norms of rationalist thinking. After all, rational thought has imprisoned Central Americans by insisting that development can only happen along Western parameters. Yet such a system of thought is untenable when one contemplates the misery and exploitation in which most Central Americans live.

The rupture with the traditional novelistic form based on the rationalist cause-and-effect model becomes a delirious negation of the Enlightenment heritage, and of its narrow demands for always operating within the schemes of formal logic to be considered a "mature society" as Kant had argued. In *A Performance With Mobiles and Stick Puppets* all this plasticity free from any logical presuppositions becomes part of a search for new alternatives of being, becomes part of the affirmation of freedom extending from the author's country and region to the larger human world beyond.

The illusion that this phenomenon generates in the text is the effort to go beyond language itself. However, it is more than ever within the confines of language, always alluding to a sensation that will not be found within the margins of the text itself that *A Performance With Mobiles* accepts and reproduces the impossibility of its own project: to substitute the oral languages present in the text by an experience, a sensation of a society that is absent, that appears only by inference or deduction on the part of the implicit reader. The text pretends to be unreal, illogical, self-destructive; it blocks the dualist relationship between social history and writing; but places itself surreptitiously and subversively in the frame of a kind of masked pastiche of social reality that textuality itself builds from within language, from within the multiplicity of fragmentary discursive practices that proliferate all over without any apparent reason.

The case of Gioconda Belli is different. After shining during the seventies with a poetry that was simultaneously erotic and politically committed, she published two novels that have had a great impact during the ensuing decade, *The Inhabited Woman* (*La mujer habitada*) and *Sophia of the Forebodings* (*Sofía de los presagios*). In both cases the plot flows in a linear fashion, without interruptions, from start to finish. Everything that the novel has to say appears within the narrative matrix and not around it. Stories are privileged as such, instead of a meta-discourse that appears almost separate or else as an obstacle to the linear development. All the meditations about political participation or the problematics of identity appear within the narrative action, or else dialogized within scenes in which one can perceive movement and relationship between sequences.

However, underneath such apparent stylistic convention, we find an ideological rupture that defies traditional notions of the subject and questions the marginality of woman. In this process, it discovers that male identity is also a fabrication, an ideological artifice, as it happens to Sophia with Rene in *Sophia of the Forebodings*.

Freedom in the postmodern world comes from analyzing and subverting all ideologically constructed identities, especially those that place any subject in a condition of oppression. Women still have to deconstruct the patriarchal image that paints them as submissive, silent beings, objects of pleasure and possession. Also, this portrait generates a crisis when it is confronted by a subject that seeks to build her own identity after being the object of the other's gaze. The same thing happens with indigenous peoples, gays, Afro-latinos and any other group marginalized from the social parameters that defined modernity.

What Belli's novels stage is the metamorphosis of identity, that new process of development of the subject's consciousness. Lavinia and Sophia both break with the identity conferred upon them by "the other," and rediscover a new identity that enables them to harmonize, through their own vital experience, the different polarities of their own lives. Lavinia's and Sophia's process is one of self-realization and of conciliation with themselves. Both discover at first the limits and the confinement of the other's gaze. It objectifies them and prejudices their own being. Both struggle inwardly to place themselves ideologically in a situation that confronts such a gaze. Both are transformed when they realize their conscious will to change. Both grow as self-sufficient people, setting up a new ethical/ideological space of their own, separate from the confinement of a society that pretends to continue denying them. Finally, they project themselves towards the world with energy and self-affirmation.

Both women's quests are ethical searches. These ethics, however, are not found in the plane of conscious realization but at the instinctive level, at the level of aesthetic perception. Their process is therefore one of breaking away from the rationalist dichotomy that forces them to define themselves as one thing or the other, but without any control over their own destiny and without recognition of the singularity of their particular place in the world. It is a process in which they have to reactively find all the ethical-cognitive determinations that make it possible for the subject to make sense of reality and define its own identity. This displacement happens to a large degree because Central American novelists have opted for a writing style in which the ideological challenge has been transferred towards the libidinal space by way of language. Distancing itself from the passive consumption of realist discourse, the new Central American narrative forces the reader to wrestle with language. This wrestling match is inscribed within the space of both sensuality and linguistic sensibility.

Another case in point that confirms this assertion is *The World Begins in Xibalbá* (*El mundo principia en Xibalbá* 1985) by the Guatemalan Luis de Lión. In this text, the village, the town, is assumed as a chronotopic space that defines identity. It is emblematic of the ethnic group that is not named directly by the text, but whose point of view is assumed from the very first line. The narrative voice speaks for the people, for the ethnic group. That is why it does not carry any individualizing traits. No characters are named.

The narrative voice speaks with the Mayas, mixing its enunciations with the enunciations of the village's inhabitants in a never-ending hybridization process. In this way, orality is staged as a trait of Mayan identity. The novel is a polyphony of utterances that articulates sense only to the degree that the utterances dialogize among themselves and at no point require either their own individualization or a separation among interlocutors.

Also, there is no visible action in the plot. Since there are no characters, there are no actions that these characters unchain either, there is no crisis between a protagonist and an antagonist, etc. The movement of the text is determined by the flux of utterances.

The individualization emerges at the moment in which eroticism breaks out with the powerful phrase, "The Virgin of Concepción was a whore." In fact, this phrase punctures the climate previously created by the linguistic flow and it starts a descent towards carnivalization in which the narrator is even more singularized: "I never met her. But I remember her."

This is another innovation by Luis de Lión. Traditionally, Guatemalan narrative has been characterized by its lack of eroticism. The stereotypical image has been that Mayan peoples, as mountain people, are not erotic, unlike coastal peoples. However, the very first Mayan novel written in Spanish is erotic (and *machista*).

We have, therefore, a text with changes of identity through the symbolic inversion of the characters. We have the narrative flow firmly controlled by the narrative voice that gives the text virtually its only movement. Without question, we are very far from testimonios such as those by Rigoberta Menchú or Víctor Montejo.

We could quote other examples to illustrate this--for example, *Divine Punishment* (*Castigo divino*) by Nicaraguan Sergio Ramírez, *Diary of a Multitude* (*Diario de una multitud*) by Costa Rican Carmen Naranjo, or else *Leviathan's Asthma* (*El asma de Leviatán*) by Salvadoran Roberto Armijo. However, the gist of the point has already been made and these new examples would not deviate from the norm established by our previous affirmation.

4. Literary Parodies, Postmodern Traits

What particular traits distinguish at present the testimonio from the novel? For me, there is a basic distinction. For the testimonio, as for the realist 19th-Century or early 20th-Century novel, there is no epistemological distinction between the narrated event and the scientific document, between science and art, between the ideal projection of the nation and the reality of integrationist projects (Sommer 1991: 7). However, for the contemporary Central American narrator this epistemological distinction is present.

In the context of the 1990s, in which the transition to postmodernism in the conceptual space is articulated in the region with the end of revolutionary utopias (some would say revolutionary opiates), productive reconversion, cultural de-territorialization, the affirmation of ethnic cultures, the emergence of feminism and attempts to occupy the public space and appropriate it through micropolitics, as well as with the need to reformulate the present-day state of crisis in terms of new theories that can redefine the values usually articulated by the humanist liberal tradition that emerged from the Enlightenment. Central American writers no longer believe in the possibility that literature can be instrumental in the formation of class-consciousness nor that it is a privileged space to formulate projects for social transformation with a nationalist bent.

Influenced directly or indirectly by various contemporary theories and hybridizing them in their very own tropical way, Central American writers have interiorized and articulated discourse-centered approaches where linguistic utterances, which enact myth and ritual to conform identities and convey cultural memory, are also the focus of the creative act; they are the performance of the text, so to speak.

This means a basic change in the understanding of how meaning is produced. It also ties up with the concept of identity, since when meaning production is transformed the conformation of a given identity is also changed. That is, reality is codified symbolically in a new way. Going even further, it is codified with full consciousness of the impossibility of language to signify, to fix essential meanings. That is why at present Central American writers are preoccupied with showing the many ways in which different languages operate as discursive practices and dialogize among them, as well as the type of interaction that such dialogization generates. So in texts as different as *A Performance With Mobiles and Stick Puppets*, *The Inhabited Woman*, *The World Begins in Xibalbá*, *Leviathan's Asthma* or *Divine Punishment*, the central problem of textuality becomes the problem of artistically representing discursive practices, the problem of representing the image of language without any intentions of fixing its meaning.

The orchestration of voices registers how within those voices different types of convictions, beliefs, behaviors and systems of thought resonate. They place at center stage their obsessions, predilections, and ways of using language, so that the many systems of thought at odds with each other within Central American societies are conformed through them. In these compositions, the texts usually value positively the subversive element of carnivalesque language in opposition to the stifling decorum of official discourses. That is why they are built on the basis of irony and parody.

It is my belief that the ironic games employed by contemporary Central American narrative provides an entry to certain contemporary ways of re-thinking writing in which the basis for reading is the play of signifiers. As a result, indeterminate discourses are generated that question the very nature of the novel as a genre.

As we know, literature is hazardous. Whereas the philosopher struggles to prevent accidents and to control chance, literature tries to provoke accidents by staging the creative power of chance (Smyth 1983: xiii). Irony is, after all, a rhetorical mechanism that breaks the systematic understanding--the Aristotelian reading--of a literary text. Its ludic indeterminacy opens the space for transgression. It is an oppositional practice much as de Certeau (1984) construed and used the concept to signify the subversion from within done by the colonized to colonizers, subaltern to hegemonic sectors, and, to focus on Latin America, indigenous peoples to colonial and postcolonial law, practices and representations. These were primarily used as metaphors in order to respond to a different order from the dominant one, and thus to function in a different register.

Ironic discourse never means what it says, or what it pretends to say; it allows not only different levels of meaning, but also different levels of incompetence and propensity for error, a process that concerns both the author and the text's narrative voice (cf. Smyth: 3). After all, irony is a relative of deception. When functioning as parody it is transformed into a humoristic instrument that satirizes the notion of aspiring to order. Language itself puts in evidence its lack of veracity.

185

According to Tynianov, parody is a very marked stylized form, a game of styles in which both the style of the language being parodied and the style of the parodying language are plainly clear. The game is built through mechanisms such as humor, satire, irony, deliberate fragmentation of the text, allegorization of reality. These are all elements of parody.

At the same time, parodic humor is not the type of humor that relaxes you; it is not the Aristotelian cathartic laughter, but rather it is the Bakhtinian carnivalizing laughter that escapes the control of the existing power, whether ideological or literary, acquiring its vigor in the process of denouncing, breaking illusions and questioning traditional values when it makes evident the literariness of literature, staging in such process the ideological nature of the discourses that constitute it. Parody is the perfect vehicle for staging ideologies without appearing to be ideological.

Finally, parody as employed by contemporary Central American literature suggests important prying into the hyper-real, schizoid conditions of human subjectivity, now openly identified as key inflections, or infections, of postmodernity.

5. The End

Central American literary discourse originates in the overall struggle for power. Its objective was to build a national-popular culture that eventually would appropriate itself of the nation. This culture would build the necessary consensus that would lead to the take-over of the state. However, these knowledge/power relations have been altered by the historical change taking place in Central America in the context of even bigger changes on a global scale. Therefore, it is not entirely surprising that discursive practices that attempt to build a certain type of "truth" in relationship to a political struggle for power are themselves suffering changes.

After all, literature has generally been conscripted to the service of nationalism especially because of its capacity to promote a popular identification with a certain territory and a certain history, and because of its ability to plant national symbols in everyday practices. In other words, when it has operated as a foundational discourse in the way that Doris Sommer (1991) refers to 19th-Century Latin American narratives.

However, the ruptures that begin the present historical period in Central America and that have introduced in a clearly discernable way many postmodern traits have fundamentally changed the nature of literary discourse. Literary discourse can no longer fulfill its previous functions, if it ever did.

It is in this moment that testimonial discourse begins to operate in analogous fashion, as a new type of foundational discourse. Presently, it is testimonial discourse that provides the narrations that promote popular identification with certain "truth-effects" and that present a process in which one can visualize a progression towards a qualitatively more satisfactory self-realization.

Without attempting to push this point any further, as it would merit an essay of its own, I wish only to underline here that testimonial discourse represents powers that are not personal nor individual, but symbolic. The discourse comes from what the subject represents as personification of a specific practice (i.e. labor union leader, peasant organizer, survivor of a massacre, etc.). In this sense, testimonial discourse manages to create a new identity over the ruins and fragments of past experiences, identities and spaces with the specific purpose of transmuting memory into discursive practice as a strategy for resistance. For the subject of the testimonio, the movement proceeds from the peripheral silence to verbal representation, to the self-constitution that re-territorializes a displaced identity, a space of subjectivity, that now allows him/her to participate in the re-structuring of power. It is a discourse that is constituted with the purpose of empowering the symbolic subject, either at the local or national level.

On the other hand, literary discourse is being disempowered, even though it probably aspires to accumulate or exercise power in the transnational or postnational space, as well as in the hegemonic centers of cultural decision-making. Testimonial textuality constitutes another type of truth, a different system of knowledge, than the one comprised by "formal literature." As a result, the emergence of testimonial narrative indicates the arrival of a new epoch in which marginalized Central Americans repossess themselves of the consciousness of their past traumas with the purpose of opening the way for a new social dynamic with new strategies for action. This situation is, now, further away from the linguistic-carnivalesque orientation in which we can place "formal literature," although we have "bridge-texts" that attempt to bring both tendencies together (e.g., the later novels of the from El Salvador, as well as *Lords Under the Trees* (*Señores bajo los arboles* 1994) by Mario Roberto Morales from Guatemala. We now have to verify if this tendency will continue as we approach the end of

187

the century, or else if it only comprised an element of momentary interest in the framework of political-ideological debates around the crisis traversed by the region during the 1980s.

Elizam Escobar, *Heurística uno*, 1992.
Acrylic, photo painting and collage on masonite- 16"x18¼"
Courtesy of the artist. photo by Tom Kelly.

THE FEIGNED BATTLE: ECHO-NARCISSISM OR TRANSFIXION[1]

Elizam Escobar

We should conclude, but the debate is interminable. The divergence, the *difference* between Dionysus and Apollo, between ardor and structure, cannot be erased in history, for it is not *in* history. It too, in an unexpected sense, is an original structure: the opening of history, historicity itself. *Difference* does not simply belong either to history or to structure. [Derrida 1978: 28]

For we have reached the point which Marx said we were capable of reaching: i.e. the point at which the material basis of private appropriation and the law of profit itself are too weak to resist the growth of the collective individual. [Negri 1987: 57]

Althusser's incorrect understandings, however, are instructive. They demonstrate the extent to which our lives and thought are dominated by the dualisms of liberal theory, and make clear the difficulty of maintaining the dialectical tension between Marxism as a theory of liberation and Marxism as a systematic analysis of capitalism. For Marx, to describe the social relations of capitalism is at one and the same time to justify revolution. But as should be clear, the unity of theory and practice is not an identity but a set of distinctions within a unity. [Harstock 1991: 12]

A.

We live in a new historical moment within the frame of capitalist domination where ideological and class struggle are going through a series of convulsions, *not* terminations, as claimed by the ideological mouthpieces at the service of dominant classes. In the terrain of artistic creation, that which contains the new and necessary truths forges itself in the heat of contradictions; it nurtures from the paradoxical strength of present nihilism and determines itself in the manner in which its course pierces through the

---

[1]All translations from Spanish to English are the responsibility of the author. This is an edited version of an article which, though initially drafted for this volume, first appeared in Spanish–cf. Escobar 1995.

merely epochal and ideological, actively resisting the seductive attraction of that culture of simulacrum that functions, as never before, as screen where the imaginary fulfillment of unsatisfied necessities and the explosion of contradictions under controlled conditions are allowed to take place. Bourgeois culture in its cultural imperialist phase, re-baptized in this new moment as "postmodernism," has once again opened its doors to make space for the war of signs and discourses generated by the sublime soldiers of culture, art and ideologies. All of us--who somehow understand the importance of the ideological, the theoretical and the symbolic--participate in this war of phantoms.

If "postmodernism" could be conceived (and I am already quoting myself [cf. Elizam Escobar 1991]) as the ambiguous "revolt" and reification-of-confusion of this new economic-cultural international order, every artist that refuses the reduction of art to an instrumentality, as well as to a mere surface design or ornamental trivialization, must, by necessity, simultaneously distinguish and connect art praxis and social-political role.

It is always dangerous to make an entry in this war. Straitjackets and devices which defuse the political power of the imagination, and which affect all processes of liberation and practices of liberty, abound in all different places and forms. Within these forms there exist the practices and ideologies that, under the generic sign of "postmodernism," wish or demand from the artist to become once again a populist, sociologized or conditioned to the models that the critic, the theoretician and the ideologue have prepared for him or her.

But let's clarify from the onset that our stand should not be confused with the "anti-postmodernist" stand in favor of continuing the "unfinished project" of "modernity." It is too late for that, or better said, the critique (or self-critique) of modernity is irreversible. And if much of that critique has been placed arbitrarily under the banner of "postmodernism," it's because the dominant mode of thinking and historicizing is imbued in the easy solutions of the metaphysics, politics and logic of the sign. One of the tasks, in order to unravel this confusion, is to enforce the concreteness of subjectivity ("subjectivity of *objective* essential powers, whose action, therefore, must also be something *objective*" [Marx 1964: 180]) through the inclusion and connection of everything that has been separated and excluded.

B.

As the self-consciousness of this new moment (false antithesis or false negation of cultural imperialism), "postmodernism" develops unequally: it dies here and resurrects there; and in each cultural space, whether theoretical, ideological, or practical, a new approach is re-born aspiring to supersede the previous mode, sometimes revisiting earlier authors or movements to extract and re-think those other more hopeful or fascinating conceptions within art and cultural practices. Among the thinkers of cultural disciplines, it acts as a panacea to re-vitalize the old tired blood of culture, or to make it look as if it contains what the specific period demands, that otherness of life, needed to supply and fulfill all imaginary and real demands of individuals and societies. The problem--the eternal conflict--is that art cannot be reduced to an *imitation* of life since it is an extraordinary force *to continue* life through other means, in spite of new modes, ideologies and other interferences that could either enrich or impoverish its praxis.

C.

The importance of the best of what had been done in the name, or placed under the sign of "postmodernism" consists in how it precipitates and accelerates--even unwillingly--the paradoxical movement of nihilism. A fundamental aspect of this nihilist movement is the power to reveal how superficial (though not necessarily weak) ideologies are. Or rather, the astonishing lack of real convictions within all kinds of social and political causes: when all accepted or imposed values, beliefs and representations of reality are "liberated" either by a new analysis/theory, by the collapse of social projects and its leadership, or the strength of the destructive force of nihilism, the masks fall, leaving instead the real, transparent ugly faces of individuals and groups hungry for crude domination and empty of any passions for all virtuous life, practice and aspirations.

The following passage from the young Marx, although its references have a specific historicity, is probably the more relevant today in order to understand in a more "metaphorical" sense the events taking place in the closing years of this century:

This movement of opposing universal private property to private property finds expression in the animal form of opposing to *marriage* (certainly a *form of exclusive private property*) the *community of women*, in which a woman becomes a piece of *communal* and *common* property. It may be said that this idea of the *community of women* gives away the *secret* of this as yet completely crude and thoughtless communism. Just as woman passes from marriage to general prostitution, so the entire world of wealth (that is, of man's objective substance) passes from the relationship of exclusive marriage with the owner of private property to a state of universal prostitution with the community. In negating the *personality* of [hu]mankind in every sphere, this type of communism is really nothing but the logical expression of private property, which is its negation. General *envy* constituting itself as a power is the disguise in which *greed* reestablishes itself and satisfies itself, only in *another* way. The thought of every piece of private property--inherent in each piece as such--is *at least* turned against all *wealthier* private property in the form of envy and the urge to reduce things to a common level, so that this envy and urge even constitute the essence of competition.... Crude communism is only the culmination of this envy and of this leveling-down proceeding from the *preconceived* minimum. It has a *definite, limited* standard. How little this annulment of private property is really an appropriation is proved by the abstract negation of the entire world of culture and civilization, the regression to the *unnatural* simplicity of the *poor and undemanding* man who has not only failed to go beyond private property, but has not yet even reached it.... The community is only a community of *labor*, and of equality of *wages* paid out by communal capital--the *community* as the universal capitalist. Both sides of the relationship are raised to an *imagined* universality--*labor* as a state in which every person is placed, and *capital* as the acknowledged universality and power of the community. [1964: 133-34]

The generic sign of "postmodernism"--moving indeterminately from joke to necrophilia--results in a test of temptations in a desert of ethical principles. No wonder too many of us have preferred to walk by or suspend judgment. But too many of us have also taken simplistic and unilateral positions *for* or *against* the odious or, otherwise, seductive carapace of "postmodernism."

Because of the fundamental defining importance given by occidental culture to the category of *mode* (and *model*), those in opposition to the imperializing ambitions of "postmodernism" have reduced the debate to the same logic of *mode*: mode-replaces-mode-replaces-mode-dialectics. Others, suddenly enamored and uncritically taken by "postmodernism's" seductiveness, have discovered here and there all kinds of "proto-postmodernisms" and have arbitrarily, capriciously and missionarily baptized previous and contemporary work in its name.

The important thing--the power of art and the concrete work of art--has been devaluated and ignored. Only mode, and mere mode, is the single category and value, the absolute criterion "to historicize," to pass judgment, and ordinate hierarchically. However, it is not mode as mode itself that must be denounced but rather this obsession and fixation, this structural abstraction of the concreteness of art that must be dealt with.

When art is understood as an end in itself that, notwithstanding, exceeds itself, because it's more than itself, and more than mere form-and-content, art, then, in its connection with the world, pierces through all obstacles. It pierces through all reductive and dogmatic impositions under any label, category or theory in order to become the force that it is: the liberating force of liberty within the dimension of the imagination: *the political of the imagination.*

Is it contradictory to propose both art as an end in itself and art with a finality? No, if it is understood that the work is always directed to another--a reader, a viewer, a listener; and if we make the leap once again to the social and the political.

The artist is a social being, and all art is social. Even when the artist might be a misanthrope. There is always that value of the work as the liberty of the being, the body, of subjectivity, or the collective individual.

Says John Berger:

> That which has become part of one's own experience and life is already other people. If one wants to put it in a rather cheap aphorism: the self is already collective. That collective is made of all those people with whom one has interacted positively or negatively, it is made up of pain and pleasure, of hope and fear, of security and risk. Think, for example, of how we dream, and in particular of how we dream of people, either of people who are dead but whom we knew, or people who we once knew and are still alive. We say that they come back to us in our dreams, but what it means is that they are already within us. Writing about other people at the most primarily and deep level, is writing about those who are already inside us. [In Papastergiadis 1992: 87]

It is the utopian aspect of art that faces as *the political of the imagination,* the metaphysical idealization of the structures of domination or the pseudo-utopian social visions that end up imposing a regime of false limits. And it is the artist who cannot differentiate him/herself from his/her work--the artist as a work of art--the radical political being, the rebellious revolutionary who adds to the political (direct) the political of the imagination. For the artist of liberation it is impossible to separate-- euphemistically, opportunistically--his/her social being from his/her conscience and consciousness, from his/her subjectivity.

D.

"Structure" appears to be just a yielding to a word that has a perfectly good meaning but suddenly becomes fashionably attractive for a decade or so--like "streamlining"--and during its vogue tends to be applied indiscriminately because of the pleasurable connotations of its sound. [A. L. Kroeber, 1962; cited by Derrida 1978: 301]

Since the late 80's, when the word "postmodernism" definitively invaded the pages of the commercial dominant press, the panacea-prefix the "post"-- enchanted and enchanting--transforms itself, more and more each time, into the empty sign of the status of the sign; that which within the critique of the political economy of the sign Baudrillard (1981) calls *sign value*: difference as status.

Beyond this artificial saturation of signs and floating narratives that seduce all of us begins to appear the repulsion of the literal "repetition-with-difference" of triviality and emptiness: structure that becomes boring, an embroilment of displaced and juxtaposed slogans; a Tower of Babel of discourses and ideologies gone mad in their logic and metaphysics of the sign that only lead to vacillation and confusion. In that artificial "pluralism" the debate takes place between the politics of cultural imperialism's simulacrum and the politics of marginality's aspirations and the world of the excluded seeking the center.

These remarks do not seek to devalorize our moment's theo-retical/cultural debate, a necessary debate to which many of us have contributed our dose (the excluded's medicine and poison). It might be unavoidable and useless to ignore the seductiveness of this debate or to get infected in the ideologizing interstices. Nevertheless, one asks oneself if the debate only seeks a life of its own within that cultural war of signs in order to expand itself in its own self-preservation, and, at the same time, to suffocate a creative force that criticism and cultural analysis seek to reduce and confine to an "object of study"; or, if the debate is a true palaestra, a space of struggle from which we return to the praxis of art (or to social praxis), fortified, cured from ghosts, purged by the fire of the temptations of the concept-without-passion, the concept-without-suffering, without-material/sensual-body

Today, it is clear, cultural theory and criticism wish to be more seductive than their "object." The same thing happens with "the debate." And, ironically, it also happens to be the case with the artist him/herself: his/her attention turns, obsessively, to that special attraction exerted by criticism in relation to the work of art. Then, the artist--"postmodernized" or not--goes to drink from the momentous "fecundity" of *the isolated form.*

E.

Form fascinates when one no longer has the force to understand force from within itself. That is, to create. --Derrida [1978: 4-5].

Derrida specifically refers to structuralism and to cultural criticism in general. In this manner, there is a diagnosis parallel to what is set forth in this paper from within first-world occidental culture's moribundity--and this from one of its lucid analysts. Most cultural criticism knows itself to be *separated* from creative force, and tends in its turn to separate the artist from his/her own. But we know--and we have to also declare it with some *force*--that the seduction is mutual: the artist and the critic seduce each other reciprocally. The official critic's premeditated absence and ignorant prejudice with regard to the art of the excluded is based on creative impotence, or even the sign's envy of the symbol, etc. The excluded's place is not based on their "posture"--though, in fact, self-exclusion might be a genuine choice for some, or merely a pose to obtain a certain aura or status-- but on the fact that as testimonies abound, dominant structures are neither *capacitated* nor sufficiently *illustrated* so that they may be dealt with "objectively." In other words, without their economic power (and politics = concentrated economy) the cultural power of the elites crumbles because it is fundamentally supported and legitimized by their economic weight. And this circumstance has also contributed to the excluded's taking on both critical and theoretical activity in a more systematic and intense way. This course can as easily mislead as illuminate the praxis of art. If artists are made aware of the dangers, if artists are not "careful," they can end up with a new "sociologization" of art (and the cases abound today) or with a "new" kind of populism.

F.

Although postmodernism interprets the ideal crisis of our epoch in eclectic terms, nevertheless, it has a high degree of descriptive power.... The positive aspect of the theoretical contribution made by postmodernism consists precisely in registering this fundamental discontinuity: it pin-points and emphasizes that moment in which the problem of human society is posed in completely new terms- -not only in the field of production, but also, and above all, in the field of communication. --Negri (1987: 202-203)

My own experience of adversity leads me to propose an anti-theoreticist theory which purports to be a combat weapon derived from the praxis of art. My proposal opposes theory-*about*-art with theory-*from*-art. My intention is far away from repeating the doctrines or theoretical works of many artists within modernism (European as well as our Occidental Hemisphere--the Americas) which ended up dogmatizing art praxis under one style, a movement or aesthetic school. Neither style, movement, school, nor "regional language," but praxis of art is at the center of my work. It is not about displacing the critic or the theoretician that is separated from the praxis of art, but about self-determining that praxis through an understanding of the difference between *model* and *example*: to cultivate self-knowledge so that we can be able to reject--theoretically as well as practically--any imposed model or style, any arbitrary prescription prepared (even if done with "good intentions," and precisely for that reason) in the theoretical laboratories of ideologies. Our liberty must nurture and orient itself in self-knowledge and in the knowledge of the relations and differences of cultural practices. In this sense, our theorizing removes the veil of theory itself, of theoretical determinism about art, of that theoreticism that is not finished until it has devoured its "object of study" reducing it to a bag of bones, gristle, joints, bowels, liquids and mucosity.

By "de-theorizing" art, by "de-ideologizing" it, we adjudicate the theoretical to art itself: the force of the image as theory; the symbolic in art as theory of art; the work of art itself as *its* theory; the superseding of the possible in the possibilities of artistic practice; and beyond the theoretical as

197

symbolic (artistic) insistence of life's problematic. Only in this manner can we talk of the power of the imagination as that which rejects the reduction of reality to an ideology of reality (or art as inoffensive entertainment), because the symbolic is the only thing that escapes codification, the sign's arbitrariness as metaphysics. And, paradoxically, the symbolic is the only true metaphysics (meta-matter's language and materiality of language versus the being's metaphysical-philosophical representation as ontological "science"), the only true language that discourses, elapses and moves by the mystery and knowledge through self-knowledge's lucidity and the obscure regions of the unconscious. In short, the most complete and higher space of liberty: sane madness and tender cruelty.

With this knowledge from art praxis (a praxis that cannot be conceptualized as a thesis, an antithesis or synthesis of life but the continuation--discontinuous or insistently paradoxical--of life by other means and of its otherness: death), from this subjectivity, we face society and the world, tragically, joyfully or ironically, politically or ideologically, from within the work of art and its discourse. Thus, it is not only possible to overcome the-theoretical-*about*-art, but to *pierce through* (transfix)--heuristically--the debate itself.

To pierce through in this case means to allow the "modernism"/"postmodernism" debate to annul and annihilate itself and for us to continue our course independently of theoreticist and culturalist production, or in the "worst" of cases, to debate *de tú-a-tú* (as equals).

G.

Not too long into this debate, the first-worlders "discovered" (they had no other alternative) that the term "postmodernism" (in Spanish without the *t*: posmodernismo) was coined by the Spaniard critic Federico de Onís in relation to a reaction within the Latin American poetic movement of *modernismo* from the beginning of the twentieth century. I have chosen to write the Spanish word with a *t*, not because I want to go against the current but because I want to differentiate it from the poetic movement to which the Spanish term refers (cf. my essay of 1991).

Within that vein of "discovery," we can appreciate Víctor Fuentes's positing "that the historical Hispanic modernismo and posmodernismo could be updated and/or utilized with the meaning these terms have in contemporary international criticism" (1990: 16). "In ... the 1930s," continues Fuentes, "Borges begins to write the tales of his *Ficciones*, already considered ... as the origin of the postmodernist literary code's invention in its present sense" (ibid.). Fuentes adds that, "since the beginning of the 50s and well advanced into the 80s" Octavio Paz "has been theorizing about the end of the art of modernity and the beginning of a distinct epoch, that ... because of its characterization, corresponds with postmodernity" (16).

Since "postmodernism" can be anything we want it to be, maybe Fuentes is right. Mr. Paz is an apologist for capitalism, though not all apologists for capitalism are like Mr. Paz: a lucid poet-thinker, but one who for his own political and social-status good, usually does not make very convincing connections between causes and effects and their interrelationships. When it comes to diagnosing our past, present and uncertain future, Paz seems to imply something different from Fuentes's characterization, as in this passage from *The Other Voice*, and published in *The New York Times Book Review*: "We are witnessing not the end of history, as a certain professor in the United States has claimed, but a re-beginning. The resurrection of buried realities, the reappearance of what was forgotten and repressed, which can lead, as it has at other times in history, to regeneration. Returns to the origin are almost revolts: renovations, renaissances." [1991: 36]

Latin America, or Fuentes seems to prefer, Spanish-speaking America, has, then, two "retroactive" claims within "postmodernism": the historical claim based on previously named poetic movements and the literary one based on characteristics of boom and *the post-boom* writing. But Latin America, from the "tragedy of development as well as the absence of the development of modernity" as Juan Carlos Venturi explains, also resists and repudiates "postmodern" ideology, usually from within the defense of that "incomplete project" of modernity. Says Venturi:

If for European and North-American society of consumption postmodernism acquires any sense as self-satisfactory (and ambiguously critical) ideology, in Latin America and in the so-called Third World, where under-consumption is the quotidian and overburdened presence, it could only be explained as a product of cultural colonization or as an extreme case of negation of reality by certain intellectuals, used to mimic within the doubtful brilliance of the North's cultural shop windows. [1991-92: 37]

In the presence of this double attitude of claim/rejection, and its variations or bifurcations that we find today, in Latin America, the debate is about the identity of the myth as well as the myth of identity. In this regard, critic and historian Ticio Escobar argues:

> The issue of the identity of Latin American art was first addressed in the 1920s, and since then it has been a topic of continuous interest for artists and, especially, critics. This is a reasonable obsession. Latin American cultures, self-defined as dependent, had to define their specificity constantly and justify their image vis-a-vis powerful foreign models. The "national being," conceived as a compact and homogeneous, and "latinoamericano" element, its projection on a continental scale, served as effective substitutions for local identities. Each national culture was understood as the specific difference of a supra-identity emerging from a similar indigenous and colonial past, from similar conditions of dependency and seeking the same dream. On the one hand, brown America, identical to itself, striving to imagine its deepest essence, on the other, an abstract conqueror who unceasingly modernizes his harquebuses and greeds. [1992: 23-24]

Culture's "ungrateful" necessity is to profane and renew its myths,; the stubbornness of modernity admits no other myths than her own ones. The only problems is that myths lose their relevance and then "the spell disappears and the solution of sacred metaphors obscenely appears" (25).

From my point of view, we shouldn't confuse the mythical power of art--as a knowledge founded in the symbolic, critical of social reality, subversive against any intentions of codifying the real movement of the symbolic and the symbolic of reality--with the "social myth"--i.e., the realistic fantasies employed by, and at the service of the epochal and ideological interests of the power of the day.

Hence, to Escobar's question, "[In Latin America], do we need new myths to fill the imaginary void left by former myths?" (26), we may answer from within art's mythical knowledge: "No, if it's a question of the concept of identity as social myth that only renews fictions in complicity with classist society and its ideologies." On the contrary, art's mythical power is the spearhead against the fastidious trivial-repetition-with-"difference" of the structures that hide the true relations of power. The imaginary void is not the imagination's void but the void of dominant culture, a void that is only filled through robbery (euphemistically called "appropriation," a word that should be reserved for art which is always human appropriation in the good sense of the word) as well as through historicization and "criticism" that are privileged by the inequality of the national and global orders in which they are undertaken.

In Latin America, as in any other place, the social myth--or ideology, as imaginary (or false) limit of real possibilities--cannot be subverted by direct, political strategies alone, since without the ethical truth that surges from the liberty offered to us by artistic praxis (seen as an "aesthetic of existence"), the cultural, social and political strategies always turn out to be too ingenuous. Probably this is what resounds most in this passage from Ticio Escobar:

> The theory of Latin American art frequently found itself [caught] in a blind alley of absolute disjunctions. Pressed to choose between cultural dependency and backwardness, this theory has hesitated in the face of too many false alternatives, leaving it with more feelings of guilt and recrimination than concrete results. [27]

While some structuralist Marxists (e.g., Jameson) equate art with ideology, some "post-marxists" (e.g., Baudrillard) equate culture with ideology. Are not the ideologies of "modernism" and "postmodernism" those "absolute disjunctions" to which we are pressed by occidentalist ideology? Only through the power given to us by art as ontic force, as an ethic that cannot be bribed, or as ironic smile, can we face the "blind alleys" created by the ideologization of art itself

H.

Culturally, the ideologization (or sociologization) of art emerges in imperialist consciousness as it does in the anti-imperialist one, in the Right, in the Center, as well as in the Left. In a recent article on "post-literature" (1992), John Beverley tells us about "the anxiety of the North American new Right in the face of the academic proliferation of 'theory' and multiculturalism":

Perhaps the most interesting aspect of testimonio ... is that it offers the theoretical model and the concrete practice of a new possibility for a relation between intellectuals (academicians or not) and subaltern subjects, a model that could be generalized to other forms of social and cultural practices. But it is not just about *our* appropriation of subalternity. Testimonio also produces, as in Rigoberta Menchú's case, a new deterritorialized modality of a subaltern organic intellectual, capable of acting with efficacy in the global circuits of power and representation. [1992: 11-12]

Here, it is fitting to remember Raymond Williams' observation that the history of the aesthetic response is in large part "a protest against the forcing of all experience into instrumentality...and of all things into commodities" (cited in McNay 1992: 4). Beverley himself cites Gayatri Spivak's warning (1988b) about this intellectual/subaltern subject relation:

Testimonio can be a kind of trap: the illusion of experts on texts' analysis of having "direct" access to the subaltern that do not oblige them to change much their own situation of enunciation. [1992: 13]

In his answer to Beverley in the Puerto Rican postmodern journal *Postdata*, Juan Duchesne characterizes the former's proposition of "post-literature" as an example of a neo-populist intellectual's suffering with the grand problem of shame and guilt feelings. For Duchesne, Beverley's negation of literature is a trap in that "to be a true intellectual according to his project, he should cease to be an intellectual, he should negate the conditions of the possibility of his practice and therefore, he should negate his practice. He should commit suicide" (1992: 7). Duchesne asks if this is going to be the basis of a new "subaltern realism" (1992).

With Beverley, we have, alongside the Right's "anxiety," the progressive intellectual's commitment to Latin America as well as to the "relative democratization" of literature. Beverley's article possesses great illuminating power about literature and its relation to structures of domination. However, independently of the article's merits, it implicitly reveals first that Latin America continues to be mainly an "object of study"; and second that "literature" is not the concrete literary work, but, preferably, "the theoretical model" whose purpose seems to be to maintain the cultural theoretician-critic busy. In this regard, wouldn't it be more accurate to talk about "para-literature" than about "post-literature?" Or to talk, also, *from* and not only *about* the new literature?

The matter is not the value of the "new deterritorialized *modality* [my emphasis] of a subaltern organic intellectual, capable of acting with efficacy in the global circuits of power and representation," or the value of a specific book from the testimonial genre (Duchesne, for example, considers Menchú's book with Debray to be wonderful). The problem here is language's function.

The ideologization or forcing of the political-direct's logic into art's internal dialectics can only *impoverish* art. Art ends up as ideology's echo, either of some category or social construct. *It is not enough* to be subaltern, minority or excluded in order to be able to make literature or art (something that Beverley does not say nor does he deem it necessary to deny from within his "post-literature" project). Neither is it enough to be a professor or a revolutionary; nor to embrace the peripheral for the sake of embracing it nor to adopt marginality's modes of life nor Foucault's "limit-experiences." None of that assures anything. As a matter of fact, the mastering or virtuosity of poetic or symbolic language, either expressed or structured in "existent" or "new forms," is not even enough. What is determinant or overdeterminant is the interrelationship of the total living conjunction of all these elements or aspects and experiences.

The danger that exists in the systematic practice of the "intellectual/ subaltern subject" model is the unconscious continuation--with good intentions and by other means--of the colonial relation--in this case, the mental colonialism in the creative and subversive terrain of the activity of the subject and of art. The theoretician's requested purity ends up, as Duchesne points out, in the production of "innocent authentic popular texts" (1992: 5).

Let's end this section with the ("modernist"--or are they "postmodernist"?) words of Monique Wittig:

> Without a reexamination of how language operates in the domain of ideology and in art, we still remain in what the Marxists precisely call "idealism." Form and content correspond to the body/soul division, and it is applied to the words of language and also to ensembles, that is, to literary works. Linguists speak of signifier and signified, which comes to the same distinction. Through literature, though, words come back to us whole again. [1984: 73]

I.

Fortunately, testimonio does not only exist as "theoretical model and the concrete practice of a new possibility for a relation between intellectuals...and subaltern subjects." Testimonio is a double-edged sword through which we could denounce the role of subalternity as the model to which the new relations of power want to reduce us either in the name of "modernism," "postmodernism" or "third-worldism."

Sebastián López, a Latin American artist living in the Netherlands, denounces this subjection to a "subalternism" (which may be seen as euphemism for mental colonialism) that prohibits foreign artists "from getting out" of their cultures:

> While European artists are allowed to look into other cultures and enrich their own work and perspectives, artists coming from other cultures are expected to deal only with that background and those artistic traditions in which they were born.... If foreign artists do not conform to this separation, they are regarded as inauthentic, Westernized, and as just followers or mere copyists. [López 1992: 24]

The same thing happened under "modernism": Europeans "enriched" their art with motifs from, and references to, other cultures; on the other hand, Latin American artists, according to certain cultural regionalisms' point of view and the ignorantist myopia of critics and historians in first-worldist Occident, ended up being "inauthentic," "derivative," and culturally "impoverished."[2]

---

[2] In a sense, the Americas (apart from the original peoples and cultures) are, on the one hand, an extension of Europe through colonization, cultural and biological reproduction (mixed or not); and, on the other hand, they are extensions of other peoples and cultures brought by force as slave labor and cheap labor power (Africans and Asians). Likewise, Europe is also an extension of Asia, the Middle East and North Africa. In the Americas, the most significant cultures and ethnic groups of the globe meet and develop under the hegemony of the European; and "the European" is the result of the evolution of so-called Judeo-Christian/Greco-Latin cultures; and these, in their turn, are at least in part the result of the cultures of the Middle East and North Africa. Add to this the elements of the Far East; the interpolation and the relative "originality" of all of the traditions and regions, etc., etc. With this in mind, think again—in terms of dominant ideology—about "authenticity," "derivative," "appropriation," "foreign," "westernized," etc.

In France, the "international" exhibition *Magiciens de la terre*, at the Centre Pompidou and La Villette in Paris

placed work from Africa, Asia and Latin America beside the work of famous First World artists in what the organizers called "the first global exhibition of contemporary art." The problems of *Magiciens* have been minutely discussed.... *They* put together practitioners working not just at different points on the global map, but in different cultural, religious, sociological and aesthetic contexts, without articulating those differences. By taking folk, shamanistic, popular and village artists out of an anthropological category, the organizers thought they would be correcting a Western prejudicial and hierarchal system of classification. With a simple label giving name and country of origin, they thought they would be treating all practitioners globally as the Western professional artist is treated. The irony was that in the event this neutralized both bodies of work, both forms of "magic." The particular, collective conditions in which folk art is created were ignored; and the individual struggle of many professional artists against the institutional containment and dilution of their insights was hidden. [Brett 1992: 17]

Rasheed Araeen, a Pakistani artist with residence in England since the decade of the 60s and a participant in *Magiciens*, expressed his displeasure with the organizing and rationale of this exhibition, denouncing the non-European traditional cultures' manipulation by the forces opposed to a radical transformation of, or within these cultures. According to him, the exhibition was based on two different categories: the modernist avant garde represented only by European artists; and the traditions, attributed only to non-European people. This attempt to reduce non-European cultures to the folkloric and religious traditions render them weak in the presence of the West's continual imperial ambitions. In the face of this reduction, Araeen asks himself:

If all kinds of art produced during the same period or time should be considered contemporary art of that time, why have we not included folk or traditional European art in this exhibition? Where are the folk and traditional artists of Europe? If you are really interested in folk or traditional art, why do you have to go in search of it all over the world? Why don't you look for it in the villages or towns of Europe--in fact, it still exists in Paris. Is it because it is not exotic enough and does not represent the Other? [1991: 8]

In fact, one thing is the good intentions of a cultural ideology or the new structurations taking place in the institutional ambits of the world of art, culture and the means of communications. A different thing is the concrete cultural policy that predominates in practice. That is, the cultural "realpolitik" under the sign of "modernism" or "postmodernism" continues its practice of *cultural apartheid* under the dissimulation of a multiculturalism understood from within the ideology and discourse of power's point of view; or from within alternative positions that still drag along mental colonialism's poison and reproduce in their bosom dominant ideology, alienated from their own intentions of "liberation."

Multiculturalism from within the non-dominant sectors whose intention is to resist cultural imperialism's hegemony and/or to interfere in the mainstream is still saturated with subtle paternalistic, myopic, missioneristic, defensive postures; such supposedly resistant multiculturalism is gloomily imprisoned by the politics of representation, where the represented becomes a mere shadow of the sign. This ventriloquist's politics is universal and ubiquitous. To escape from it is almost impossible, unless at the personal level, at the level of an ethical praxis of liberty enthroned in the re-invention of the self as the work of art.

There is a problem faced by certain practitioners of multi- or cross-culturalism. Basing themselves on performance art and other forms of populist "postmodernism," while seeking a direct-exit mode to ridicule the status quo, consumer society and the values/beliefs/representations of occidentalist culture or national cultures, they make a ridiculous spectacle of themselves reifying those same practices and ideologies that they pretend to criticize, devalue or reject.

Iván Silén, a Puerto Rican poet living in the Bronx, argues that the work of certain representatives of the contemporary generation of Puerto Rican literature embodies "the spirit of democracy's crisis that by seeking the popular, it cannot achieve a lyricism that can counterbalance it.... This is a nihilism that attempts to become a literature of laughter" (1992a: 1). Silén's characterization could very well apply to this populist "postmodernism," a populism that forgets that "all laughter is the ontological tearing of that that we felt as sublime" (5).

On multiculturalism, the editors of *Third Text* (#18) comment:

> The dispersal of signs across the modern world has done little to undermine the basic opposition between the centre and the periphery.... The term

multiculturalism is now commonplace throughout all the political corridors of Europe, but does it have the same meanings in each location?... In the art world multiculturalism is synonymous with two processes which are essentially conservative: a rejuvenation of the parameters of its dominant frame--modernism--by the admission of "foreign" elements--a logic which seems to subscribe to the axiom that a small ... amount of poison can act as medicine for an ailing body; and secondly, we are witnessing a new wave of sentimental realism which appeals to the pathos of the liberal conscience as it aestheticizes the condition of the oppressed. This latter mode is particularly disturbing when it involves a domestication of deconstruction in which the "other" is repeatedly "represented" in the position of lack. [Spring 1992: 4-5]

Not only this representation but also the state of the "comic" contributes from within self-parody to the state of pathetic alienation of the oppressed-- this is what the editors consider to be at stake here. However, although the "gift" of [multiculturalism may be pregnant with irony, "its paradoxes must not lead to uncritical rejections or acceptances," since the "struggle for change and the function of critical engagement require multiple levels of action" (5).

The paradoxical, as I understand it, is paradoxical not because reality may seem paradoxical to us, but because it *is* paradoxical. While the polemic in Latin America moves in between acceptance/rejection of the assumed antitheses "modernism"/"postmodernism," in Europe, some foreign artists seem to understand that in practice the antithesis is false--though as seen from within postmodernism's own logic, there is no contradiction if one works within the assumed antitheses simultaneously.

In his article, "How I discovered my Oriental Soul in the Wilderness of the West," Araeen notes:

I have been reminded of the belief, quite common in the West, that modernity is harmful for other cultures and that they should refrain from it... that they should remain in a state of innocence and purity. It seems that the idea of multiculturalism in Europe is very much part of this thinking. [1992: 101]

As it is also very much part of naive multiculturalism to think that a true atmosphere of equality or non-hegemony is possible within classist societies. This knowledge should not lead us to pessimism, defeatism, cynicism or to embrace the "eternal present" of the status quo and the hyper-reality of synthetic "neo-liberalism" that schizophrenic society offers us. On the contrary, it is from within the profound knowledge of the force that represents nihilism where we can consolidate ourselves in the present in order to take all that is necessary from this force, and with it, against it, and in spite of it, to construct "our subjectivity by going beyond the material conditions of its expansion" (Negri 1989: 50).

Multiculturalism, cross-culturalism or transculturalism without class struggle is like movement without contradictions, like non-problematic existence, without tension or crises. It is not to say that culture must be understood or wanted as "class culture." On the contrary, it is against classism, against all alienation, that art works; and as we know, social class is a form of alienation, another prison, another false limit of humanity. As Eagleton notes:

> It is sometimes forgotten that social class, for Karl Marx at least, is itself a form of alienation, canceling the particularity of an individual life into collective anonymity. Where Marx differs from the commonplace liberal view of such matters is in his belief that to undo this alienation you had to go, not around class, but somehow all the way through it and out the other side. [1990: 23]

In order to supersede the alienation and false limit pertaining to class that has been naturalized by ideology, we have to first affirm ourselves in a revolutionary subject capable of leading to the transformation of classist culture into a human culture that is harmonically universal and diverse--a culture which, using the prefix in vogue is "post-classist," "post-eurocentric," "postmodernist," etc.

In this sense--or against this sense--multiculturalism may be a force as well as a weakness; and to a great extent this depends on the lucidity of its participants. Negri points out a paradox that serves as a challenge for those who struggle against alienation and its contemporary forms:

> that the great increase in our ability to understand power--its extension described by Foucault, its molecular penetration described by our closest teachers and comrades, etc., etc.--has been imputed to us and almost used against us: as if the awareness of its complexity, instead of making possible a higher destructive capacity, were a maze from which we could no longer extricate ourselves. [1989: 159]

208

J.

It is in this maze where we move unequally, seeking the orientation towards an exit. Art is one of those subversive forces whose heuristic power works all the time as a light in the ideological and political fogginess of our contemporary world: "the affirmation/of a terrible/ and, moreover, implacable necessity" (Artaud), it operates "as a permanent force" (Derrida 1978: 233).

The artist, that permanent god or goddess of revolution, of that cruel truth that demands a "double nature" and, more than a "separation," the co-penetration and enmatrixation of totality from within the ontic ("that which is lived so intimately that it is inaccessible to ontology" [Spivak 1992: 15]), needs, today more than ever, to clarify his/her social role in the arts but also in politics, as a political being--a task as conflictive as the creative process itself.

I believe that it has been demonstrated to satiety that any art that functions as *Narcissus* (art for art's sake, formalism, market art, etc.) or as *Echo* (political-direct art, ideologism, ventriloquist/dummy dialectics, etc.) works against the subversive permanent force of the political of the imagination. It is only from within the political of the imagination--that positive force of destruction which through symbolic forms unites negation to affirmation, non-being to being, nothingness to the whole, the political to the ontic, the absurd to liberty, etc.--that the artist should construct his/her social role.

The ironic thing in this case is that those ideologues, philosophers or critics of art and politics who have made the call to political and social commitment to the artist have not understood very well the problematic of the conflict between desire and duty. They always end up separating them metaphysically (either under the idealist or materialist ideological-philosophical flag), or subordinating one to the other. The knowledge that liberty is conflictive, or better said, that liberty is a reciprocal, inclusive, circular, boomerang-like movement, is always missing. Hence, no artist who understands or senses that "the imagination is our most intelligent faculty," that all "prohibited pleasure, as political problem, is linked to the imagination" because in "the imagination being always dreams that which it lacks" (Silén 1992: 10), could conform with the strategized or tacticized truth of the political-direct and ideologism.

To "permanenticize" the artist's social role with art's permanent force it is necessary above all to affirm that force in the personal, in subjectivity, in the collective individual who rejects mercantilistic individualism as well as cretinous and echonarcissistic collectiveness. My subjectivity constructed by my (self) consciousness in relation to the knowledge flowing from my reflection and my objectivity (my experience) engages in dialogue with other subjectivities equally "close" or "far away." Thus I might feel, then, that that *new social subject* which, already in the Paris of 1986, Negri visualizes, is also effervescent in our hemisphere.

The question for Negri is an *ethical subject* in the sense that "it becomes political while rejecting the political--that is, the whole machine and the individual cogs of a state which is dominated by parties; it reappropriates political methods, using them in the service of truth" (1989: 48). In this manner--as in a double rapier stabbing--the political of the imagination rejects the political-direct in art; and, at the same time, as the artist decides to participate in the direct political struggle, he/she injects force, the unceasing power of liberation, of the subversive within that which almost innocently is self-named the "progressive" or "liberation" movement. So it is that the liberation movement receives in its bosom--inadvertently?--a praxis of liberty that engages in liberating it from its obsolete and dusty concepts, its values, beliefs, representations and identifications, its "innocence" and "myths." Either it liberates itself or to hell with it.

In this conflict--an alienating, distressing, cruel one--different languages or tongues are spoken. But in the same way that the two hemispheres of the brain are united, so in discourse, a link or common passage unites both languages. A subjectivity that grows up in this conflict has a power that Negri says "cannot be expropriated under any circumstances" (1989: 51).

It doesn't matter if the artist finishes up martyred or destroyed because he/she has accepted in his/her bosom the unmerciful intensity of the movement of permanent contradiction. For what is important is his/her life as a work of art, as "aesthetic existence," or as an offering to the other; what is important is his/her liberty beyond the commodity's or ideological sign's exchange/use value--his/her liberty as mythic and utopian power, and therefore, his/her liberty as a work of art that is an agency of the politically profound. Yes, and of the ethical.

If the subject described by Negri is an imminently intellectual labor force, it will also be, inevitably, multiracial/national and international/racial,

210

arisen "within and against those old and new ideologies of inequality and negative value: neo-liberalism and postmodernism" (55). But the permanent dream and desire of the imagination cannot wait for the political-direct's dream and duty; its immediacy is its own realization in the course of events--an immediacy non- vulgarized in the licentiousness of the "eternal present" of schizophrenia and the impotence of conformism; an immediacy that cannot be stopped by either social utopia nor political myopia-- because it is the force itself that moves everything else: the force of the living before and after death. It is not the sciences or philosophy that deliver the whole human being to us; it is the mythic power of artistic expression and invention.

K.

Art as liberation and as liberty has to refuse any intervention to reduce it to the Narcissus/Echo relation, which transforms the mythic power of art into the social myth's ideological power through the populist or elitist socioligization of art.

If "postmodernism" could be conceived as "modernism's self-consciousness," and the mystifying mentality/ideology of this new economic-cultural moment of late capitalism, then this "self-consciousness" is not just *any* self-consciousness. In this new moment, Narcissus not only thinks that he has seen himself as he himself is, in the mirror of his own image; he has also decided that all of us--the "subalterns," colonial, neo-colonial, post-colonial, derivative and peripheral species; all kinds of invisible-excluded subjects--should be converted in his imitation or "beloved" Echo.

We, guests of the "postmodernizer" Narcissus, should transform ourselves into the pluralistic echo of his image. That should be our maximum aspiration. Otherwise, we should preserve ourselves within our autochthonous, folkloric cultures, the culture of tourism, as relics, etc. All this culminates in the narcissistic cult of echo or in the regionalization of artistic language. Of course, due to the confusion and interpolation of languages and discourses identified with one or the other pole of the "antithesis," we clash frontally against the useless and the absurd unless the work could speak louder than criticism and theoretical reflection.

L.

If there are real as well as false limits in reality, we shouldn't limit ourselves more than we already are limited, in that liberty which art offers us. All unnecessary limitation is unnecessary. In this path, search, realization or actualization toward, for, of and in a "radical aesthetics," there are those who:

1. *resist* critically by continuing the "political art" tradition within the existent or experimentational practices.

2. *intervene* critically by using the same "postmodern" devices (tactical/strategic homeopathicism) in order to "undo" "postmodernism" itself.

3. *pierce through* these two, understanding that the antithesis is not only false in this case, but that in art the epochal is not the fundamental thing if we have well understood the relationship between the permanent and the passing, and between the passing and the passenger.

The role of art transcends the epochal. Here, mode/model belongs to the epochal. "Postmodernism" as ideology thinks of itself as the end of the epochal--as the "post-epochal." However, in spite of all the fuss, it is simply the "sublime" effort of an epoch that does not want to end and has found in the simulacrum and camouflage the most sublime form (or mode) for self-preservation.

The definitive liberation of art and the artist claims the rejection of any doctrine or ideology that prescribes *a priori* art praxis, or that subordinates or reduces the concrete work to the conceptual abstraction; that is, structuration at the service of the law and order logic of sciences and philosophy. It is from here that we irrupt into the cultural debate as well as we construct or invent the artist's social and political role. There are no formulas; or better said, there are for those who seek easy solutions.

We should conclude, but the debate is interminable...

Elizam Escobar
9 February 1993; revised December 1996.
Oklahoma, Necrópolis

212

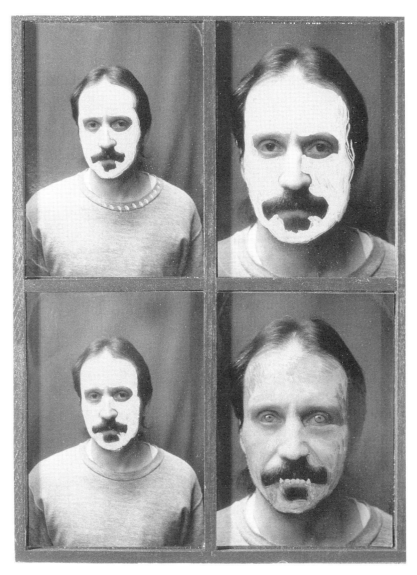

Elizam Escobar, *El terrorista,* 1992.
Acrylic on photos- 10½"x7¼"
Courtesy of the artist. photo by Tom Kelly.

YOUR APPROPRIATIONS ARE
NOT OUR APPROPRIATIONS:
TOWARDS A RADICALIZED AESTHETIC

Michael Piazza

"Eduardo, you put this stuff on your canvases, and Julian Schnabel does the same thing in New York, but your work seems diametrically opposed to Schnabel's. Can you talk about that?"
"Who is Julian Schnabel?"--Jimmie Durham, quoting his interview with Chilean artist, Eduardo León. [1988-1989: 32]

1.

Alas, the Western modern hero has been shattered (or has been shattering for some time now) and may spend forever trying to gather up all that has been lost except the opportunity to tell us about it over and over again like a broken record, summer reruns, or a glitch in the software. Depending on one's point of view, postmodernism can be said to be where alienation of the bourgeois individual collapses into (or is repackaged as) the death of the subject. Indeed, Jameson has made the case that the autonomous subject "never existed in the first place but constituted something like an ideological mirage" (1991: 15).

Euphoria and numbness replace what was left of any real emotion. Affectations come by means of thrills and spills--a giddiness coupled with "blind and uncritical enthusiasm or else condemned with a new Olympian remoteness and contempt" (Berman 1982: 24). Pastiche replaces parody, which no longer can find a subject to parody; hence, there is an "implosion of the real" and the end of history. "And how long will this 'no future' last into the future, if you'll excuse the paradox?" (Hall 1985: 45).

In 1980, North American artist Julian Schnabel ironically and arrogantly entitled a painting, "Exile" (figure 1) in which he tried to locate himself amongst trophied memories: antlers framing a youthful image of the Mannerist painter, Caravaggio and a wooden doll. The painting is self-consciously rendered as though to convince the artist, himself, that the painted gesture can still sustain a self-referential. According to Heartney, Schnabel has attempted "to secure at least temporary refuge" by

214

appropriating sources that are "profoundly Other and thus seem to promise a kind of mysterious wholeness that Western culture seems to lack" (1988: 32).

Analyses such as Heartney's present the illusion of the Western modern as almost romantically lamentable. Meanwhile, diametrically opposed to Heartney's Schnabel is Eduardo León. A Chilean painter living in Mexican exile because of his political activism in his own country, León continued to paint in Mexico City, appropriating Mexican popular and acculturated images of the mythology that confronted him every day in the streets. As a stranger, he could search for identity and express solidarity, "with the Mexican people and their ridiculously schizophrenic situation" (Durham 1988: 28.) Not unlike Schnabel's painting, León's piece, "Untitled" (figure 2) places disparate images next to or on top of each other on what is left of the flattened surface of the canvas. At first glance, their works seem quite similar to one another; and one is tempted to adapt Jorge Luis Borges's story, "Pierre Menard, Author of Don Quixote" to portray the relation.

In typical Borges fashion, Menard's "aim was never to produce a mechanical transcription of the original; he did not propose to copy it. His admirable ambition was to produce pages which would coincide--word for word and line for line with those of Miguel de Cervantes" (Borges 1962: 49). Given the different time periods during which the works by Cervantes and Menard were written and the different sensibilities of the two authors, it is certainly Borges' somewhat tongue-in-cheek assertion that one could perceive a "contrast in styles" by which "the archaic style of Menard--in the last analysis, a foreigner--suffers from a certain affectation" (ibid. 53).

Borges points to the slippages that exist between the author and the meaning, the signifier and the signified, vis-à-vis the word--the sign. The application of Menard's technique across the board "would fill the dullest books with admiration. Would not the attributing of *The Imitation of Christ* to Louis Ferdinand Céline or James Joyce be a sufficient renovation of its tenuous spiritual counsels?" (55).

Perhaps it is not all that ironic that North American and European artists and critical theoreticians claim their indebtedness to Borges, given the Argentine author's deep-seated desire to be European by distancing his own country from the rest of Latin America in his own mind. Borges denies, and hence flattens out, the polyvalence of history and ethnicity which makes up Latin America in order to be recognized as one of the "Big Boys" of the dominant culture. We can see this more clearly by taking up Borges's offer and slightly altering his concept of "the copy."

What if by freakish coincidence, both León and Schnabel, unaware, as in fact they are, of each other's existence, produced identical works at roughly the same time. In the ideal world of Borges, the preference of one over the other would induce an existential chuckle, but in the actual world this could only instill a tragic sigh. For, given the present U.S./Eurocentric situation, we regrettably know that Western cultural hegemony will favor Schnabel's effort while dismissing León's as derivative, underdeveloped, and dependant. So, it is the discourse of power that is missing from Borges's story, and it is precisely this discourse which sets up a hierarchy of privilege.

From a point of view of privilege, Schnabel can appropriate real geographical exiles and internalize them, so that he can metaphorically become a privileged exile within his own culture while denying any self implication as part of the dominant cultural power structure. Schnabel's identification with real exile lets him off the hook in regards to his own country's implication in matters which led to, in this case, León's exile.

Identification becomes the absorption of the exile, the dispossessed, the marginalized, and the excluded while sliding through all the connotations of the "possession"--territorially, bodily, and spiritually. Schnabel as agent for Western cultural hegemony which must acquire the exile to satisfy its drive for completeness, in turn, displaces and pressures the real exile into becoming (or at least feeling like) what Schnabel actually is (a construction which the dominant culture favors and disseminates)--a quotidian tourist.

2.

Is postmodernism a global or a Western phenomenon? Is postmodernism the word we give to the rearrangement, the new configuration, which many of the elements that went into the Modernist project have now assumed? –Hall (1985: 46)

Hall asks the question cited to counter the notion that postmodernism represents a new epochal rupture beyond history. The global economy can be seen as the economy of transnational capitalism positing a continuation of the same scenario only now more severe with less space from which to offer any resistance. The arena of resistance in an occupied zone, and must be taken into consideration in order to rearticulate a radicalized aesthetic or an aesthetic of resistance against the latest guise of bourgeois aesthetics-- namely postmodernism.

Postmodernism claims that all essentialist discourses of universal values have disintegrated or were mere illusions brought on by the Enlightenment. "Any discourse can be dominant and oppositional at the same time; hence we are left 'decentered' as subjects and can only ... gaze in wonderment at the diversity of discursive species" (Lyotard 1991: 29). This situation should, and to some degree has, led to the emergence of discourses that were previously excluded in order to fill the gap left by essentialist discourse. Here, one could hope for the inevitable breakdown of the power apparatus constructed therein. But, in fact, the dominant power structure is still intact. For if there had truly been a definitive rupture, we would not be witnessing the cultural discrepancies that continue or emerge today.

The contradiction can still be best explained by hegemonic relations. It was on the terrain of the cultural that Gramsci developed his concept of hegemony to articulate the complexities and overlappings of relations in society which eluded both various reductionist and essentialist discourses. So, as a "society constructs the image and the management of its own impossibility" (Laclau and Mouffe 1985: 191), so it is such illusions of righteousness, determinism, morality, etc. that galvanized otherwise disperse elements of society which in turn reinforces an ethnocentrism that defines both itself and, more importantly, what is not itself. An ethnocentric culture projects all that it lacks and fears out onto that which it perceives as outside, i.e. on the periphery.

Cuban artist and critic Gerardo Mosquera defines Eurocentrism as "the global hegemony of this Western culture [that] has imposed ethnocentrism as a universal value" (1992: 6). With regards to those neo-colonial, neo-exotic tendencies of dominant Western hegemony, there is a kind of perverse strength behind the claim of key intellectuals that the notion of a dominant center exerting control over its peripheries is in disintegration; and that what we are witnessing is the fragmentation of the master narrative into a heterogeneous plurality of meanings, accommodation for all differences and the emergence of micro-narratives. In fact, the critical stance (resistance, radicality) or dialogical exchange that those of the periphery, the marginal, the excluded could undertake, becomes blended in the sameness of

217

difference. Nelly Richard notes that "no sooner are these differences--sexual, political, radical, cultural--posited and valued, then they become subsumed into the meta-category of the 'undifferentiated' which means that all singularities immediately become indistinguishable and interchangeable in a new, sophisticated economy of sameness (1987: 11). Ahistoric pluralism, which may well be disguised homogeneity, then, only veils the still existing unequal power structure. The center is masked as a non-center from which the non-center is excluded.

The game of catcher-catch-can is what artists such as Eduardo León are up against; but it is precisely within these circumstances that a stand must be taken. It is against the communication model of the sign--transmitter to receiver--that radicalized aesthetics can begin to be articulated within the space of the symbolic as part of what Laclau and Mouffe refer to as "discursive discontinuity" set against epistemological universals (1991: 191).

Coco Fusco is very much aware of the new postmodernist configuration. She writes that young Cuban artists whose work utilizes innovations not unlike those in the U.S. and Europe "reject the paternalism of the assumption that their borrowing is necessarily a symptom of dependency while similar gestures in the first world enrich the vocabulary of High Art" (1988: 1). The Cuban artists' subversive reciprocity undermines U.S. and European claims of authority over culture especially in terms of contemporary culture. Elizam Escobar warns "not to reduce the new and authentic to only reacting per se against "Western Art" or to the "modernism of the mainstream," for this reduction only perpetuates the resentment perspective of the colonized (1988: 27). When referring to Latin American artists in particular, he states, "We must depart from Latin America (in the Caribbean, South America, Central America, in exile), not to stay in Latin America, but to take an ontological and political walk, to go wherever necessary--in thematics, space, time, style, etc." (ibid.).

Cuban artist, José Bedía, has taken such an ontological and political walk. In his work, he borrows from many sources making no distinction between high and low culture, drawing from Afro-Cuban roots as well as Western Culture to address the complexities which make up "the "mestizo" nature of his cultural foundation" (Mosquera 1992: 7). In his painting "Va caminando, ya son las horas (He's Walking, It's Time to Go)," Bedía paints a contoured figure of a male nude on the move armed with a ballpin hammer and a machete. The ground is covered with hatched symbols and crosses along with the boldly written title. The canvas is a large one bound by chains as though packaged. In this picture as well as the one presented in this book, "Llega a pie" (see Part I of this book), Bedía confronts Western paternalistic hegemony (and perhaps Eastern paternalistic hegemony as well) in a conceptualized and intellectualized "primitive" manner. As Mosquera argues,

> the point in question is how to produce contemporary art in relation to our own values, sensibilities, and interests. The de-Euro-centralization of art does not consist of retreating to some pre-colonial "purity" but rather of assimilating post-colonial "impurity" so as to liberate ourselves in our own terms. [ibid.]

Baddeley and Fraser note that the regression to some sort of pure past has been proposed by Western Marxists before; at bottom it implies the same sort of neo-colonial dictates of Western Hegemony at large. The idea of "pure" or authentic art is a subjective value which can be imposed by the dominant culture as a form of neo-colonial trap (1989: 91). One could in fact argue that the sort of hybridity apparent in artists such as Bedía has represented a way of life for people in the periphery feeling the effects of the U.S. and European culture. Again no one has studied the effects that hybridity has had on the West as part of a transculturated process. It is the West's appropriations of the periphery's appropriations that have been examined with an eye for the ironic. As Rasheed Araeen puts it:

> In the beginning, it was Modernism, modernism for everybody all over the world irrespective of different cultures. When others began to demand their share of the modern pie, modernism became postmodernism: now there is "Western" culture and "other" cultures, located within the same "contemporary" space. The continuing monopolization of modernism by Western culture (particularly in the visual arts) is to deny the global influence of modernism, and to mask its function as a dominant force of history to which peoples all over the world are increasingly subjected. [1989: 6]

In his painting, "Senay Ke Chirya/Golden Bird," Araeen includes contemporary strategies which reject the Eurocentric notion that the traditional art forms of "other" cultures are pure and authentic while contemporary art forms are contaminated. Araeen uses everything from Karachi commercial images to Western minimalist codes which defy any sort of mapping sources to the point of utter absurdity. Still the game continues, thwarting the entry of such works at every turn.

Artist Raúl Quintanilla, who was the administrator at the National School of Plastic Arts in Managua, Nicaragua, speaks of the recent "triumph of neoliberal capitalism" as the latest turn in Latin America. The present situation undermined the Nicaraguan artists' attempts to construct a new dialogical process which entailed a combination of "social commitment and visual experimentation" that included everyone (1992). At present, the trend is towards, the "trivialization of art and culture to levels of inconsequentiality," where art only "serves the demands of the Western art transnationals for touristic ethnic eccentricities" (ibid.). In the post-Sandinista period, Quintanilla and a group of Nicaraguan artists formed a new collaborative team called *Arte Facto* to begin again the dialogical process as a way of remembering the identity that was being forged during Sandinista hegemony, while at the same time figuring a way out of being considered some kind of "'sociological joke' in a Babylonian context" (ibid.).

Cherokee artist, Jimmie Durham recognizes only too well this idea of a "sociological joke." Nevertheless, he continues to reclaim his cultural identity and prepares for the clashes along the way. In his "Self-Portrait" (figure 3), Durham truthfully builds on his shattered subject-as-a-subject, no less, to forge an ironic representation by writing words from the imposed colonizer's language over the image of his body which at once mocks the connotations that the words signify. Although Durham doubts anyone would "read" his work, it is precisely this interjection of repressed history back into the social (amnesia), this neo-narrative which brackets the non-narrative that is desperately needed to rearticulate a radicalized aesthetic--to rearticulate a counter-hegemony (Durham and Fisher 1988: 99).

3.

It is the being of non-being taking place mockingly, politically, in liberty. We are the self portrait. This is the truth and this is the joy; in spite of hell they have not been able to destroy us. We laugh at our own tragedy ... in the game that claims scandalously the liberation that we are." --Iván Silén [1992: 51]

From the complexities and diversities which make up the world, it would be detrimental to reduce our situation to any simple equation which as we know has only damaged progress in the past. We must take advantage of the space opened in postmodern discourse and practice, and nurture the emergence of voices that had previously been silenced. Within the terrain of a multiplicity of discourses, a "discursive discontinuity", or a cacophony, if you will, there may be points of convergence which would allow for new articulations and open up new possibilities for change. As Laclau and Mouffe conclude:

> The decentering and autonomy of the different discourses and struggles, the multiplication of antagonisms and the construction of a plurality of spaces within which they can affirm themselves and develop, are the conditions *sine qua non* of the possibility that the different components of the classic ideal of socialism--which should, no doubt, be extended and reformulated-- can be achieved." [1985: 192]

It is at some moment when the Laclau-Mouffean conditions may fully pertain that Elizam Escobar turns on the light in his painting, "La misa del nuevo mundo" (figure 4), to reveal all those who have gathered armed with their particular historical and political counter-narratives with which to confront the hegemonic master (non) narrative.

For the moment, the cast seems to be locked on stage like characters in a Becket play. "We Are Waiting For You To Become One Of Us," proclaims another title from Escobar in order to play out the narrative in the shadow of the ever-present noose. In an essay on Escobar's work, Silén points to a radicalized aesthetic that is beyond bourgeois aesthetics, beyond the commodification of the market:

> We can confront the world, imperial art, imperial consciousness philosophy, linguistically, poetically and pictorially because we have gotten rid of fear. We have lost to much already and we do not want to lose anymore. And this triumph over the colony and neo-colony, is the victory of our works of art, of our artistic (= human) liberation. [1992: 51]

Although our attempts at rearticulations are doomed to be incomplete, we can only, on this side of despair, hope (like a tragic-comic figure) that all of our activities, discourses, and arts are needed preparations for something else.   Perhaps it is for some unforeseen desires brewing in the many unconsciousnesses of the world waiting to spring forth at some unexpected moment and provide the missing ingredient to our stew. We can only hope, and until then continue to dissent in our various fashions (self-consciously? mimically?) For we all know that overwhelming desire when we feel it, somewhere in our memory, when old hairsplitting suddenly dissipates and new bridges are miraculously and marvelously forged.

Fig. 1. Julian Schnabel, *Exile,* 1980.
Oil and antlers on wood- 90"x 120"
Photo courtesy of Pace Gallery, New York.

Fig. 2. Eduardo León, *Untitled*, 1986.
Reproduced from *Third Text* no. 5 (winter 1988/89)
Photo courtesy of *Third Text*.

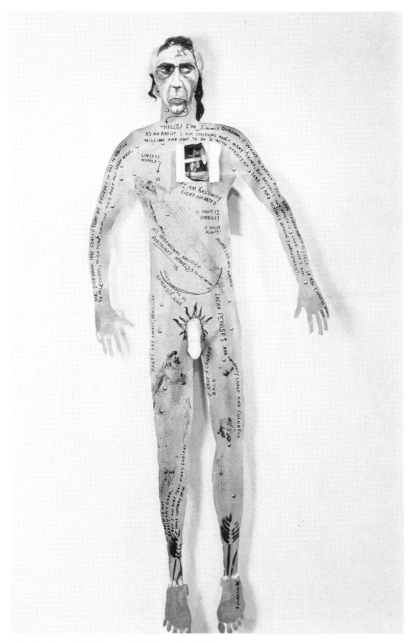

Fig. 3. Jimmie Durham, *Self Portrait*, 1987.
Canvas, wood, mixed media- 72"x 36"x 12"
Private collection- photo courtesy of Nicole Klagsbrun Gallery, New York.

Fig. 4. Elizam Escobar, *La misa del nuevo mundo*, 1990.
Acrylic on canvas
Courtesy of the artist. photo by Tom Kelly.

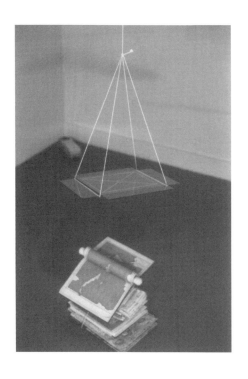

IV. Final Subaltern In(tro)spections
and (B)order Specifications

BETWEEN CYNICISM AND DESPAIR: CONSTRUCTING THE GENERIC/ SPECIFYING THE PARTICULAR

Ileana Rodríguez

I detect in all these reports on exchanges between tourists, [ethnographers] and others a certain mutual complicity, a co-production of a pseudo-conflict to obscure something deeper and more serious: namely that the encounter between tourist and "other" is the scene of a shared utopian vision of profit without exploitation, logically the final goal of a kind of cannibal economics shared by ex-primitives and postmoderns alike. [Dean MacCannell, *Cannibal Tours*, cited in Price and Price, 1992: 100]

For the Eurocentric discourses traversing the film [*Crocodile Dundee*], the outback is a perfect Other to the ultimate urban jungle; historically an "empty" (that is, violently depopulated) space for the enactment of colonialist fantasy. The perfection of the outback for this purpose is its supposed "remoteness" from cities (learning, modernity) and, unlike other legendary wastes, its "isolation" in the middle of a monster island--prime territory for Darwinian fancies of throwbacks, remnants, mutants, the (primitive) origin, and the (apocalyptic) of life. The outback is an ideal site for the staging of knowledge conflicts. Its value is reversible: it can be invested with romantic, pretechnical wisdom (Roeg's *Walkabout*, Herzog's *Where the Green Ants Dream*) or surreal, degenerative ignorance (Kotcheff's *Outback, a.k.a. Wake In Fright*, Mulcahy's *Razorback*) and a zone of life-and-death struggle over what it means, in extremis, to be human (*The Road Warrior, Beyond Thunderdome*). The shuttle between opposites, the disintegration of categories, is the outback's power for metamorphosis: from the midst of it surges, usually, "the beast"--savage black, crazed white, man-eating pig, crocodile, dingo. It's from this space that what one neoconservative columnist calls the "muscular innocence" of Mick Dundee--the survivor with no opinions--is born. [Meagan Morris 1988: 115]

1. Two Texts and Subaltern Specificities

In their analyses of the postcolonial condition, postmodern critics in English Departments or Cultural Studies Programs produce generic ideas of worlds abroad and overseas, or of what Latin Americanist critics during

229

"the Marxist phase" called the periphery. Two examples, selected at random from the writings of Dean MacCannell and Meaghan Morris, provide us with lexemes which illustrate a relationship of difference between the first critics and those whose perspectives emerged in the context of "Third World" area studies. The relationship engages tourism and the definition of geographical areas where investment is to take place as the generic outback. The two examples in question signal the shift in, and merging of, discursive practices: Marx merges with Foucault; economy merges with biology. The merging of discursive practices explains what Foucault terms the threshold, that is, that point of intersection which identifies the new rules of formation of discourse that have come into effect (cf. Foucault, in Burchell, Gordon, and Miller, ed. 1991).

MacCannell's constructive lexemes underscore a model of a postmodernized mode of production. His vocabulary ("tourists," "ethnographers," "other," "ex-primitives," "postmoderns," "complicity," "co-production," "profit without exploitation," "cannibal economics"), encodes the specific in the generic, and while in context we know that he is theorizing about a trend, the place described in this passage can be any place, and the people any people. In Morris' piece, the lexemes denote discursive production as mode of production. Here adjectives are as telling as, if not more indicative than, nouns, and contribute to the identification of Foucault's episteme, that is, the "space of dispersion," the "open and doubtless indefinitely describable field of relationships, ... a simultaneous play of specific remanences" (Foucault, ibid.: 55).

The citation from MacCannell involves a more complete set of terms and a more typical prose in the sense that all the key verbs, nouns and adjectives are germane to a specifiable yet general periphery called the outback, the "ultimate urban jungle," marked by its "remoteness from the cities," "historically an `empty' space," apt for the "enactment of colonialist fantasy." The outback is "the apocalyptic," a space to be colonized, although it is one where knowledge must be precisely invested, for it is "prime territory for Darwinian fancies of throwbacks, remnants, mutants, the primitive," the world of unknown species, of "muscular innocence," "the beast, savage black, crazed white, man-eating pig, crocodile, dingo," all intended to be narratable in terms of mere geography and biology. Potentially this is the terrain Cannibal Tours will colonize and transform into some kind of industry.

Based on these two samples, I would have to conclude that one aspect of the postmodern critic's production is to erase the specific and put forth the generic, so that speaking about the periphery or even from the periphery loses its epistemological value. Reading this tendency in reverse, or what for these examples would specify the concrete--territoriality, solidarity, transmission, modality, ambiguity--is one of the applications of Indian Subaltern Studies, particularly of Ranajit Guha's work, to Latin America (cf. Guha 1992). The relationship between specific and generic identifies only one locus of tension of postmodern cultural studies, but a significant one.

The primary sources of these two narratives quoted here, emanating from a "Eurocentric discourse" staging "a perfect Other," are not made explicit by the authors of the samples whose postmodern vocabulary has borrowed terminology from a whole host of discourses: Marxism, narratives of exploration, business journals, all to produce the proper mixture to be accepted by the industries of representation. The two works quoted above fall squarely into what Guha calls "elite" as a means of signalling geographic and class, gender and ethnic loci of production as power (Guha 1988: 37-44). The two works also indicate the predicament of being located within the hard realities produced by the unavoidable mode of production of corporate capitalism which furnishes any concept or production with its content. They also mark the lack of dialogism among intellectuals who, because of their national cultural base, still look at social phenomena differently. The difference between the U.S. mainstream critics and the Latin Americanist critics (whether from Latin America or the U.S.) resides, I will argue, in that the latter group *places emphasis on* the specific wherein lies the empowering of cultural production today; and the specific, as Achugar argues in his article in this volume, is not a uniform space. Although the corporate world aims at erasing all differences, the local is still singularly unique.

I also want to notice the irony and despair which constitutes the tone of these two citations. Both critics feel trapped in a spiderweb, and want to distance themselves from the power of the concepts constituting their context, the colonial archive, while both of them feel the despair of reading the realities of colonialism in their own discursive production. Here then, is where the continually reiterated dilemma of representation again presents itself. How does one represent the totality outside the totality? How does one represent the totality with a logic which is different from the logic of the totality? To address the question of representation within postmodernity brings us by necessity to the debate on endings, mainly to that of the end of ideology and of history. That is why any cultural statement today *must begin* by acknowledging the victory of capitalism over socialism which discapacitated structural opposition, and tightened up the space in which the production of culture as systemic criticism was viable. The demise of socialism produced a theoretical and political surge/overflow/meltdown/glut which hardened and confused our conditions of production. More so than ever, the production of counterdiscourse and dissention came to be located directly within the domain of supply and demand. The market mechanism intervened in the universities, transforming them from centers of learning into centers of training. Like any space at any other center, in our productive space neoliberalism means balancing budgets and the remodeling of resources of financial assistance from state support to corporate financing. The consequence is a drastically altered site whose conditions of production are pervaded by despair, fear, or cynicism, leading us back to a discredited Marxism, a Marxism converted from the philosophy of praxis into the praxis of philosophy.

2. Theories of Endings: A Vicious Hermeneutical Circle

According to Fredric Jameson, the world is caught up between the belated Modernism pervading the Third World and the Postmodernism of advanced countries. During the pre-postmodern era, this discrepancy, explained in terms of uneven development and debated as the center/periphery, still granted the periphery a certain degree of cultural autonomy. Today, the national cultures of the Third World are being intervened upon by global commercial production. As a result, their neotraditional images are being dissolved. In his essay on testimonial literature, for instance, Jameson argues this principle in the production of testimonials and points out the similarities between testimonial narratives and the *Bildungsroman* (cf. the summary by Beverley 1996). Postulating that testimonials are instances of the representation of identities in the periphery, Jameson then asks provocatively if subjectivities are exportable.

232

But, if subjectivities are able to be exported, they can no longer be predicated in national terms. Hence, the idea of the end of the national state is here invoked. Postcolonial studies debates over the nature of the nation-state have come to the same conclusions and this explains the production of "abroad and overseas" as a generic space. But to think of that space as saturated space is to eradicate the notion of agency. If agency is erased, who or what performs the role of the subject? How would we read the actantial function which blocks or impels the workings of events as history? What, then, is to be done?

In his paper "`End of Art' or `End of History'"? delivered at the Fall 1995 Midwest Modern Language Association convention, Jameson took the opportunity to remind us that the ideology of endings was epistemologically untenable. To make his point, he revisited Hegel to see what he could tell us about our particular juncture of now. This long route was taken in order to highlight the radical difference in endings between Hegel, Alexander Kojeve (1994), and Francis Fukuyama (1992).

Jameson explains first that in Hegel's polymorphous system, what is important is not any conceptual relationship which involves certainty or as stasis, but rather the breakdown in the relationship--that is movement, dialectics, discrepancy and difference. Second, he points out how Hegel's triadic way of thinking interrupts any smooth conceptual glide from religion into art and from art into philosophy, and leads to a "system crash." Art, which is thought of as symbolic, classic and romantic, suffers a logical collapse at the moment it is to pass into philosophy. Philosophy, in turn, is defined as "the historical self-consciousness of an absolute present" (that is, the end of history), and as "the shaping power of the human collectivity over its own destiny" (that is, utopia). The end of art thus coincides with the end of history. We are then to conclude that in aborting the step from art into philosophy, there is neither an end of art nor an end of philosophy.

Jameson then attributes this break in terms to the emergence of the sublime, the moment in which philosophy is superseded by positivism. In Hegel's system, the end of art is the beginning of philosophy; however, the transit between the two forms is aborted and instead of art becoming philosophy , the end result is more art--i.e., the art of Modernism which is predicated on progress, science, development and the age of mechanical reproduction. Art or aesthetics was split into the beautiful, which becomes decorative and deprived of truth, and the sublime, which is Modernism or

233

the "transaesthetic." Adorno's phrase that "philosophy, which once seemed obsolete, lives on because the moment to realize it was missed," comes in to tie Marx into Hegel, and to introduce Marx's idea of the end of history as a systemic change, that is, not the end of history but the end of pre-history, which is, utopia--"the shaping power of the human collectivity over its own destiny." In this way, Jameson inverts Kojeve's and Fukuyama's logic of endings--of ideology, of history--as a way of declaring the absolute and definitive triumph of capitalism. Via Hegel and Adorno, he comes back to the basic Marxist belief in liberation. The end of history is then predicated on ending exploitation.

If Modernism is the threshold signalling the intersection of art and philosophy in the Hegelian system, in Jameson's it comes to signify a point of reference for the end of history in Fukuyama's and Kojeve's systems. Far from predicating the Hegelian conversion, in which the end of one category (art), becomes the fulfillment of the other (philosophy--as end of history, that is, "the shaping power of the human collectivity over its own destiny" in the present) they predicate the triumph of the market system and thus become the prophets of doom, that is, of dystopia.

If there is an end of something, Jameson proposes, it is the end of Modernism and the sublime. Within the emergence of theory, and the de-differentiation theory makes, in a return of consciousness as self-consciousness, whose central theme is the dynamics of representation itself, Jameson locates hope. He hopes that theory will take humanity, via the figural, to praxis itself. The question is, can theory crack open the commodification implicit in the beautiful? Faithful to Marxist theory, Jameson sees the end of history as predicated only on systemic changes, concretely on modes of production. By a logical tour de force, then, he goes back to Marx and posits that the change from one mode of production (capitalism) to something else (socialism or communism) will bring to an end not history but the pre-history of humanity. Is Jameson predicting the end of capitalism when he tells us that today there is an end to the Promethean conception of production; that it is impossible to imagine "development", or rather "progress", without the conquest of nature, and that the conquest of nature is no longer possible because there is an ecological limit to expansion? Is his tour de force not the transference of the question of history as time to the question of history as space?

The reason why Hegel's neat triadic system crashed was not epistemological but political. What disillusioned Hegel was the French Revolution. What disillusioned Adorno was Modernism as Fascism. What *re-illusions* Jameson, or even hopes to supersede illusioning, is theory, that is, the absolute certainty that we still remain within the capitalist mode of production, and that only a systemic change can bring to fruition the transition between the sublime and utopia. In ecology he finds the notion of a limit which has already brought the system to checkmate.

My perplexity is then to think of the injunction placed on Marxism, parallel to those on Hegel and Adorno. If Marxism is the theory of praxis, Marxist analysis cannot do without the concept of class struggle, or without the role of the working class--Marx's agents for changing pre-history into history (utopia). Marxism is not Marxism if we remove from it the notion of agency. So my question is, has globalism succeeded in placing an injunction on Marx similar to that imposed by the French Revolution, the Prussian State, and Fascism on Hegel and Adorno? Has capitalism in its last stage succeeded in putting a halt to Marx's narrative of history, that is, on that which makes his theory of praxis work? If the answer is no, then what is our forecast on the capacity of the human collective (agency) to possess control over its own destiny, to bring about utopia? If the answer is yes, then can we conclude that we have reached an end, Marxism defeated by capitalism in its last stage, and consequently a reversal of utopia into dystopia? This brings us back to the representation of the generic periphery and of agency. Our predicament on endings seems to have reached representation itself.

3. Agency and Action in Subaltern Studies

In contrast to a large majority of recent texts which speak about closures and fragmentations and constitute narratives of despair, the work of the Indian Subaltern Group presents us with a clean bill of health. By centering their studies on the subaltern, they have synergetically worked out the antinomies of class, gender, ethnicity, nationality, poverty and subordination. They represent subordination in a way which accounts for the transformation of capital and labor in relation to the question of the subaltern subject as the agent of history. They represent a criticism after Foucault and Derrida which still has the toughness of a Marxist criticism and the weight of writing as an act of power. They are not afraid of politically engaging a theoretical paradigm that directly addresses the possibilities of plotting collective action. Their works enable a reading of texts in reverse, or from the perspective of the subaltern, that is, as the potential and real victims and hence agents of capital in each of its historical phases.

The Latin American Subaltern Studies Group has been inspired by them, and brings their own theoretical apparatus to engage the postmodern debate with Marxism. Our take comes from Guha's dictum that elite historiography cannot properly explain the world "for it fails to acknowledge, far less interpret, the contribution made by the people on their own, that is, independently of the elite" (Guha 1988: 39). In our field, debates on subalternity can be properly said to have begun in the postmodern era with the centering of testimonial as a genre, mainly the polemic generated by Elizabeth Burgos Debray's book on Rigoberta Menchú. Rigoberta was subsequently constituted into an "transcendental signifier" because in her were coalesced several aspects of subalternity as Guha specifies it, namely "the general attribute of subordination ... expressed in terms of class, caste, age, gender and office or in any other way" (ibid.: 35--cf. Carr 1992).

In this debate one can already discern some of the theoretical predicates of the group, the most important of which being that of solidarity with the marginalized, and the acknowledgement of their own contribution to all areas of culture. In Guha's dictum, quoted above, we find stated questions concerning representation and its limits which, in the case of Rigoberta, centered on the categories and hierarchies of ethnicity, gender and political commitment. The Rigoberta represented as such opened up whole new worlds and enabled critics to play within the epistemological domain by combining the categories of ethnicity, class and gender; class, nation and ethnicity; gender, class and nation.

The fundamental methodological premise of the group, implicit in its name, "Latin American Subaltern Studies," finds then in Rigoberta an example which includes the subjugated, the un-, and the under-represented to be represented, and from there, to take up current debates analyzing absent theoretical spaces such as sexual orientation, substance abuse marginality, alienation in post-work society, debates over pre-Hispanic indigenous cultures, inclusion of migrant populations in the era of neo-liberalism, Latino studies, theories of the absent state, governability and citizenship (cf. Latin American Subaltern Studies Group 1993: 135-146). Guha's work on peasant insurgencies underscores questions relative to agency as government or administration and civic or human rights. Government and human/civic rights are related to agency through the reading of insurgency as an ungovernable space or what he terms the unfamiliar, the inversion, the world upside down, the unanticipated--that is, that which constitutes the antithesis of colonialism as governance. Ungovernability is the insurgent opposition to the dominant, that which introduces consciousness as an indispensable aspect of subaltern contestation of power, and hence, the affirmation of civic and human rights. Guha's point is precisely to acknowledge the negation of the subaltern as subjects of history in their own right.

Therefore ungovernability, coupled with citizenship, is one of the great producers of culture. It produces the official documents of colonialism, the careers of the officers, part of its historiography, and cultural criticism. In this way, subaltern agency becomes central to any such debate. For instance, via the articulation of the subaltern into the narratives of agrarian disturbances and insurrections, the Indian Subaltern Studies Group reintroduces a mode of production discussion which links state formation, officialized hegemony, and power to elite discourse. Although their moment of theoretical intervention is the Raj, that is, the period of English rule of colonial India, there is also a polemic with postcolonial organizations such as the Indian Party Congress and the Indian Communist Party. Thus as Guha notes:

> The formative layers of the developing state were ruptured again and again by these seismic upheavals until it was to learn to adjust to its unfamiliar site by trial and error and consolidate itself by the increasing sophistication of legislative, administrative and cultural controls. [Guha 1992: 2]

But Guha also speaks about peasant insurgencies as a discourse. In true Foucauldian fashion, Guha is also interested in mode of production as discourse production, the technologies of which constitute knowledge as power. He takes on many of the elements of everyday life encoded in the colonial documents and reads them as metaphors of power, thus unveiling how subordination and dominance as well as the logic of causality and the production of culture are harnessed to counterinsurgency as government.

Security of the state, preservation of power, and a maintenance of hegemony are as central to the narratives of governance and administration as ungovernability and human rights are to those of insurgency, for "subordination can hardly be justified as an ideal and a norm without acknowledging the fact and possibility of insubordination" (ibid.: 11). To identify knowledge as a technology of power which excludes subaltern practices is to delimit the domains that must be read in reverse. Although the whole work of Foucault has dealt with epistemology and subaltern studies, madness and the mad, discipline and punishment, sexuality and the deviant--that is, those subalternities which are in his immediate cultural environment--the radical difference is that Guha is more interested in the technologies of resistance whose production is insurgency. To underline this relationship, Guha answer's Foucault's title *Discipline and Punishment* with his "Discipline and Mobilize." Seen from each other's reverse, their strategies are clear: in one, demobilization by example; in the other, mobilization by example. In sum, Foucault's domain is less directly politico-insurgent and more directly politico-technological. Foucault is already situated within the postliberal moment.

We can read the position of the subaltern within the Latin American field using Guha's methodologies. I will argue, for instance, that his distinction between structured and unstructured models is very pertinent. "Structured" refers to the theoretical model of orthodox Marxism premised upon an organized program and a leadership as a precondition of insurgency, that is, on the existence of the Communist Party as a vanguard party. "Unstructured" refers to Guha's notion of insurgency, as a revised Marxism. The rift concerns subaltern participation within the debate of modes of production. Guha argues against a one-model theory of organization as a precondition of agency. His discussion with leftist political parties is argued within the field of historiography through the conception of the "pre-political" which Hobsbawm (1959) advocates to explain peasant rebellions. It is his dissatisfaction with the orthodox model and his efforts to better approximate the social realities of the periphery, or what he calls the postcolonial in India, which explains Guha's theoretical shifts towards a Gramscian version of Marxism, and the substitution of Lenin for Mao's militant appraisal of rebellion. Thus, the group's theory is premised more on the concept of subalternity than on the concept of class. In fact, in their works, the concept of class in itself is rendered inoperative.

Gramsci's analysis of Italy, in fact, follows the model of the *18th Brumaire*--that is, of political mobilization understood as class struggle. But he broadens the concept of struggle to accommodate other forms of mobilizations relevant to less industrialized spaces. Here is where Guha's insurgency and the distinction between criminality and uprising, consciousness and spontaneity take hold. Thus, he notes:

> To acknowledge the peasant as the maker of his own rebellion is to attribute ... a consciousness to him.... This amounts ... to a rejection of the idea of such activity as purely spontaneous.... But as ... Gramsci... has said, there is no room for pure spontaneity in history. This is precisely where ... [elite historiographers] ... err who fail to recognize the trace of consciousness in the apparently unstructured movements of the masses. The error derives ... from two nearly interchangeable notions of organization and politics. What is conscious is presumed in this view to be identical with what is organized in the sense that it has, first, a `conscious leadership,' secondly, some well-defined aim, and thirdly, a program specifying the components of the latter as particular objectives and the means of achieving them. [1992: 4-5]

The snag here lies in the old notion of uneven development (today represented by the Modernism/Postmodernism divide), the polemic on social formation and how, in India,

> capitalist development in agriculture remained merely incipient and weak throughout the period of a century and a half until 1900. Rents constituted the most substantial part of income yielded by property in land.... In other words, it was a relationship of dominance and subordination--a political relationship of the feudal type. [5]

The polemic over the organization and development of capitalism is very similar to that undertaken by Celso Furtado (1972) and Andre Gunder Frank (1972) over dependency theory, in which Frank argued for a dependent capitalism, whereas Furtado argued the totality, that is, the impossibility of thinking the system outside the logic of the system, unless a shift in the mode of production is entertained.

The transition between hacienda and latifundia was discussed as a transition to capitalism in Latin America, but the relation between latifundia and labor produced disagreements concerning the proper nature of political organization and mobilization. This is the chasm between the Communist

Parties and the guerrilla movements of the 60s. The motto, "only workers and peasants will reach the end," points to a revised version of Marxism inspired in China and applicable to several Latin American struggles. Moving towards a conclusion, the tension between seeing mode of production as economic or discursive, as endings or continuations of a history predicated on struggle, obviously comes from an exhausted base/superstructure debate still current in a new form. However, our decision in defining which model/paradigm is primary will place either political economy or cultural agendas in the forefront. In this, as in many other aspects, I believe the Indian Subaltern Group tries to mediate. They make their discussions on historiography inimical to cultural studies by enabling the conversion of historical documents and political actions into culture, and culture back into politics. They uphold that it is part of elite historiography to reduce insurgency and politics to carnival, to the "mere embellishment, a sort of decorative and folklorist detail serving primarily to enliven the curricula vitae of indigenous and foreign elites," when

the actual volume of evidence yielded by the songs, rhymes, ballads, anecdotes, etc., is indeed very meager... compared to the size of documentation available from elitist sources on almost any agrarian movement of our period. This is a measure... of their concern to watch and record every hostile gesture among the rural masses. [Guha, 1992: 14]

They also point to more political ways hegemony and power come to bear upon culture, affecting the lives of the people in insidious ways. Such is the case of disglossia as verbal abuse, kinesics and proxemics as the politics of carrying the body in public, dress habits, all domains administered by law-enforcing agencies.

In India, the complicit collaboration between colonial power and rural elite in the enforcing of authority and punishment parallels Latin America where the corresponding structures also govern or manage the lives of the subaltern. Both maintain a vigilante-style attitude over the cultural practices of everyday life, of

snatches of conversation, ... chunks of prose addressed to this purpose...designed primarily to indicate the immorality, illegality, undesirability, barbarity, etc., of insurgent practice and to announce by contrast the superiority of elite on each count. [ibid.: 16]

By positing subaltern consciousness as a viable theoretical positivity, Guha brings back the assurance that, even under the harshest conditions, there has always been consciousness of oppression and hence a possibility of insurgency; that subaltern agency is always a precondition of discourse production; and that the role of the intellectual as elite has been to erase subaltern agency. His challenge to us is to reverse those practices to enable rebel consciousness to dominate the academic exercise and thus

emphasize its sovereignty, its consistency and its logic in order to compensate for its absence ... and to act, if possible, as a corrective to the eclecticism common to much writing on this theme. [13]

Carlos Cortez (with Michael Piazza), *Caged sin fronteras*, 1997.
Recycling of scratchboard and collage images of Fusco and Gómez-Peña, 8"x 10"
Courtesy of the artists.

PASSAGE TO AMERICA:
FUSCO, GOMEZ-PEÑA AND
LATINO BORDER PERFORMANCE

Kartik Vora

"Passage to more than India...."
--Walt Whitman

1. From Kafka's Academy to a Museum Cage

Honored members of the Academy! You have done me the honor of inviting
me to give your Academy an account of the life I formerly led as an ape. --
Franz Kafka "A Report to an Academy" [1979: 245].

Kafka's story is about an aboriginal captured from the Gold Coast of
Africa and brought to Germany for display as a primate. Kafka's play on the
irony of having to demonstrate one's humanity alludes to many ethnographic
exhibitions of human beings that have taken place in the west over the past
five centuries. The tradition of exhibiting non-white peoples as freaks
probably started with Columbus returning from his 1492 voyage with
several Arawaks, one of whom was left on display at the Spanish Court
(Fusco 1994: 148)--this at the same time as the Conquest, genocide and
other disorders continued in the "New World." In the second half of the
nineteenth century, objects from colonies were repeatedly assembled in
displays at international exhibitions. Their transience and ephemerality set
them apart as extraordinary phenomena. These exhibitions created a unitary,
though not uniform, landscape of discourse and practice, that situated the
colony within a single analytical field.
   As a major cultural industry, the exhibitions made a significant
contribution to consolidating the political economy of the empire; at the
same time, they forged and then made use of a social construction involving
a very specific notion of the cultural other. What is involved, historically
and in this paper, is a movement from the initial travels of "discovery," to
voyeuristic displays and gazing, to our presentday stagings of "postcolonial
othering" or exile.

As a key instance of the latter phase, Coco Fusco and Guillermo Gómez-Peña came to Chicago in 1993, set up their showcage in front of the city's Field Museum and presented their own recreation of the human exhibition routine, "The Guatinaui World Tour," which they had been staging outside of various anthropological museums and other public places in London, Washington D.C., Madrid Spain, Sydney Australia, Los Angeles and Minneapolis during the early years of the decade (see Gómez-Peña 1993: 136-137; 1996: 98).

For Gómez-Peña, the Tour dramatized the unconscious of "New World" conquest and colonization--an unconscious which supposedly grounded and justified genocide, enslavement and the seizure of lands through the "naturalized" splitting of humanity along racial lines (Fusco 1994: 152). He and Fusco lived in their gilded cage for three days, presenting themselves as supposedly undiscovered Amerindians from the recently discovered island of Guatinau (a "spanglishization" of "what now") in the Gulf of Mexico that had somehow been overlooked by Europeans for five centuries. Gómez-Peña was dressed as a kind of Aztec wrestler from Las Vegas and Fusco as a Taina straight out of *Gilligan's Island* (Gómez-Peña 1996: 97). They performed "traditional" tasks, which ranged from sewing voodoo dolls and lifting weights, to watching television and working on a laptop computer. They were hand-fed by fake museum docents and taken to the bathroom on leashes. A donation box in front of the cage indicated that for a small fee, the aboriginal woman would dance (to rap music), and the male would tell authentic Amerindian stories (in a nonsensical language); and both would pose for polaroids with the visitors.

The original intent of the performers was to create a satirical commentary on the western concepts of the exotic, primitive Other. But they confronted "two unexpected reactions" in the course of developing the performance: First, a significant segment of the public took their fictional, parodic identities as real ones; and second, other reproached them for faking their identity and misguiding the public. In Washington D.C. an angry visitor phoned the Humane Society to complain and was told that human beings were out of their jurisdiction (Fusco 1994: 157); elsewhere, as Fusco notes, certain intellectuals, artists, and cultural bureaucrats "sought to deflect attention from the substance of our experiment to the `moral implications* of our dissimulation, or in their words, our `misinforming the public about who we are'" (143).

244

Fusco's use of "we" highlights the complexity of self identification, which is necessarily done in terms of what it is *not*—i.e., the other. In many cultural traditions the other is thematized as dark, uncertain, chaotic--a threat to be reduced. The paradigmatic conception in western thought is that of the `quest' in Chivalric romances, where the adventurous knight leaves King Arthur's court--the realm of the known--to confront some form of otherness. The conquest is brought to an end when this alien has been reduced to the same, or nearly the same. In other words, the *raison d'etre* of the crusade--the search for the dragon (including its eventual slaughter by the hero [always, a male]), and for the grail itself--is ultimately symbolic of the *inner* search for hidden treasures. This archetypal myth is indicative of the location where the final resolution of all external searches for the other end: where they began--*within*.

As Edward Said notes, the realization that the other is not an ontological given, but is historically and culturally constituted, is a requisite step in "erod[ing] the exclusivist biases we so often ascribe to cultures, our own not the least" (1989: 225). Self/other relations are determined by the fact that we do not see ourselves as we are seen by others, and this difference in perspective informs and embodies our self-image. Since the body is what others see but what the subject cannot, the subject becomes dependent upon the Other in a way that ultimately makes the body the focus of a power struggle with far-reaching ramifications. Involved in this interpretative struggle is the Lacanian question of the relationships among the self, its mirror-image, and the other. In normal situations the mirror image and the other are distinct from the self, constituting its integrity and sanity. But how determine the basis for these entities and relations? Seeing something is contingent on not seeing something else. This not seeing stems from socially-constructed blindspots whose recognition through critical or hermeneutic analysis would alter the entire field of perceptions. The existence of blindspots points to perceptual relativity; locating them is essential to understanding what we see and why. But it is almost impossible to perceive and locate blindspots within a shared cultural frame. Given the self's social construction, the questions of cultural as well as individual identity are inherently implicated.

Gómez-Peña (1991: 126) considers three sources of cultural identity: those imposed from above, those that come from below, and hybrid or transitional identities. The first kind, he argues, "is fictitious and responds to the agendas of the governments that enforce it." The second kind, which comes from the traditions and "often enters into conflict with the one from above[,] ... is much more fluid and, because it is open to fusion and cultural negotiation, it is constantly changing." It is the last category of hybridity--with its multiple and hyphenated identities--that interests Gómez-Peña because of what it says about "the future of this country" and beyond:

> As a conceptual and performance artist raised in two cultures, I am affected by Latin American novelists, Chicano poets and artists as I am by Beuys and Fassbinder. This double source of imagery and methodology appears in my work. What I do is a hybrid... [ibid.]

Gómez-Peña has worked with his many collaborators in exploring ethnic-looking objects and decontextualized rituals with the eye of a conceptual artist and the humor of a Chicano comedian. The "ethnic look" of his work is intentionally "dismantled in front of the audience" (ibid.).

Working together in the early 1990s, Fusco and Gómez-Peña concentrated on the "zero degree" of intercultural relations in an attempt to define a point of origin for the debates that link "discovery" and "Otherness." Their specific performance was specifically based on the once popular European and North American practice of exhibiting indigenous peoples from Africa, Asia, and the Americas in zoos, parks, taverns, museums, freak shows, and circuses. Emerging at the time when mass audiences were barely literate and hardly cognizant of the rest of the world, the displays were an important form of public "education." They were the spaces where most whites "discovered" the non-Western sector of humanity. Fusco argues that such human displays were the origins of intercultural performance in the West—living expressions of colonial fantasies that helped to forge a special place in the Euro-American imagination for non-white peoples and their cultures (1994: 148).

2. *Expositions and Fairs/ Exiles and Itineraries*

> The truth of a human situation is the itinerary of not being able to find it. -- Spivak [1987: 77]

The study of expositions and world's fairs from the point of view of the colonized is an important aspect of the interpretation and indeed the politics of representation--above all, the construction of an orientalized discourse that describes and defines the `other' culture. The notion of collecting and exhibiting artifacts expanded considerably in the post-Enlightenment era. With the emergence of nineteenth century imperialism, the collection activities, repositories and showplaces--the expeditions and digs, the decipherings, surveys and censuses, the folk-lore collecting and ethnography, the archives, libraries, museums, and galleries--developed an aura of scientific status. This obsession for collecting objects should be understood within a larger context of mapping, surveying, recording, classifying, and evaluating as travels, commerce, and politics widened horizons; but the obsession also raised questions about borders as well as about every fundamental category of phenomena and their conceptualization--even as people clamored to exhibitions and expositions which were supposed to represent and perhaps make some sense of it all.

Walter Benjamin considers these public showings as key elements characterizing nineteenth century urbanity. Expos and exhibitions "are sites of pilgrimages to ... `commodity fetishes'" which "open up a phantasmagoria that people enter to be amused" as social subjects "submit to being manipulated while enjoying their alienation from themselves" (Benjamin, quoted in Buck Morss 1989: 83-87). According to Clifford (1988), modernists and ethnographers of the early 20th century projected coded perceptions of the black body as imbued with vitalism, rhythm, magic, and erotic power.

Also defining the irrational as the primitive and libidinal during the same period to which Clifford refers, Freud, saw "the other" or the double in the function of "the alien and the uncanny"--i.e., phenomena which result from a morbid anxiety that is not new or foreign, but familiar and old and which is established by the process of repression (Freud 1974: 241). Freud's essay on the uncanny tracks the double gesture by which the familiar (or *heimliche)* becomes frightening (*unheimliche*). Thus, paradoxically, the unfamiliar is for Freud nothing other than the *familiar* in disguise, and the alien is the symbol of the same. This confounding of the identical with the foreign, or the same with the other, is also about disguised or faked identity that causes fear and discomfort.

Long before Freud, during the Enlightenment period itself, Kant had discussed the alien as a simple and absolute otherness that inspires fear and sublimity and thereby evokes a border problem no amount of patrolling could completely control. The alien in Kant, like the alien that would emerge in Freud, is a strangely complicated figure--as it is, with great variance, in Kafka, Benjamin and other modernist thinkers. It is the mark both of the absolute other and of otherness transgressed; it is both spoken by human discourse and not spoken by it; it takes place without ever taking place. Thus, the borders in Kant that keep the human from the sublime can never be completely closed and secured; for Kant's figure of the other finds itself in a mutually parasitic relationship with that which misrepresents it. In other words, the alien always positions itself somewhere between pure familiarity and pure otherness, between the speech of the same and the speech of the other. With Freud and other twentieth century figures, the alien, taking its place on the borders between identity and difference, marks those borders, articulating while at the same time disarticulating and confusing the very distinctions for which the borders supposedly stand.

Another appropriation of the uncanny is offered by Homi Bhabha to speak of the diaspora and return of migrants and minorities who destabilize traditional notions of center and periphery by crossing over boundaries which now "imperceptibly turn into a contentious liminality that provides a place from which to speak" (1990: 319-320). After Heidegger, we can recognize transcendental homelessness as the predicament of the postmodern cultures. As Said points out, migrancy and exile involve a "discontinuous state of being." Over a few decades they have been transformed from a form of controversy about where you come from "into a potent, even enriching, motif of modern culture" (1990: 365).

All our major thinkers of recent times--those whom Bhabha refers to as "comedians of culture's non-sense"--have stood, for a brief moment in that undecidable enunciatory space where culture's authority is undone in colonial power; they have taught culture's double lesson (1990: 136). For the uncanny lesson of the double, as a problem of intellectual uncertainty, lies precisely in its double-inscription and indeterminate border location.

3. *To Amerika and Beyond*

"Visit the U.S. before the U.S. visits you."
--Message on a Mexican T-Shirt

The discussion developed herein takes us now to our present period which Foucault, dying as its postmodern contours fully emerged, attempted to characterize in terms of a dichotomized view involving utopias and heterotopias[1] as two sites that "have the curious property" of being related to all other sites, but in such a way as to suspect, neutralize, or invert the relational set "they happen to stagnate, mirror or reflect" (Foucault 1985-86: 12). The sites are linked with all the others, but primarily by a relation of contradiction.

Heterotopias, like boundaries, are established "in the very founding of society," and stand as "counter sites" in which all the other real sites that can be found within a culture "are simultaneously represented, contested, and inverted" (ibid.).

A system of openings and closing isolates heterotopias and at the same time, makes them penetrable. This principle is very significant, because it deals with the edges and openings of the heterotopic construct that performs the magical function of linking everyday reality with utopian ideals. One does not enter heterotopic spaces by one's own will. One is either forced, as in the case of barracks or prison; or one must submit to the purification rites.

Heterotopias have in relation to the rest of space, a function that takes place between two opposite poles. On one hand they perform the task of creating a space of illusion that reveals how all of real space is more illusory, all locations within life are fragmented. On the other hand, they have the function of forming another space, another real space, as perfect, meticulous and well-arranged as ours is disordered, ill-conceived and in a sketchy state. Foucault calls these heterotopias not of illusion, but of compensation; best illustrated in the case of certain colonies where the goal was to create perfect, utopian places.

The U.S. is no longer seen as the perfect utopian heir of Western European culture and its colonizing contradictions. Instead, it is a bizarre laboratory in which all races and all continents are experimenting with identity, trying to find a new model of conviviality, in which all cultures border on each other, cross over, mix, merge, and rearticulate their similarities, their differentiations. In this process, very exciting kinds of hybrid identities and hybrid art forms are being created. In our time and condition, when God is supposed to be long dead, so are authors and human

---

[1] Foucault mentioned the term "Heterotopia" in his book of 1966; he developed it in a lecture he gave in Paris, March 1967. The transcription of the lecture finally appeared in 1984 and was republished in 1986; the key matters are also discussed in his article of 1985-86.

subjects: the victims of epistemic violence or directly physical violence--or some undelineated combination of both.

Gómez-Peña's border performances address the question of hybridity and above all the precise paradigm of migrant identity enunciated by Bhabha and Said. Between 1988 and 1992, he and his collaborators performed *Border Brujo* at the U.S.-Mexican border and other sites throughout the world, traversing back and forth, dressed in ethnic costumes, posing as cultural transvestites and spouting multilingual monologues, as they addressed key border identity issues. They were clowns, jesters and fools--vagrant/migrant artists toying with the border patrols and the Immigration and Naturalization Services.

After two years on the road, travelling from city to city and country to country, they ended their performance back at the border--burying their costumes and staging a performance funeral (Gómez-Peña 1996: 95-96). As Gómez-Peña warned at the time:

> We can no longer strive for national cohesiveness; it is an outmoded goal. We can no longer define our borders, our identities, our notion of self by opposing the cultural other...If we do not begin a systematic dialogue across borders, races, genders, and generations, we are going to arrive at the 21st century in disastrous shape.... We can no longer strive for national cohesiveness; it is an outmoded goal. We can no longer define our borders, our identities, our notion of self by opposing the cultural other (1991: 159)

With the 1992 quincentenary, Coco Fusco and Gómez-Peña sought to explore and re-discover America, seeking to fend against contemporary techniques of violence and obliteration addressed against colonial subjects. They saw their caged confrontation with the cultural other as the beginning of a dialogue that would question solidified identities and generate new perceptions able to break down old oppositions.

What Gómez-Peña and Coco Fusco intended as heterotopia of illusion served as a means of compensation for their white audiences anticipating exotic sights on the quincentenary of the New World's "Discovery." It is even possible that at least some audience members found themselves "cheated" when they found out that the "indigenous natives" were fake; for their part, the behind bars performers experienced moments of restitution which compensated for the reactive, anti-colonial aggressivity at the heart of their motivation for this performance.

Fusco and Gómez-Peña employed identity-faking as a strategy inspired by Brecht's *Verfremdung* or alienation techniques. The faking was a dramatic device to force audience reaction or participation through disorientation and discomfort. Of course, for these Latino performance artists, the goal was ultimately one of postcolonial decolonization. For both the performers and spectators the pendulum swayed from a nostalgia about the past to a nostalgia with respect to the future. The performers wanted to subvert colonial fascination with an exotic (but properly caged and domesticated) native display by putting a mirror in the face of the audience so that what it sees is not the other but itself. The cage became a blank screen onto which the audiences projected their fantasies of the savage, now rendered safe by bars. Confronted with a performance they were invited to observe, many audience members, at least initially, felt entitled to assume the role of colonizer and exercised the colonizing gaze of surveillance, appropriation and definition--only to find themselves, as the performance unfolded with all its aggressive parody and satire, increasingly uncomfortable with the implications of the game. This discomfort seemed to increase even as some of the spectators learned the game and tried to achieve complicity, and recognition of complicity, with the anti-colonizing, anti-Eurocentric semiology many came to understand themselves to be witnessing.

Indeed, even for those who identified with the performers and their game, unpleasant associations which were also very important, emerged from the performances. Above all, the central position of the white spectator, the objective of the performance as a confirmation of the position of Western whites as global consumers of exotic cultures, and the stress on authenticity as an aesthetic value, all remained fundamental to the spectacle of otherness which many in the public enjoyed even as they experienced discomfort.

A similar discomfort was used by Aronowitz and Giroux in a learning experiment in which people were asked to assume the role of students scrutinizing phenomena from subject-positions "constructed around coordinates of difference and power" (1991: 199). Such pedagogy, then, encourages students "to develop a relationship of non-identity with their own subject positions and the multiple cultural, political and social codes that constitute established boundaries of power, dependency and possibility" (200).

For Gómez-Peña, discomfort decenters the conventional relationship between performers and audience:

> Recent debates in the art world seek to redefine canons, contexts, criteria for quality and orientations to representation. These debates ... are an expression of the "other" moving into the center. This new center is the multiracial, non-Anglo-European experience. The old center, monocultural and Eurocentric, is being left behind. [1991: 159]

Increasingly, theories have restored power to the subaltern, under-privileged non-west (including the non-west in the west), granting them the power to reaffirm and self-determine their identities. Clifford argues that "now that the west can no longer present itself as the unique purveyor of anthropological knowledge about others; it has become necessary to imagine a world of generalized ethnography with expanded communication and intercultural influence, people interpreting others and themselves in a bewildering diversity of idioms (1988: 22).

On this score, Clifford invokes Bakhtin's view of "heteroglossia," which assumes that "languages do not *exclude* each other, but rather intersect with each other in many different ways. It might even seem that the very word `language' loses all meaning in this process--for apparently there is no single plane on which all these `languages' might be juxtaposed to one another." And Clifford adds that what is said of languages applies equally to "cultures" and "subcultures." This ambiguous, multivocal world makes it increasingly hard to conceive of human diversity as inscribed in bounded, independent cultures" (23).

Performative comedians and jesters of postmodern culture's non-sense, Fusco and Gómez-Peña seek to elude the epistemological border patrols who would like to settle once and for all what and who belong where and when, here or there, now and then. In their enactment of colonial othering, they create their own charged, ambiguous, multivocal and unstable language to represent or, rather, relate to the unsettled and unsettling turbulence which is the predicament of our times: the mobility of relations, the nomadic schizophrenia of social being and knowing, and, of course, the persistent instability of naming and of language itself. The heterotopic spaces that find expression in the ever-proliferating heteroglossia of their performances lead to other languages and other spaces which are indeed "other," and which help to configure their as yet incomplete and uncharted journey to an unknown America. The "New World" that Fusco and Gómez-Peña seek to explore is, after all, not a place--and hence it is neither a non-place (utopia) nor an other place (heterotopia)--but rather, the *itinerary* for its search composed of a checkered network of criscrossing paths that delineate the veritable palimpsest of passages to Americas.

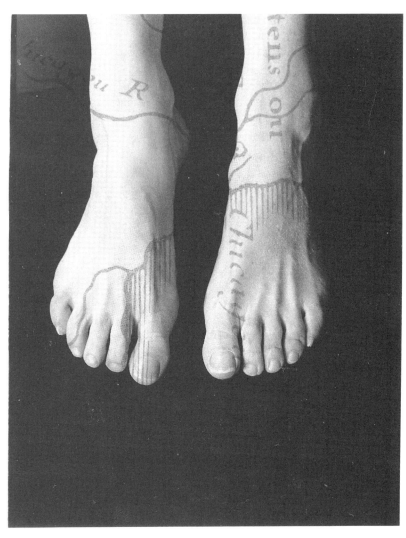

Diana Solís, *Untitled 2*, from *Intersticios* (installation) 1997.
Silver gelatin print-20"x24"
Courtesy of the artist.

WORKS CITED

Achugar, Hugo. 1990a. "Postmodernidad y postdictadura: Fin de Siglo en Uruguay." *Revista de Crítica Cultural.* May. 1. 1: 18-19.
_____. 1990b. "Postmodernity and Fin de Siecle in Uruguay." *STCL.* Vol. 4 no. 1: 45-59.
_____. 1990c. "De Maracana a la cultura del reciclaje." *Cuardernos de Marcha.* Montevideo. Septiembre.
_____. 1991. "Representar lo popular." *Graffitti.* no. 10 Montevideo.
_____. 1992. *La balsa de la Medusa: Ensayos sobre identidad, cultura y fin de siglo en Uruguay.* Montevideo. Ediciones Trilce.
_____. 1994. "Fin de siglo. Reflecciones desde la perferia." Herlinghaus and Walter, eds.: 233-255.

Ahmad, Aijaz. 1987. "Jameson's Rhetoric of Otherness and the 'National Allegory'." *Social Text* 16: 3-25.

Ahumada, Eugenio et al. 1989. *Chile, La memoria prohibida.* Santiago. Editorial.

Aldunate, Adolfo, Angel Flisfich and Tomás Moulián. 1985. *Estudios sobre el sistema de partidos en Chile.* Santiago. FLACSO.

Allende, Salvador. 1975. *Discursos de Salvador Allende.* La Habana. Editorial de Ciencias Sociales. Ediciones Políticas.

Althusser, Louis. 1970. *For Marx.* New York. Vintage.
_____971. *Lenin and Philosophy and Other Essays.* New York. Monthly Review Press.

Anderson, Benedict. 1983. *Imagined Communities. Reflections on the Origin and Spread of Nationalism.* London. Verso.

Anzaldúa, Gloria. 1987. *Borderlands/La Frontera: The New Mestiza.* San Francisco. Spinsters Aunt Lute.

Appadurai, Arjun. 1996. *Modernity at Large: Cultural Dimensions of Globalization.* U. of Minnesota Press.

Araeen, Rasheed. 1989. "Our Bauhaus Other's Mudhouse." *Third Text,* 6. Spring: 3-16.
_____. 1991. "Art is Not Magic, Magic is Not Art; When They Meet They Destroy Each Other" in Escobar, ed.: 1-10.

_____. 1992. "How I Discovered My Oriental Soul in the Wilderness of the West."
Third Text, 18. Spring: 85-102.

Archeti, Eduardo, Paul Cammack and Bryan Roberts. 1987. *Sociology of Developing
Societies: Latin America.* New York. Monthly Review.

Arias, Arturo. 1990a. "Changing Indian Identity: Guatemala's Violent Transition to
Modernity." In Smith, ed.: 230-257.
_____. 1990b. "Nueva narrativa centroamericana." In *Centroamericana, Studi di
Letteratura Ispanoamericana,* I. Roma. Bulzoni: 9-23.
_____. 1991. "Literary Production and Political Crisis in Central America." *Revue
Internationale de Science Politique.* Vol. 12, no. 1. Janvier: 15-28.
Arias, Arturo, ed. 1993. *Postmodernism and New Cultural Tendencies in Latin
America: 500th Anniversary of the Encounter of Two Worlds.* San Francisco. School
of Humanities. San Francisco State U.

Aronowitz, Stanley and Henri Giroux. 1991. *Postmodern Education: Politics, Culture,
and Social Criticism. Mpls. U. of Minnesota Press.*

Arrate, Jorge. 1986. *Siete ensayos sobre democracia y socialismo en Chile.* Santiago.
VECTOR. Centro de estudios económicos y sociales.

Arriagada Herrera, Genaro. 1988. *Pinochet, the Politics of Power.* Boston. Allen and
Unwin.

Arriagada Herrera, Genaro, ed. 1986. *Democracia Cristiana y Partido Comunista.*
Santiago. Editorial Aconcagua.

Aylwin, Patricio. 1988. *Un desafío colectivo.* Santiago. Planeta.

Aylwin, Mariana et al. 1985. *Chile en el siglo XX.* Santiago. Emisión.

Baddeley, Oriana and Valerie Fraser. 1989. *Drawing the Line: Art and Cultural
Identity in Contemporary Latin America.* New York. Verso.

Bakhtin, Michael. 1993 *Towards a Philosophy of the Act.* Austin. U. of Texas Press.
Baudrillard, Jean. 1981. *For a Critique of the Political Economy of the Sign.* St.
Louis. Telos Press.
_____. 1991. "The Reality Gulf." *The Guardian.* 11 January.
_____. 1992. *El extasis de la comunicación en la postmodernidad.* México. Kairos.
187-189.

Bayce, Rafael. 1992. "El exito de los pai de santo de *Brecha*." *Brecha*. Montevideo. 24 de avril.

Becker, Carol, ed. 1994. The *Subversive Imagination*. New York. Routledge.

Belli, Gioconda. 1990. *Sofia de los presagios (Sophia of the Forebodings)*. Managua. Ed. Vanguardia.
____. 1994. *The Inhabited woman (La mujer habitada)*. Willimantic, Conn. Curbstone Press.

Bell, Daniel. 1973. *The Coming of Post-Industrial Society: A Venture in Social Forecasting*. New York. Basic Books.
____. 1978. *The Cultural Contradictions of Capitalism*. New York. Basic Books.

Berman, Marshall. 1982. *All That Is Solid Melts Into Air The Experience of Modernity*. New York. Simon and Schuster.

Bertens, Helmut. 1986. "The Postmodern Weltschaung." In Fokkema and Bertens: 7-22.

Beverley, John. 1991. "Postmodernism in Latin America." *Siglo XX/ 20th Century (1991-92)*: 9-29.
____. 1992. "¿Post-literatura? Sujeto subalterno e impase en las humanidades." *Postdata*. Vol. 2, núm. 5: 1-19.
____. 1996. "*The Real Thing: Testimonial Discourse and Latin America*." In Gugelberger, ed.: 266-286.
Beverley, John and Hugo Achugar, ed. 1992. *La voz del otro: Testimonio, subalternidad y verdad narrativa*. Lima, Peru/Pittsburgh. Latinoamericana Editores.
Beverley, John and José Oviedo. 1995. "Introduction." In Beverley, Oviedo and Aronna, eds.: 1-17.
Beverley, John, José Oviedo, and Michael Aronna, eds. 1995. *The Postmodern Debate in Latin America*. Durham and London. Duke U. Press.
Beverley, John and Marc Zimmerman. 1990. *Literature and Politics in the Central American Revolutions*. Austin. U. of Texas Press.

Bhabha, Homi. 1989. "Of Mimicry and Man: The Ambivalence of Colonial Discourse." In Rice and Waugh, eds.: 234-241.
____. 1990. "Articulating the Archaic: Notes on Colonial Nonsense." In Collier and Ryan: 165-212.
Bhabha, Homi, ed. 1990. *Nation and Narration*. London. Routledge.

Bitar, Sergio, ed. 1980. *Chile, liberalismo económico y dictadura política*. América Problema 11. Lima. Instituto de Estudios Peruanos.

257

Borges, Jorge Luis. 1962. *Ficciones*. London. Weidenfeld and Nicholson.

Bourdieu, Pierre. 1984. *Distinction: A Social Critique of the Judgement of Taste*. Cambridge. Harvard U. Press.

Boyle, Catherine. 1992. *Chilean Theater 1973-1985. Marginality, Power, Selfhood*. London. Associated U. Press.

Breton, André. 1936. *What is Surrealism?* London, Faber and Faber.

Brett, Guy. 1992a. "The Limits of Imperviousness." *Third Text*, 18. Spring: 15-25.
____. 1992b. "Venice, Paris, Kassel, Sao Paulo and Havana." *Third Text*, 20. Autumn: 23-32.

Brown, Doug. 1990. Sandinismo and the Problem of Democratic Hegemony." In Chilcote, ed.: 39-61.

Brunner, José Joaquín. 1981. *La cultura autoritaria en Chile*. Santiago. FLACSO.
____. 1987. "Los debates sobre la modernidad y futuro en America Latina." In Martner, ed.
____. 1987. "Notas sobre la modernidad y lo postmoderno en la cultura latinoamericana." *David y Goliat*, 17, 52. Sept.
____. 1990. "6 preguntas a José Joaquín Brunner." Interview conducted by Karin Eitel. *Revista de Crítica Cultural*. May. No. 1. Año 1: 20-25.
Brunner, José Joaquín and Alicia Barrios. 1987. *Inquisición, mercado y filantropía. Ciencias Sociales y autoritarismo en Argentina, Brasil, Chile y Uruguay*. Santiago. FLACSO.
Brunner, José Joaquín, Alicia Barrios and Carlos Catalán. 1989. *Chile, transformaciones culturales y modernidad*. Santiago. FLACSO.
Brunner, José Joaquín and Enrique Gomariz. 1991. *Modernidad y cultura en América Latina*. San José, Costa Rica. FLACSO.

Buck-Morss, Susan. 1989. "The Dialectics of Seeing." Cambridge. MIT Press.

Burchell, Graham, Colin Gordon, Peter Miller. eds. 1991. *The Foucault Effect. Studies in Governmentality: with Two Lectures by and an Interview with Michel Foucault*. Chicago. U. of Chicago Press.

Bürger, Peter. 1983. *Theory of the Avant-Garde*. Mpls. U. of Minnesota Press.
Caffarena, Elena. 1945. *Algo acerca del proyecto de ley sobre el voto femenino*. Santiago. Zig-Zag.
____. 1952. *Un capítulo en la historia del feminismo*. Santiago. MEMCH.

Calderón, Fernando. 1987. "América Latina: Identidad y tiempos mixtos. O como tratar de pensar la modernidad sin dejar de ser indios." *David y Goliath*, 52. Sept. Trans.: Beverley, Oviedo and Arrona, eds.: 55-64.

Calderón, Fernando and José Luis Reyna. 1990. "La irrupción encubierta." *Nuevo Texto Crítico*. Año III. No. 6: 17-30.

Calinescu, Matei. 1987. *Five Faces of Modernity*, Durham. Duke U. Press.

Callinicos, Alex. 1989. *Against Postmodernism: A Marxist Critique*. Cambridge. Polity Press.

Cammack, Paul, David Pool and William Tordoff, eds. 1988. *Third World Politics. A Comparative Introduction*. Baltimore. John Hopkins U. Press.

Canovas, José. 1990. *Memorias de un Magistrado*. Santiago. Emisión.

Carías, Marcos. 1980. *Una función con móbiles y tentetiesos (A Performance With Mobiles and Stick Puppets)*. Tegucigalpa. Editorial Guaymuras.

Carr, Robert. 1992. "Re(-)presentando el testimonio: Notas sobre el cruce divisorio primer mundo/tercer mundo." In Beverley and Achugar, eds.: 73-94.

Carrasco, Eduardo. 1988. *Quilapayún, La revolución y las estrellas*. Santiago. Ornitorrinco.

Cash Molina, Jorge. 1986. *Bosquejo de una historia*. Santiago. Copygraph.

Casanova, Guillermo. 1988 "Mama era punk" (video). Montevideo. CEMA.

Catalán, Carlos, Rafael Guillasasi, Guiselle Munziaga. 1987. *Transformaciones del sistema cultural chileno entre 1920-1973*. Santiago. CENECA. (no. 65).

Catalán, Carlos and Gisselle Munizaga. 1986. *Políticas culturales estatales bajo el autoritarismo en Chile*. Santiago. CENECA no. 79.

Certeau, Michel de. 1984. *The Practice of Everyday Life*. Berkeley. U. of California Press.
Chaui, Marilena. 1986. *Conformismo e resistencia*. Sao Paolo. Editora Brasiliense.
Chilcote, Ronald H. 1990a. "Post-Marxism: The Retreat from Class in Latin America." In Chilcote, ed.: 3-24.
_____. 1990b. "Tensions in the Latin American Experience: Fundamental Themes in the Formulation of a Research Agenda in the 1990s." In Chilcote, ed.: 122-128.

259

Chilcote, Ronald H. ed. 1990. *Post-Marxism, the Left, and Democracy. Latin American Perspectives*. 65, Spring. Vol. 17, no. 2.

Cifuentes, Luis. 1989. *Fragmentos de un Sueño*. Santiago. Logos.

Clifford, James. 1989. *The Predicament of Culture: Twentieth Century Ethnography, Literature, and Art*. Cambridge, MA.: Harvard U. Press.

Clifford, James and Marcus, G., ed. 1986. *Writing Culture: The Poetic and Politics and Ethnography*. Berkeley. U. of California Press.

Colás, Santiago. 1994. *Postmodern Latin America: The Argentine Paradigm*. Durham and London. Duke U. Press.

Collier, P. and H. Ryan. 1990. *Literary Theory Today*. Cambridge. Polity Press.

Collins, Randall. 1992. *Sociological Thought*. Oxford. Oxford U. Press, 2nd edition.

Cornblit, Oscar. 1967. *Inmigrantes y empresarios en la política argentina*, 2da. edición, Doc. de trabajo. Centro de Investigaciones Sociales, Instituto Torcuato Di Tella.

Correa, Raquel, Malú Sierra and Elízabeth Subercaseaux. 1983. *Los generales del régimen*. Santiago. Aconcagua.

Covarrubias, Paz. 1978. "El movimiento feminista Chileno" in *Chile, Mujer y Sociedad*. Santiago. Covarrubias/UNICEF.

Cueva, Agustín. 1989. *América Latina en la frontera de los años 90*. Quito. Planeta.

Dawes, Greg. 1991. "Hacia una reartculación del posmodernismo en América Latina: El caso de la poesía nicaragüense." *Nuevo Texto Crítico*. Año IV. No. 7: 85-109.

_____. 1992. *Asethetics and Revolution: A Historical Materialist Analysis of Nicaraguan Poetry, 1979-1990*. Mpls. U. of Minnesota Press.

De Imaz, José Luis. 1970. *Los que mandan (Those Who Rule)*. Albany, NY. SUNY Press.

Deleuze, Gilles and Félix Guattari. 1987. *A Thousand Plateaus. Capitalism and Schizophrenia*. Mpls. U. of Minnesota Press.

De la Maza, Gonzalo and Mario Garces. 1985. *La explosión de las mayorias. Protesta nacional 1983-1984*. Santiago. Educacion y Comunicaciones.

260

Derrida, Jacques. 1978. *Writing and Difference.* Chicago. U. of Chicago Press.
_____. 1994. *Specters of Marx: The State of the Debt, the Work of Mourning, and the New International.* New York. Routledge.

De Shazo, Peter. 1983. *Urban Workers and Labor Unions in Chile. 1902-1927.* Madison. U. of Wisconsin Press.

Di Tella Torcuato. 1990. *Latin American Politics: A Theoretical Framework.* Austin. U. of Texas Press.

Dinamarca, Manuel. 1987. *La Republica Socialista de Chile: Origenes legítimos del Partido Socialista.* Santiago. Ediciones Documentadas.

Dorfman, Ariel, and Armand Mattelart. 1975. *How to Read Donald Duck: Imperialist Ideology in the Disney Comic.* New York. International General.

Drake, Paul. 1978. *Socialism and Populism in Chile. 1932-1952.* Urbana. U. of Illinois.

Duchesne Winter, Juan. 1992. "Notas sobre neopopulismo, literatura e intelectuales (Respuesta a John Beverley)." *Postdata* 2, 5: 1-15.
Duchesne, Juan, et al. 1997. "La estadidad desde una perspectiva democrática radical: Propuesta de discusión a todo habitante del archipiélago puertorriqueño." *Diálogo.* Febrero: 30-31.

Durham, Jimmie. 1988-89. "Here at the Centre of the World." *Third Text,* 5. Winter: 21-32.
Durham, Jimmie and Jean Fisher. 1988. "The Ground Has Been Covered." *Artforum.* Summer: 99-105.

Dussel, Enrique. 1990. "Marx's Economic Manuscripts of 1861-63 and the 'Concept' of Dependency." In Chilcote, ed.: 62-101.

Eagleton, Terry. 1983 *Literary Theory: An Introduction.* Mpls. U. of Minnesota Press.
_____. 1988. *Nationalism, Colonialism, and Literature: Nationalism, Irony and Commitment.* Derry, Northern Ireland. Field Day Theatre Co.
_____. 1991. *Ideology.* New York. Verso.

Echevarría, José, Susana Regent and Jorge Ruetalo. 1987. "Reflexiones acerca del espacio juvenil barrial." *Participación* #6. February.

Escobar, Arturo. 1984. "Discourse and Power in Development: Michel Foucault and the Relevance of his Work to the Third World." *Alternatives* 10, no. 3: 377-400.
_____. 1992. "Imagining a Post-Development Era? Critical Thought, Development and Social Movements." *Social Text* 31/33 (1992): 20-56.

Escobar, Arturo, and Sonia E. Alvarez, eds. 1992. *The Making of Social Movements in Latin America: Identity, Strategy, and Democracy*. Boulder, Colorado. Westview Press.

Escobar, Elizam. 1988. "Havana Biennial and Art in Latin America." *Panic*. 3: 25-38.
_____. 1991a. "The Empty Coffin of 'Post-Modernism'" in Elizam, ed.: 25-82.
_____. 1991b. "International Art, Yes, But No Imperialism, Please!" In Elizam, ed.: 13-22.
_____. 1995. "La batalla fingida: econarcisismo o transfixión." In Rivera and Gil, eds.: 387-418.
Escobar, Elizam, and the Axe Street Arena Collective, ed. 1991. *Disparities and Connections: The Excluded on Postmodernism*. Chicago. Axe Street Arena.

Escobar, Ticio. 1992. Identity and Myth Today." *Third Text*, 20. Autumn: 23-32.

Evans, Peter. 1979. *Dependent Development: The Alliance of Multinational, State and Local Capital in Brazil*. Princeton, Princeton U. Press.

Falcoff, Mark. 1989. *Modern Chile 1970-1989: A Critical History*. New Jersey. Transaction Publishers.

Featherstone, Mike, ed. 1990. *Global Culture: Nationalism, Globalization and Modernity*. London. Sage Publications.
Featherstone, Mike, Scott Lash and Roland Robertson, eds. 1995. *Global Modernities*. London. Sage Publications.

Fergusson, Russell, Martha Gever, Trinh T. Minh-ha and Cornell West, eds. 1990. *Out There: Marginalization and Contemporary Cultures*. New York and Cambridge. New Museum of Contemporary Art and MIT Press.

Ferman, Claudia. 1993. Paper on Arturo Arias, *Itzam na*, presented at First International Congress of Central American Literature. Granada, Nicaragua. Feb..
_____. 1994. *Política y postmodernidad: Hacia una lectura de la anti-modernidad en Latinoamérica*. Buenos Aires. Editorial Almagesto.
Ferman, Claudia, ed. 1996. *The Postmodern in Latin and Latino American Cultural Narratives: Collected Essays and Interviews*. New York and London. Garland Publishing Company.

Fernández Retamar, Roberto. 1979. *Calibán y otros ensayos (Nuestra América y el mundo)*. La Habana. Editorial Arte y Literatura.
_____. 1989. *Caliban and Other Essays*. Mpls. U. of Minnesota Press.

Fish, Stanley. 1980. *Is There a Text in this Class?: The Authority of Interpretive Communities*. Cambridge, Mass. Harvard U. Press.

Fleet, Michael. 1985. *The Rise and Fall of Chilean Christian Democracy*. Princeton. Princeton U. Press.

Flores, Juan. 1992. *Divided Borders*. Houston, TX. Arte Público Press.
Flores, Juan and George Yúdice. 1992. "Living Borders/Buscando América: Languages of Latino Self Formation." In Flores: 127-146??

Fokkema, Douwe and Bertens, Hans, eds. 1986. *Approaching Postmodernism*. Amsterdam and Philadelphia. John Benjamins.

Fontaine-Aldunate, Arturo. 1988. *Los economistas y el Presidente Pinochet*. Santiago. Zig-Zag.

Foster, Hal, ed. *1983. The Anti-Aesthetic: Essays in Postmodern Culture*. Port Townsend, Wash. Bay Press.

Foucault, Michel. 1971. *The Order of Things: An archeology of the human sciences*. New York. Penguin Books.
_____. 1973. *Madness and Civilization: A History of Insanity in the Age of Reason*. New York. Random House.
_____. 1984. "Des Espaces Autres." *Architecture-Movement-Continuité*. 73. October: 6-9.
_____. 1985-86. "Other Spaces: Principles of Heterotopia." In *Lotus International*. 48/49: 9-17.
_____. 1986. "Of Other Spaces." *Diacritics* 16:1. Spring: 76-84.
Foxley, Alejandro. 1988. *Chile puede más*. Santiago. Planeta.

Franco, Jean. 1989. *Plotting Women: Gender and Representation in Mexico*. New York. Columbia U. Press.
_____. 1990. "Contemporary Latin American Fin de siécle." *Studies in 20th Century Literature*. 14, 1. Winter: 5-7.
_____. 1992. "Going Public: Reinhabiting The Public." In Yúdice, George, Jean Franco and Juan Flores, ed.: 65-84.

Freud, Sigmund. 1974. "The 'Uncanny.'" *Standard Edition*. XVII. J. Strachey, ed. London: Hogarth Press.

Frank, André Gunder. 1972. *Lumpenbourgeoisie; Lumpendevelopment: Dependence, Class, and Politics in Latin America.* New York. Monthly Review Press.

Fuentes, Carlos. 1969. *La nueva novela hispanoamericana.* Mexico. J. Mortiz.

Fuentes, Víctor. 1990. "Deslindes sobre el posmodernismo hispánico." *Claridad.* Feb. 23-marzo 1: 17; abril 6-12: 20-21.

Fukuyama, Francis. 1992. *End of History and the Last Man.* New York. Free Press.

Furci, Carmelo. 1984. *The Chilean Communist Party and the Road to Socialism.* London. Zed Books Inc.

Furtado, Celso. 1972. *Breve historia económica de América Latina. La Habana.* Editorial de Ciencias Sociales, Instituto Cubano del Libro.

Fusco, Coco. 1988. Signs of Transition: 80's Art From Cuba." In Fusco, ed. 1988: 1-5.
_____. 1994. "The Other History of Intercultural Performance." *The Drama Review.* 38,1 (T141). Spring: 143-167.
Fusco, Coco, ed. 1988. *Signs of Transition Exhibition Catalogue.* New York. Museum of Contemporary Hispanic Art.

García Canclini, Néstor. 1984. "Gramsci con Bourdieu," in *Nueva Sociedad,* 71: 62-78.
_____. 1988. *La producción simbólica. Teoría y método en sociología del arte.* 4th edition. Mexico. Siglo XXI.
_____. 1990. *Culturas híbridas: Estratégias para entrar y salir de la modernidad.* México. DGP-CNCA/Grijalbo.
_____. 1991. "¿Qué nos queda de Gramsci?" *Nueva Sociedad.* Caracas. Sept.-Nov.
_____. 1992. "Museums, Airports and Garage Sales: Identity and NAFTA." Paper presented at the Borders/Diaspora Conference organized by the U. of California-Santa Cruz, April 3-5.
_____. 1995a. *Hybrid Cultures: Strategies for Entering and Leaving Modernity.* Mpls. U. of Minnesota Press.
_____. 1995b. *Consumidores y ciudadanos: Conflictos multiculturales de la globalización.* México. Grijalbo.
García Canclini, Néstor, ed. 1996. *Culturas en globalización. América Latina--Europa--Estados Unidos: libre comercio e integración.* Caracas. Nueva Sociedad.
García Canclini, Néstor and Patricia Safa. 1989. *Tijuana: La casa de toda la gente.* INAH-ENAH. Programa Cultural de las Fronteras. UAM-Iztapalapa/CONACULTA.
García Márquez, Gabriel. 1976. "Ramírez Amaya, cazador de gorilas." In Ramírez Amaya, ed.: 22-31.

264

Garretón, Manuel Antonio. 1984. *Dictadura y democratización en Chile*. Santiago. FLACSO.
____. 1987. *Reconstruir la política. Transición y consolidación democrática en Chile*. Santiago. Andante.
____. 1989. *Propuestas políticas y demandas sociales*. Santiago. FLACSO.
Garretón, Manuel Antonio and Tomás Moulián. 1983. *La Unidad Popular y el conflicto político en Chile*. Santiago. Minga.

Gertz, Clifford. 1983. *Local Knowledge. Further Essays in Interpretative Anthropology*. New York. Basic Books.

Giddens, Anthony. 1990. *The Consequences of Modernity*. Cambridge, England. Polity Press.

Gil, Carlos. 1995. "Elizam Escobar o la pérdida de la utopía (Reflexiones en torno a un sentimiento plano). In Rivera Nieves, Gil, eds.: 237-244.

Goldman, Shifra. 1994. *Dimensions of the Americas: Art and Social Change in Latin America and the United States*. Chicago. U. of Chicago Press.

Gómez-Peña, Guillermo. 1987. "Wacha ese border, son." *La Jornada Semanal*. 162. 25 de octubre: 23-24.
____. 1990. "Death on the Border: A Eulogy to Border Art. *High Performance*. Vol. 14, no. 1. Spring: 8-9 (Trans. of Gómez-Peña ____. 1987).
____. 1991. "On Nationality." *Art in America*. Sept.: 124-131.
____. 1992. "The New World (B)order." *High Performance*. Vol. 15, no. 2-3. Fall: 58-65. Republished in Gómez-Peña 1996.
____. 1993. *Warrior of Gringostroika*. St. Paul, MN. Gray Wolf Press.
____. 1996. *The New World Border*. San Francisco. City Lights Books.

Gómez-Quiñones, Juan. 1982. "On Culture," in Kanellos, Nicolás, ed.: 290-308.

Gugelburger, Georg, ed. 1996. *The Real Thing: Testimonial Discourse and Latin America*. Durham, NC. Duke U. Press.

Guha, Ranajit. 1988. "On Some Aspects of the Historiography of Colonial India." In Guha and Spivak: 37-44.
____. 1992. *Elementary Aspects of Peasant Insurgency in Colonial India*. Delhi. Oxford U. Press. (first publication, 1983)
Guha, Ranajit and Gayatri Chakravorty Spivak, ed. 1988. *Selected Subaltern Studies*. New York. Oxford U. Press.

Habermas, Jürgen. 1983. "Modernity--An Incomplete Project." In Foster: 3-15.
_____. 1988. "Modernidad versus postmodernidad." In Pico, ed.: 87-103.
_____. 1990. *The Philosophical Discourse of Modernity*. Cambridge, Mass. MIT Press.

Halebsky, Sandor and Richard L. Harris, eds. 1995. *Capital, Power, and Inequality in Latin America*. Boulder. Westview Press.

Hales Dib, Jaime. 1986. *Los caminos de Chile*. Santiago. Emisión.

Hall, Stuart. 1986. "On Postmodernism and Articulation. An Interview with Stuart Hall," ed. Lawrence Grossberg. *Journal of Communication Inquiry*. 10, 2: 45-60.

Harrington, E. and M. González. 1987. *Bomba en una calle de Palermo*. Santiago. Emisión.

Harstock, Nancy. 1987. "Rethinking Modernism: Minority vs. Majority Theories." *Cultural Critique*. 7. Fall: 187-206.
1991. "Louis Althusser's Structural Marxism: Political Clarity and Theoretical Distortions." *Rethinking Marxism*. Winter: 10-40.

Harvey, David. 1989. *The Condition of Postmodernity*. Oxford. Basil Blackwell.

Hassan, Ihab. 1987. *The Postmodern Turn: Essays in Postmodern Theory and Culture*. Columbus, Ohio. Ohio U. Press.

Heartney, Eleanor. 1988 "Charlatan or Savior: Julian Schnabel at the Whitney." *New Art Examiner*. March: 30-32.

Henríquez Ureña, Pedro. 1976. *La utopía de América*. Caracas. Biblioteca Ayacucho.

Herlinghaus, Hermann and Monika Walter, eds. 1994. *Posmodernidad en la perferia: Enfoques latinoamericanos de la nueva teoría cultural*. Berlin. Langer Verlag.

Hicks, Emily. 1992. *Border Writing*. Mpls. U. of Minnesota Press.

Hobsbawm, Eric. 1959. *Primitive Rebels: Studies in Anarchic Forms of Social Movements in the 19th and 20th Centuries*. Manchester, England. Manchester U. Press.

Huidobro, Vicente. 1978. *Altazor*. Santiago. Editorial Nacimiento.
_____. 1988. *Ecuatorial*. [Bilingual edition, trans. Eliot Weinberger]. St. Paul. Gray Wolf Press.

266

Husband, Bertha. 1997. "La obra de Diana Solís." *Zorros y Erizos*. Núm. 1. Junio 15: 16-17.

Hutcheon, Linda. 1988. *A Poetics of Postmodernism*. New York. Routledge.

Inselmann, Andrea. 1997. Introduction. *Silvia Malagrino Between Times--Between Worlds*. [Exhibition Catalogue]. Sheboygan, Wisconsin. John Michael Kohler Arts Center.

Jackson, Michael. 1994. "Phenomenology, Radical Empiricism, and Anthropological Critique." Unpublished. Indiana U. Bloomington, Indiana.

Jameson, Fredric. 1984. "Postmodernism, or the Cultural Logic of Late Capitalism." *New Left Review* 146: 59-92.
_____. 1987. "Third World Literature in the Era of Multinational Capitalism." *Social Text*, 15: 65-88.
_____. 1987. "A Brief Response." *Social Text* 17: 26.
_____. 1988. "Cognitive Mapping." In Nelson and Grossberg, ed.: 347-357.
_____. 1989. "Foreward." Fernández Retamar: ii-xii.
_____. 1991. *Postmodernism, or the Cultural Logic of Late Capitalism*. Durham, NC. Duke U. Press.
_____. 1992. "De la sustitución de importaciones literarias y culturales en el tercer mundo: El caso del testimonio." In Beverley and Achugar: 117-133. Translated and published in Gugelburger, ed. 1997: 172-191.
_____. 1995. "'End of Art' or 'End of History'?" Plenary Session. MMLA Convention. Saint Louis. Fall 1995. n.p.

Jara, Joan. 1984. *An Unfinished Song. The Life of Victor Jara*. New York. Ticknor and Fields.

Kafka Franz. 1979. *Collected Short Stories*. New York. Random House.

Kanellos, Nicolás, ed. 1982. *A Decade of Hispanic Literature: An Anniversary Anthology*. Houston. Arte Público Press.

Keen, Benjamin and Dale Wasserman. 1988. *A History of Latin America*. 3rd edition. Geneva, Illinois. Houghton Mifflin Co.

King, Anthony D., ed. 1991 *Culture, Globalization and the World System: Contemporary Conditions for the Representation of Identity*. London. Macmillan.
King, John. 1985. *El Di Tella*. Buenos Aires. Ediciones de Arte Gaglianone.

Kirkwood, Julieta. 1986. *Ser política en Chile*. Santiago. Cuarto Propio.

Kojeve, Alexandre. 1994. *The Roots of Post Modern Politics.* New York. St. Martin's Press.

Kroeber, A.L. 1962. *Anthropology: Race, Language, Culture, Psychology.* New York. Harcourt, Brace.

Labarca, Amanda. 1974. *Feminismo contemporaneo.* Santiago. Zig-Zag.

Laclau, Ernesto. 1971. "Feudalism and Capitalism in Latin America." *New Left Review* 67. May-June: 19-38.
_____. 1977. *Politics and Ideology in Marxist Theory.* London. New Left Books.
Laclau, Ernesto and Chantal Mouffe. 1985. *Hegemony and Socialist Strategy: Towards a Radical Democratic Politics.* London. Verso.

Larsen, Neil. 1990. "Posmodernismo e imperialismo: teoría y política en Latinoamérica." *Nuevo Texto Crítico.* Año III. No. 6: 77-94.
_____. 1995. *Writing North by South: On Latin American Literature, Culture and Politics.* U. of Minnesota Press.

Latin American Subaltern Studies Group. 1995. "Founding Statement." In Beverley, Oviedo and Aronna: 135-146.

Lavín, Joaquín. 1987. *Chile, Revolución silenciosa.* Santiago. Zig-Zag.

Lethen, Helmut. 1986. "Modernism Cut in Half: The Exclusion of the Avant garde and the Debate on Postmodernism." In Fokkema and Bertens: 233-238.

Linz, John, Alfred Stepan, ed. 1986. *The Breakdown of Democratic Regimes.* Baltimore. John Hopkins U. Press.

Lión Díaz, Luis de. 1970. *Su segunda muerte.* Guatemala. Nuevo Signo Ediciones.
_____. *1985a. Pájaro en mano.* Certámen Permanente. Guatemala. Ed. Serviprensa Centroamericana.
_____. 1985b. *El tiempo principia en Xibalbá.* Guatemala. Ed. Serviprensa Centroamericana.

López, Sebastián. 1992. "Identity: Reality or Fiction?" *Third Text,* 18. Spring: 7-13.

Lowenthal, Abraham (ed). 1991. *Exporting Democracy. The United States and Latin America.* Baltimore. John Hopkins U. Press.

Lyotard, Jean-François. 1984. *The Postmodern Condition. A Report on Knowledge.* Mpls. U. of Minnesota Press.

268

_____. _1991. Economie libidinale._ Paris. Minuit.

Machin, Horacio. 1991. "Conversación con Fredric Jameson." _Nuevo Texto Crítico_ 7: 3-18.

McCabe, Colin. 1987. Foreward. Spivak: ix-xix

Maira, Luis. 1988. _La Constitución de 1980 y la ruptura democrática._ Santiago. Emisión.

Malloy, James and Mitchell Selligson. 1985. _Authoritarians and Democrats, Regime Transition in Latin America._ Pittsburgh. U. of Pittsburgh Press.

Mandel, Ernest. 1987. _Late Capitalism._ London. Verso.

Marcuse, Herbert. 1978. _The Aesthetic Dimension: Toward a Critique of Marxist Aesthetics._ Boston. Beacon.

Marras, Sergio. 1988. _Confesiones._ Santiago. Onitorrico.

Martín[-]Barbero, Jesús. . 1984. _Cultura popular y comunicación de masas._ Lima. Materiales para la comunicación popular 3.
_____. 1987a. _De los medios a las mediaciones._ México. Gustavo Gili. Translated as _Communication, Culture and Hegemony: From the Media to Mediations._ London, Newbury Park and New Delhi. Sage Publications. 1993.
_____. 1987b. _Procesos de comunicación y matrices de cultura. Itinerario para salir de la razón dualista._ México [Lima]. G. Gili.

Martner, Gonzalo, ed. 1964. _Diseños para el cambio._ Caracas. Nueva Sociedad.

Marx, Karl. 1964. _The Economic and Philosophic Manuscripts of 1844._ Edited/Introduction by Dirk J. Struik. New York. International Publishers Co., Inc.

McCafferty, Larry, ed. 1986. _Postmodern Fiction: A Bio-Bibliographical Guide._ Westport, Conn. Greenwood Press.

McClintock, Cynthia and Abraham Lowenthal, ed. 1983. _Exporting Democracy. The United States and Latin America._ Princenton. Princeton U. Press.

McNay, Lois. 1992. "The Problems of the Self in Foucault's Ethics of the Self." _Third Text_, 19. Summer: 3-8.

Mattelart, Armand. 1974. *La cultura como empresa multinacional.* México. Ediciones ERA.

Mattelart, Armand and Michele Mattelart. 1992. *Rethinking Media Theory: Signposts and New Directions.* Mpls. U. of Minnesota Press.

Morales, Mario Roberto. 1994. *Lords under the Trees* (Señores bajo los arboles). Guatemala. Artemis y Edinter.

Morandé, Pedro. 1984. *Cultura y modernización en América Latina.* Santiago. Universidad Católica de Chile.

Morris, Meaghan. 1988. "Tooth and Claw: Tales of Survival and Crocodile Dundee." In Ross, ed.: 105-127.

Morris, Nancy. 1984. *Canto porque es necesario cantar: The New Song Movement in Chile, 1973-1983.* Research Paper Series No. 16. Albuquerque. Latin American Institute, The U. of New Mexico.

Mosquera, Geraldo. 1992. "The Marco Polo Syndrome: Some Problems Concerning Art and Eurocentrism." Unpublished.

Moulián, Tomás. 1988. *La democracia difícil: Dificultades y dilemas actuales.* Santiago. FLACSO.

Moulián, Tomás and Isabel Torres. 1987. *Discusiones entre honorables. Las candidaturas presidenciales de la derecha, 1938-1946.* Santiago. FLACSO.

Muñoz, Oscar, ed. 1990. *Transición a la democracia. Marco político y económico.* Santiago. CIEPLAN.

Negri, Antonio. 1989. *The Politics of Subversion: A Manifesto for the Twentieth Century.* Cambridge, Mass. Polity Press.

Nelson, Cary and Lawrence Grossberg, eds. 1988. *Marxism and the Interpretation of Culture.* Chicago. U. of Illinois Press.

Newsweek Editor. 1988. "Pinochet's Chile: Eight More Years?". *Newsweek.* no. 39. September.

Norman, Richard and Sean Sayers. 1980. *Hegel, Marx and Dialectic: A Debate.* Brighton, Sussex. Harvester Press.

Norris, Christopher. 1990. *What's Wrong with Postmodernism: Critical Theory and the Ends of Philosophy.* Hemel Hemsptead. Harvester-Wheatsheaf and Polity Press.

270

_____. 1992. *Uncritical Theory: Postmodernism, Intellectuals and the Gulf War.* Amherst, Mass. U. of Massachusetts Press.

Nunn, Frederick. 1976. *The Military in Chilean History.* Albuquerque. U. of New Mexico.

Oboler, Suzanne. 1995. *Ethnic Labels/ Latino Lives.* U. of Minnesota Press.

O'Brien, Philip. 1983. *Chile: The Pinochet Decade. The Rise and Fall of the Chicago Boys.* London. Latin American Bureau.
O'Brien, Philip and Paul Cammack, ed. 1985. *Generals in Retreat. The Crisis of Military Rule in Latin America.* Manchester. Manchester U. Press.

O'Donnell, Guillermo, Philippe C. Schmitter and Laurence Whitehead, ed. 1986. *Transitions from Authoritarian Rule. Prospects for Democracy.* Baltimore. John Hopkins U. Press.

Olalquiaga, Celeste. 1992. *Megalopolis: Contemporary Cultural Sensibilities.* Mpls. U. of Minnesota Press.
Ortega, Julio. 1990. "Perú: Hacia una democracia radical." *Revista de Crítica Cultural.* May. No. 1. Año 1: 26-27.

Papastergiadis, Nikos. 1992. "The Act of Approaching: Conversation with John Berger." *Third Text,* 19. Summer: 87-95.

Paz, Octavio. 1991. "Poetry and the Free Market." *The New York Times Book Review.* December 8: 1-38.

_____. 1992. *The Other Voice: Essays on Modern Poetry.* San Diego. Harcourt Brace and Jovanovich.

Peeler, John. 1985. *Latin American Democracies. Colombia, Costa Rica, Venezuela.* Chapel Hill. U. of North Carolina Press.

Perus, Françoise. 1991. "García Canclini. *Culturas híbridas.*" Review. *Nuevo Texto Crítico.* Año IV. no. 8: 217-220.

Petras, James. 1990. "The Metamorphosis of Latin America's Intellectuals." In Chilcote, ed.: 102-112.

Pico, Josep, ed. 1988 *Modernidad y postmodernidad.* Madrid. Alianza Editorial.

271

Pinochet, Augusto. 1979. *El día decisivo*. Santiago. Editorial Andrés Bello.
____. 1983. *Política, politiquería y demagogía*. Santiago. Renacimiento.

Pollack, Bebby and Hernán Rosenkranz. 1986. *Revolutionary Social Democracy: The Chilean Socialist Party*. London. Frances Pinter.

Ponce Molina, Homero. 1986. *Historia del movimiento asociativo laboral chileno*. Primer Tomo 1838-1973. Santiago. Alba.

Price, Richard and Sally Price. 1992. *Ecuatoria*. London. Routledge.

Prisioneros, Los. 1986. "El baile de los que sobran". Song in recording, *Pateando piedras*. Santiago. Emi Odeon.

Quintanilla, Raúl. 1992. "A Suspended Dialogue: The Nicaraguan Revolution and the Visual Arts." Unpublished.

Rama, Angel. 1989. *La narrativa latinoamericana*. Montevideo. Fundación Rama.

Ramírez Amaya, Arnoldo, ed. 1976. *Sobre la libertad, el dictador y sus perros fieles*. México. Siglo XXI.

Rice, Philip and Patricia Waugh, eds. 1992. *Modern Literary Theory: A Reader*. London. Arnold.

Richard, Nelly. 1987. "Postmodernism and Periphery." *Third Text*, 2. Winter: 5-12.
____. 1988. *La estratificación de los márgenes*. Santiago. Francisco Zegers, Editor S.A.
____. 1990. "De la rebeldía anarquizante al desmontaje ideológico (crítica y poder)." *Revista de Crítica Cultural*, 2. Mayo: 6-8.
____. 1991. "Latinoamérica y la Postmodernidad." *Revista de Crítica Cultural*, 3. Año 2. Abril: 15-19.
____. 1994. *La insubordinación de los signos (Cambio político, transformaciones culturales y poéticas de la crisis)*. Santiago. Editorial Cuarto Propio.

Rivera Nieves, Irma. 1995. "Glissando a manera de prólogo." In Rivera and Gil, eds.: 17-41.
Rivera Nieves, Irma and Carlos Gil, eds. 1995. *Polifonía salvaje. Ensayos de cultura y política en la postmodernidad*. San Juan, Puerto Rico. Editorial Postdata.

Robertson, Roland. 1992. *Globalization, Social Theory and Global Culture*. London. Sage.

Rorty, Richard. 1979 *Philosophy and the Mirror of Nature*. Princeton, NJ. Princeton U. Press.

Ross, Andrew. 1988. *Universal Abandon? The Politics of Postmodernism*. Mpls. U. of Minnesota Press.

Rowe, William and Vivian Schelling. 1991. *Memory and Modernity: Popular Culture in Latin America*. New York. Verso.

Roxborough, Ian; Philip O'Brien and Jackie Roddick. 1977. *Chile, The State and Revolution*. London. MacMillan Press.

Ruffinelli, Jorge. 1990. "Los 80: ¿Ingreso a la posmodernidad?" in Ruffinelli, ed. no. 6: 31-42.
Ruffinelli, Jorge, ed. 1990. *Nuevo Texto Crítico*. Año III no. 6 y 7. *Modernidad y posmodernidad en América Latina* (I y II)

Rush, Alan, ed. 1995. *Posmodernidad y Latinoamérica*. San Miguel de Tucumán, Argentina. Instituto Interdisciplinario de Estudios Latinoamericanos.

Said, Edward. 1989. "Representing the Colonized." *Critic Inquiry*, vol. 15, no. 2. Winter: 222-235.
_____. 1990. "Reflections on Exile." In Fergusson, et al.: 327-365.

Sandoval, Chela. 1991 *U.S. Third World Feminism: The Theory and Method of Oppositional Consciousness in the Postmodern World*. *Genders*. 10. Spring: 1-24.

Sarlo, Beatriz. 1988. *Una modernidad periférica: Buenos Aires 1920-1960*. Buenos Aires. Ediciones Nueva Visión.
_____. 1990. "Basuras culturales, simulacros políticos." *Revista de Crítica Cultural*. 2. Octubre: 21-25.
_____. 1994. *Escenas de la vida posmoderna: Intelectuales, arte y videocultura en la Argentina*. Buenos Aires. Ariel.
_____. 1995. "Aesthetics and Post-Politics: From Fujimori to the Gulf War." In Beverley, Oviedo and Aronna, eds.: 250-263.

Saveter, Fernando. 1992. *Ensayo sobre Cioran*. Madrid. Espasa Calpe.

Schiller, Herbert. 1969. *Mass Communications and American Empire*. New York. A. M. Kelly.

Schiller, Nina Glick, Linda Basch, and Cristina Banc Szanton. 1992. "Towards a Definition of Transnationalism: Introductory Remarks and Research Questions." *Annals of the NY Academy of Sciences*, Vol. 645, July 6, ix-xv.

Schwarz, Roberto. 1992. *Misplaced Ideas*. London. Verso.

Silén, Iván. 1992a. "Los ciudadanos de la morgue." (unpublished).
____. 1992b. "The Citizens of the Phantom Country." *Left Curve*. 16: 43-52.

Silva, Patricio. 1991. "From the Chicago Boys to the CIEPLAN monks." *Journal of Latin American Studies*, 23: 385-410.

Smith, Carol A. 1984. "Local History in Global Context: Social and Economic Transitions in Western Guatemala." *Comparative Studies in Society and History*, 26, 2: 193-228.
____. 1990. "Conclusion: History and Revolution in Guatemala." In Smith, ed.: 258-285.

Smith, Carol A., ed. 1990. *Guatemalan Indians and the State: 1540 to 1988*. Austin. U. of Texas Press.

Smyth, John Vignaux. 1983. *A Question of Eros: Irony in Sterne, Kierkegaard and Barthes*. Tallahassee. Florida State U. Press.

Soja, Edward. 1990. *Postmodern Geographies; The Reassertion of Space in Critical Social Theory*. New York. Verso.

Sommer, Doris. 1991. *Foundational Fictions*. Berkeley. U. of California Press
Sommer, Doris and George Yúdice. 1986. "Latin American Literature from the 'Boom' On." In McCaffery, ed. 189-214.

Somerville, Siobhan. 1996. "Introduction" to *Silvia A. Malagrino. Testimony: Inscriptions from the War Zone*. [Exhibition Catalogue]. Woodstock, NY. The Center for New Photography at Woodstock.

Speaks, Michael. 1989. "Chaos, Simulation and Corporate Culture. *Mississippi Review*. 49/50 (1989): 159-76.

Spivak, Gayatri Chakravorty. 1988a. *In Other Worlds: Essays in Cultural Politics*. New York and London. Routledge.
____. 1988b. "Can the Subaltern Speak?" *Marxism and the Interpretation of Culture*. Ed. Cary Nelson and Lawrence Grossberg. Chicago. U. of Illinois Press. 271-313.

_____. 1992. "Asked to Talk About Myself." *Third Text*, 19. Summer: 9-18.

Stavins, Ilan. 1995. *The Hispanic Condition: Reflections on Culture and Identity in America*. New York. HarperCollins Publishers.

Stepan, Alfred. 1988. *Rethinking Military Politics. Brazil and the Southern Cone*. Princeton. Princeton U. Press.

Subercaseaux, Bernardo. 1984. *Notas sobre autoritarismo y lectura en Chile*. Santiago. CENECA.
_____. 1985a. *La industria editorial y el libro en Chile*. Santiago. CENECA.
_____. 1985b *Sobre cultura popular. Itinerario de concepciones operantes*. Santiago. CENECA.
_____. 1987. "La apropiación cultural en el pensamiento latinoamericano." *Mundo* 1, 3 (verano).
_____. 1988. *Fin de siglo. La época de Balmaceda*. Santiago. Aconcagua.

Taussig, Michael. 1980. *The Devil and Commodity Fetishism*. Chapel Hill. U. of North Carolina Press.

Third Text Editors. 1992. Editorial. *Third Text*, 18. Spring: 3-5.

Tulchin, Joseph and Augusto Varas (ed). 1991. *From Dictatorship to Democracy. Rebuilding Political Consensus in Chile*. Boulder. Lynne Reiner Publishers.
Tupper, Patricio, ed. 1987. *89/90 Opciones políticas en Chile*. Santiago. Colchagua.

Urzua, Germán. 1987. *La democracia práctica. Los gobiernos radicales*. Santiago. CIEDES.

Valdes, Teresa. 1988. *Venid, benditas de mi padre. Las pobladoras, sus rutinas, sus sueños*. Santiago. FLACSO.

Valdes, Juan Gabriel. 1989. *La escuela de Chicago. Operación Chile*. Buenos Aires. ZETA.
Valdes, Juan Gabriel, ed. 1989. *La campaña del no vista por sus creadores*. Santiago. CIS.

Valenzuela, J. Samuel and Arturo Valenzuela, ed. 1986. *Military Rule in Chile*. Baltimore. John Hopkins U. Press.

Varas, Augusto. 1985. *Militarization and the International Arms Race in Latin America*. Boulder. West View Press.

_____. 1989. *Democracy Under Siege: New Military Power in Latin America*. New York. Greenwood Press.

Varas, Augusto, ed.

_____. 1989b. *Hemispheric Security and the U.S. Policy in Latin America*. Boulder. West View Press.

Vasconi, Tomás A. 1992. "Democracy and Socialism in South America." In Chilcote, ed.: 25-38.

Venturi, Juan Carlos. 1991. "Una Aproximación crítica al posmodernismo. Escalera hacia ninguna parte." *Brecha*, November 15: 22-35.

_____. 1991-92. "Posmodernismo: Escalera hacia ninguna parte." *Claridad*. Dic. 13-19: 35; dic. 20-26: 33; dic. 27-enero 2: 37.

Verdesio, Gustavo. 1987. "Sobre el Rock Nacional." *Participación*, no. 22. Montevideo. Foro juvenil.

Vergara, Marta. 1974. *Memorias de una mujer irreverente*. Santiago. Mistral.

Vergara, Pilar. 1985. *Auge y caída del neoliberalismo en Chile*. Santiago. FLACSO.

_____. 1990. *Políticas hacia la extrema pobreza en Chile. 1973-1988*. Santiago. FLACSO.

Vidal, Hernán. 1991. *Dictadura militar. Trauma social e inauguración de la sociología en Chile*. Mpls. Institute for the Study of Ideologies and Literature.

_____. 1992. "La representación de tensiones culturales post-traumáticas durante la transición a la democracia en Chile. Postmodernismo y neovanguardismo." Variant version published as "Postmodernism, Postleftism, and Neo-Avant-Gardism: The Case of Chile's *Revista de Crítica Cultural*. Trans. in Beverley, Oviedo and Arrona, eds. 1995: 282-306.

Vodanovic, Hernán. 1988. *Un socialismo renovado para Chile*. Santiago. Andante.

Wallerstein, Immanuel. 1974-89. *The Modern World System*. Vols. 1-3. New York. Academic Press.

_____. 1991. *Geopolitics and Geoculture*. Essays on the Changing World-System. London. Cambridge University Press. Paris. Editions de la Maison des Sciences de L'Homme.

Welchman, John C., ed. 1996. *Rethinking Borders*. Mpls. U. of Minnesota Press.

276

Williams, Raymond Leslie. 1995. *The Postmodern Novel in Latin America: Politics, Culture, and the Crisis of Truth*. New York. St. Martin's Press.

Wittig, Monique. 1984. "The Trojan Horse." (photocopy).

Wood, Ellen Meiksins. 1986. *The Retreat from Class: A New "True" Socialism*. London. Verso.

Workshop on Postmodernism. 1986. *Approaching Postmodernism: Papers presented at a Workshop on Postmodernism; 21-23 September 1986*. Amsterdam. Benjamins.

Yúdice, George. 1985. "Central American Testimonial." Unpublished. Recast and published as "Testimonio and Postmodernism." Voices of the Voiceless in Testimonial Literature, I. Special issue of Latin American Perspectives. Issue 70. Vol. 18, no. 3. Summer 1991: 15-31. Republished in Gugelberger, ed.:42-57.
____. 1991. "El conflicto de posmodernidades." *Nuevo Texto Crítico*. Año IV. no. 7.
____. 1992a. "Postmodernity and Transnational Capitalism in Latin America." In Yúdice, Franco and Flores: 1-28.
____. 1992b. "We Are *Not* the World." *Social Text* 31/32: 202-216.
Yúdice, George, Jean Franco and Juan Flores. 1992. "Introduction." In Yúdice, Franco and Flores, eds.: vii-xiv.
Yúdice, George, Jean Franco and Juan Flores, eds. 1992. *On Edge: The Crisis of Contemporary Latin American Culture*. Mpls. U. of Minnesota Press.

Zeitlin, Maurice and Richard Earl Ratcliff. 1988. *Landlords and Capitals, the Dominant Class of Chile*. Princeton. Princeton U. Press.

Zimmerman, Marc. 1992a. "Orientaciones de la cultura popular latinoamericana: Calibán en la edad de Laclau, Mouffe y Gorbachev." *Calibán en Sassari: Por una redefinición de la imágen de América Latina en vísperas de 1992. Homenaje a Roberto Fernández Retamar*, Hernán Loyola, coordinador. *Nuevo Texto Crítico* Spanish Dept., Stanford U. 9 y 10. Enero-Dic.: 271-297.
____. 1992b. *U.S. Latino Literature: An Essay and Annotated Bibliography*. Chicago. MARCH/Abrazo Press.
____. 1995. *Literature and Resistance in Guatemala: Textual Modes and Cultural Politics from El Señor Presidente to Rigoberta Menchú*. Athens. Ohio U. Press.
____. 1998. *Tropicalizing Hegemony: Latin American Culture and Literature in Transnational Context*. Roman and Littlefield.

NOTES ON THE CONTRIBUTORS

A prize-winning Uruguayan poet and critic/theorist, **Hugo Achugar** has published innumerable books including literary studies of Donoso, Uruguayan modernism and testimonio, as well as Latin American and Uruguayan postmodernity (see our Bibliography for some of his recent texts). He holds his Ph.D. from the University of Pittsburgh and is former Full Professor of Latin American Literature at Northwestern University; he currently teaches in his native country, which he represents at innumerable conferences and in numerous publications dealing with the cultural implications of neo-liberalism and MERCOSUR.

Arturo Arias, novelist and literary critic, is a native of Guatemala. Born in 1950, he earned a Ph.D. in the Sociology of Literature from the Université de Paris; and he is currently Professor of Humanities at San Francisco State University. His best known novel is *Después de las bombas* (México. Joaquín Mortiz: 1979), later translated as *After the Bombs* (Willimantic, CT. 1990). His other novels include *Itzam na* (1981), winner of Cuba's Casa de las Américas prize; *Jaguar en llamas*. (Guatemala 1989); and *Los caminos de Paxil* (Guatemala 1990). His literary study, *Ideologías, literatura y sociedad durante la revolución guatemalteca* won him the Casa de las Américas prize in criticism; forthcoming is another fullscale literary study, *La identidad de la palabra: Narrativa guatemalteca a la luz del nuevo siglo.*

A native of Argentina, **Nora Bonnin** has become a classic case of Chicago Latino-ization since she installed with her family in Chicago's Mexican Pilsen barrio. At the University of Illinois at Chicago, she has explored literary, anthropological, political and historical approaches to cultural studies while studying Sociology and Latin American Studies and pursuing an advanced degree in History. She works on transnational relations at UIC's John Nuveen Center of International Affairs and is currently doing research on epidemics and social relations. In 1997, she participated in the UIC-ColMich program on transnational relations in Zamora, Mexico.

Robert Scott Curry, a former student at UIC, has earned a graduate degree in Comparative Literature at the University of Iowa and now moved on to Austin, Texas. A co-translator of Zimmerman and Rojas's *Guatemala: Voices from the Silence* (1998), he has written mainly on questions of post-Marxist and post-colonial theory in relation to Latin American cinema. In addition to his own essay, he is the translator of Hugo Achugar's essay in this volume.

Elizam Escobar is a Puerto Rican painter and writer imprisoned in the United States since 1980 for his participation in the struggle for the independence of Puerto Rico. He earned a B.A. in Fine Arts at the University of Puerto Rico and was a teacher at the School of Art of El Museo del Barrio in New York City. His art work has been exhibited widely, and his writings have appeared in various art and cultural journals and books, including the following anthologies: *Disparities and Connections: The Excluded on Postmodernism,* (1991), which he edited; *Reimaging America: The Arts of Social Change,* (Philadelphia: New Society Publishers, 1990), edited by Mark O'Brien and Craig Little; and *The Subversive Imagination: Artists, Society, and Social Responsibility,* (New York: Routledge, 1994), ed. by Carol Becker. Jack Hirshman and Csaba Polony are working on a collection of his essays to be published by Curbstone Press.

An Uruguayan student of anthropology, film and communications, **Marquesa Macadar** studied at UIC, and then went on to graduate work at Indiana University, Bloomington, where she has studied questions of modernity and globalization, written innumerable studies, embarked on a collective EMAIL-concocted postmodrnized novel and collaborated fulltime plus on the new Chicago cultural magazine, *Zorros y Erizos.* Inveterate traveller, she wanders the Americas and the streets of Montevideo and Chicago's Mexican/Latino barrios.

Silvia A. Malagrino, from Buenos Aires, Argentina, is an artist and professor at the School of Art and Design at UIC. Her work has been exhibited widely and is represented in collections the National Museum of American Art, Smithsonian Institution, the Art Institute of Chicago, the Milwaukee Art Museum, la Bibliotheque National de France, the Fundaçao Athos Bulçao in Brasilia, among others. Recent solo exhibitions include multimedia installations at the Rockford Art Museum, the John Michael Kohler Arts Center in Sheboygan, Wisconsin, and the Center for Photography in Woodstock, New York. She has also appeared in group exhibitions at Chicago's Museum of Contemporary Photography, the Rice University Media Center, and the Institute of Art of Chicago. **Mónica Flores Correa**, whose text is part of Malagrino's essay, is a New York-based Argentine writer and journalist who has worked with Amnesty International and is currently a correspondent for the Argentine newspaper, *Página Doce.*

Born of Chilean parents in Lima Peru (1970), **Patricio Navia** was reared in Chile, but emigrated to the U.S. as a teenager, earning degrees in Sociology and Political Science at the University of Illinois at Chicago and the University of Chicago, the latter involving a thesis on women's electoral participation in Chile in 1965. He is pursuing doctoral work at New York University with a focus on

Latin American politics and political culture. He has collaborated with Marc Zimmerman in *Guatemala: Voces desde el silencio* (Guatemala 1993), to appear in English with U. of Ohio Press in 1998.

Michael Piazza is a Chicago-based visual artist and writer who teaches Art, Culture and Education at Columbia College and De Paul University. Co-founder of Axe Street Arena Artists Collective, he holds an MFA from the School of Art and Architecture of the University of Illinois at Chicago. Recently he has been working on collaborative art projects like "At Night in the Grand Court--A Renovation," an interdisciplinary art installation with resident youth at the Cook County Juvenile Temporary Detention Center. His work has appeared in *New Art Examiner, Whitewalls: A Journal of Language and Art, Left Curve* and a volume he and other Axe Street Arena members edited with Elizam Escobar, *Disparities and Connections* (1991).

Born in Chinandega, Nicaragua and a professor in the Department of Spanish and Portuguese at Ohio State University, **Ileana Rodríguez** studied Philosophy at the Universidad Autónoma de México and received her Ph.D. in Latin American Literature at the University of California, San Diego, with a dissertation on Alejo Carpentier. Winner of various grants, she held several major positions in Nicaragua during the Sandinista years and also worked as a bibliographer for Cuba's Casa de las Américas. Her editions-in- collaboration include: *Nicaragua in Revolution: The Poets Speak* (Mpls.: MEP, 1980); *Processes of Unity in Caribbean Societies, Ideologies and Literature* (Mpls.: Institute for the Study of Ideologies and Literature, 1983). Her books include: *El primer inventario del invasor* (Managua: Ed. Nueva Nicaragua, 1984); *Registradas en la historia: 10 años de quehacer feminista en Nicaragua* (Managua: Vanguardia, 1989); *House/Garden/Nation: Representations of Space, Ethnicity, and Gender in Transitional Post-Colonial Literatures by Women* (Duke U. Press, 1994); and *Women, Guerrillas, and Love: Understanding War in Central America* (Mpls: U. of Minnesota Press, 1996). A co-founder of the Latin American Subaltern Group, she is currently at work on methods of constructing discourses defining fields of knowledge.

Kartik Vora, from Bombay, India, graduated from the College of Art and Architecture at the U. of Illinois at Chicago. He is currently working on computer technologies and cultivating his interest in postcolonial and postmodern studies. A member of the Editorial Committee of Chicago's *Whitewalls: A Journal of Language and Art*, he continues his work on performance art and border thinking, bringing his perspective even to U.S. Latino Cultural Studies.

Professor of Latin American Studies at the University of Illinois at Chicago, **Marc Zimmerman** holds his doctorate from the U. of California, San Diego (1974). He has taught at various universities and also worked in the Literature Section of the Nicaragua's Ministry of Culture in 1979-80. His books and editions in collaboration include: *Lucien Goldmann y el estructuralismo genético, and Processes of Unity in Caribbean Societies, Ideologies and Literature* (Mpls.: Institute for the Study of Ideologies and Literature, 1983 and 1985); *The Central American Quartet* (collage epics, *Nicaragua in Revolution, Nicaragua in Reconstruction and at War, El Salvador at War* and *Guatemala: Voces desde el silencio* [Mpls.: MEP, 1980, 1985 and 1988; Guatemala: Palo de Hormigo & Oscar León Palacios, 1993]). Other recent volumes include: *Literature and Politics in the Central American Revolutions* (Austin: U. of Texas, 1990--with John Beverley); *U.S. Latino Literature: An Essay and Annotated Bibliography* (Chicago: MARCH/Abrazo Press, 1992); and *Literature and Resistance in Guatemala: Textual Modes and Cultural Politics from El Señor Presidente to Rigoberta Menchú* (U. of Ohio Press). He is currently completing *Tropicalizing Hegemony: Latin American Culture and Literature in Transnational Context*, to be published by Roman and Littlefield. He directs the Chicago Latin American/Latino/a Cultural Activities and Studies Arena (LACASA CHICAGO) sponsored by MARCH/Abrazo Press; he is a fellow in UIC's Great Cities Institute.

INDEX

Goldmann, Lucien, 9, 282
Gómez-Peña, Guillermo, ix, 2, 5, 23, 28, 30, 58, 60, 242, 244, 246, 250, 251- 253, 265
Gómez-Quiñones, Juan, 8, 58, 60, 63, 266
González, M., 124, 266
Good neighbor policy, 75
Gordon, Colin, 230, 258
Gramsci, Antonio, 59, 217, 239, 264
Grass, Gunter, 92, 117
Great Depression, 106
Grenada, 42
Grossberg, Lawrence, 266, 267, 271, 275
Grove, Marmaduque, 117, 118
Guardia, Gloria, 180
Guatemala, 11, 78, 79, 81, 174, 175, 188, 269, 270, 274, 278, 279, 281-283
Guattari,Felix , 4, 39, 76, 260
Guevara, Ernesto, "Che", 27, 52
Guha, Ranajit, 16, 55, 231, 236-238, 241, 266
Guillasasi, Rafael, 120, 259
Guillén, Nicolás , 47, 49, 88
Gulf war, 89, 271, 274
Gutiérrez Alea, Tomás, 50

Habermas, Jürgen, 14, 88, 147, 266
Haber, Alicia, 28,100
Halebsky, Sandor, 4, 266
Hall, Stuart, 55, 214, 216, 266
Harlem Renaissance, 47
Harrington, E. 124, 266
Harris, Richard L., 4, 266
Harstock, Nancy, 83, 266
Harvey, David, 3, 4, 266
Hassan, Ihab, 55, 266
Heartney, Eleanor, 214, 266
Hegel, G. W. F., 10, 233-235, 271
Hegemony, ix, 1-4, 7, 12, 18, 20, 22, 25, 26, 33, 38, 39, 41, 45, 46, 52, 54,

61, 63, 103, 105, 108, 112, 114, 162, 204, 206, 207, 216, 217, 219, 220, 237, 240, 258, 268, 269, 278, 282
Heidegger, Martin, 248
Henríquez Ureña, Pedro, 89, 266
Hercules, 90
Herlinghaus, Hermann, 6, 255, 267
Hernández, 94
Heterogeneity, 32, 33, 84, 95, 161
Heterotopia, 249, 250, 253, 263
Hicks, Emily, 58, 267
Hobsbawm, Eric, 238, 267
Holland, 65
Honduras, 175, 176, 180
Huidobro, Vicente, 94, 95, 267
Husband, Bertha, 26, 27, 267
Hutcheon, Linda, 55, 92, 267
Hybridization, 3, 5, 18, 33, 57, 58, 80, 183
Hydra, 90, 91, 97

Ibañez, Carlos,117, 118, 121
ILET, 137
Imperialism, 3, 4, 33, 41, 43, 44, 54, 56, 72, 74, 192, 247, 262
India, 77, 96, 237-240, 243, 266, 281
Inselmann, Andrea, 17, 267
Inti-Illimani, 140
Iran, 60
Italy, 93, 238

Jackson, Michael, 14-16, 112, 144, 162, 163, 267
Jameson, Fredric, ix,1, 3, 4, 7, 9, 22, 39, 55, 63, 69, 70, 72, 74, 75, 80, 201, 214, 232-235, 267, 269
Jamesonian concept, 70
Jara, Joan, 138, 267
Jiménez, Jorge, 134
John Nuveen Center, x, 279

King, John, 12, 101, 109, 110, 268
King, Anthony D., 32, 268

209, 234, 235, 260, 272-274, 281, 282
Re-functionalization, 150
Re-territorialization, 5, 150
Rice, Phillip, 257, 272, 280
Richard, Nelly, 2, 5, 10, 13, 19, 21, 23, 41, 44, 83, 102, 139-142, 218, 266, 271-273, 278
Ríos Montt, Efraín, 79
Rivera Nieves, Irma, 6, 20, 265, 273
Robertson, Roland, 32, 262, 273
Rockefeller Foundation, 5, 110
Roddick, Jackie, 119, 273
Rodríguez, Ileana, viii, ix, 22, 229, 281
Rojas Guardia, Armando, 94
Romanticism, 40, 60, 66
Roos, Jaime, 94
Rorty, Richard, 83, 163, 273
Rosaldo, Renato, 62
Rosenkranz, Hernán, 117, 118, 272
Rowe, William, 66, 273
Roxborough, Ian, 119, 123, 273
Ruetalo, Jorge, 159, 262
Ruffinelli, Jorge, 6, 55, 273
Rush, Alan, 6, 273
Rushdie, Salmon, 92

Safa, Patricia, 58, 265
Said, Edward, 2, 4, 21, 30, 31, 58, 66, 88, 123, 141, 174, 179, 190, 191, 193, 209, 212, 214, 236, 239, 245, 248, 250, 252, 273
Saint Jean, Ibérico, 167
Saldívar, José D. , Ramón, Sonia., 62
Salinas, Manuel, 176
Sánchez, Rosaura, 62
Sandinismo, Sandinistas, 173, 174, 258
Sandino, Agusto César 45, 47, 48
Sandoval, Chela, 65, 274
Sarli, Isabelitta, 95
Sarlo, Beatriz, 5, 12, 23, 38, 44, 76,

101, 112, 274
Saveter, Fernando, 274
Sayer, Sean, 10, 73, 271
Schelling, Victoria, 66, 273
Schiller, Herbert, 43, 63, 274
Schnabel, Julian, 28, 214-216, 223
Schwarz, Roberto, 5, 44, 274
Sierra, Malú , 48, 124, 260
Silén, Iván, 20, 206, 209, 220, 274
Silva, Patricio, 274
Smith, Carol A., 80, 256, 274
Smyth, John V., 185, 186, 274
Social change, 113, 119, 123, 141, 265, 280
Social theory, 12, 13, 46, 273, 275
Socialism, 41, 52, 53, 88, 124, 221, 232, 234, 261, 264, 276, 277
Socialist party, 117, 147
Sociologization, 197, 201
Soja, Edward.10, 78, 275
Solís, Diana, x, 26-28, 254, 267
Somerville, Siobhan, 17, 275
Sommer, Doris, 18, 56, 184, 187, 275
South America, 218, 276
Southern Cone, 17, 114, 275
Sovereignty, 92, 241
Speaks, Michael, 5, 32, 74, 83, 86, 177, 178, 183, 220, 237, 275
Spivak, , Gayatri Chakravorty, 9, 10, 16, 19, 20, 55, 70-72, 75-78, 83, 96, 202, 246, 266, 269, 275
Stavins, Ilan, 8, 275
Stepan, Alfred, 268, 275
Structuralism, 9, 70, 196
Subercaseaux, Bernardo, 118, 120, 121, 124, 137, 260, 275
SUR, 111, 137
Surrealism, 50, 258

Tecún Umán, 47
Terrorism, 16, 76, 77
Textuality, vi, 173, 176, 179, 181, 185, 188

291

ABOUT MARCH, INC. AND MARCH/ABRAZO PRESS

The Movimiento Artístico Chicano (MARCH) was incorporated in Illinois in 1975 as a not-for-profit cultural/arts organization. Its goal was and is to promote Chicano and Latino literary and visual arts expression, with an emphasis on the Midwest and Chicago. MARCH/Abrazo Press is the publishing arm of MARCH which is dedicated to the publication of chapbooks and perfect-bound literary texts by and about Chicanos, Latinos and Native Americans. For copies of MARCH publications, as well as requests for presentations by our writers, interested parties should contact MARCH, INC., P.O. Box 2890, Chicago, IL 60690; or send a FAX to (773)-539-0013.

ABOUT MARCH'S LACASA CHICAGO
PROGRAM AND PUBLICATION SERIES

Overseen by the MARCH Board of Directors and coordinated by Professor Marc Zimmerman (Latin American Studies, University of Illinois at Chicago), the Chicago Latin American/Latino/a Cultural Activities and Studies Arena (LA CASA CHICAGO) seeks to work on given cultural projects (exhibitions, presentations, publications, etc.) with Chicago-area Latino community and academic groups and to develop Chicago Latino ties with other Latin American and Latino cultural projects and groups throughout the Americas and beyond.

LACASA Chicago seeks to publish, distribute and promote or help find the proper public venue for creative and analytical projects that address issues and concerns stemming from the recent emergence and development of Latin American and Latino Cultural Studies. Emphasizing the contributions and perspectives of Chicago-based or related artists, writers, critics and scholars, LACASA provides opportunities to neophytes in concert with more established cultural workers; the organization seeks to help build and diversify Chicago's Latino/Latin American cultural infrastructure. Above all, its aim is to project the city as a Latin American center in relation to other Latin American centers in the U.S. and Latin America for the coming century.

LACASA CHICAGO's publications include Zimmerman's *U.S. Latino Literature: An Essay and Annotated Bibliography* (Chicago: MARCH/Abrazo, 1992) and *New World [Dis]Orders and Peripheral Strains: Specifying Cultural Dimensions in Latin American and Latino Studies* (Chicago: MARCH/Abrazo 1998), edited by Michael Piazza and Marc Zimmerman. Through MARCH/Abrazo, LACASA will also help promote and distribute other books published elsewhere, with our first such promotion being *Disparities and Connections: The Excluded on Post-modernism, first published by* Chicago's Axe Street Arena. Future projects include texts portraying Chicago Latino life, culture, literature and the arts, and works on Latin American/ Latino cultural transnationalization.. To contact LACASA, write Marc Zimmerman in care of MARCH (see above) or in care of his E-mail address, Marczim@uic.edu.

293

MARCH/ABRAZO AND LACASA PUBLICATIONS LIST

I. MARCH/Abrazo Poetry Series

Carlos Cortez, *De KANSAS a CALIFAS & Back to Chicago*. ISBN 1-877636-09-6. Poems and woodcuts by a famous Chicano Wobbly bard. $6.50.

Carlos Cumpián, *Coyote Sun*. ISBN 1-877636-08-8. Biting urban poems by a Chicano in Chicago. $6.50

Olivia Maciel, *Mas salado que dulce/ Saltier than Sweet*. ISBN 1-877636-13-4. Poems in Spanish and English translation by a Chicago Mexican writer. $7.95.

Marc Turcotte, *The Feathered Heart*. ISBN 1-877636-12-6. Nature and urban struggles in these poems by a poet of Ojibwa and Irish ancestry. $7.95

Frank Varela. *Serpent Underfoot*. ISBN 1-877636-11-8. Urban meditations, some translated into Spanish, by a Chicago Puerto Rican. $7.95.

II. MARCH LACASA Cultural Studies Series

Marc Zimmerman, *U. S. Latino Literature: An Essay and Annotated Bibliography*. ISBN 1-877636-01-0. A much-praised reference to Chicano and other U.S. Latino texts. $8.95 (discount).

Michael Piazza and Marc Zimmerman, *New World [Dis]Orders and Peripheral Strains: Specifying Cultural Dimensions in Latin American and Latino Studies*. ISBN 1-877636-16-9. Essays on Latin American/Latino modernity, postmodernity and globalization. $15.95.

III. Additional Books Currently Distributed by MARCH/Abrazo and LACASA

Carlos Cumpián, *Armadillo Charm*. ISBN 1-882688-09-0. Chicago: Tía Chucha Press. New meditations and riffs by the Chicago/Chicano poet warrior. $10.95.

Axe Street Arena, *Disparities and Connections: The Excluded on Postmodernism*. An international collection of writings on postmodernity, with considerable attention to Latin American themes. $9.95.

Include quoted price plus $2.00 postage/handing for first book and $1.00 for each additional. Checks go to MARCH., Inc., P.O. Box 2890, Chicago, IL 60690.

294